Praise for
A TANGLED WEB

"An engrossing, bizarre tale of stolen identities . . . A deft, fascinating true-crime story of obsession." **—*Library Journal* (starred review)**

"A bizarre story of jealousy and stalking in the heart of the Midwest . . . Rule moves beyond the sensational aspects to investigate the lives, families, and histories of everyone involved." **—*Booklist***

"A gripping case of fatal obsession and stolen identity so bizarre it's hard to believe it's true. Rule's first true-crime book hits the mark." **—Katherine Ramsland**, author of *Confession of a Serial Killer*

"Leslie Rule artfully weaves the strands of a monstrous net that ultimately ensnared its evil perpetrator. A fascinating, incredible read." **—Diane Fanning**, Edgar finalist and author of *Written in Blood*

"Rule deftly explores the strange case of a bizarre love triangle, a cyberstalking imposter, and a terrifying fatal attraction that leads to a deadly obsession." **—Kathryn Casey**, bestselling author of *In Plain Sight*

"With a journalist's eye for detail and a storyteller's compelling voice, Leslie Rule draws readers into the world of a diabolical criminal and her victims." **—Axton Betz-Hamilton**, author of the Edgar Award-winner *The Less People Know About Us*

"Leslie Rule delivers an incredible story of obsession and deceit, a one-woman campaign of terror that could only exist in our digital age. Harrowing." **—Maureen Callahan**, *New York Times* bestselling author of *American Predator*

"Leslie Rule's recipe for *A Tangled Web* takes one depraved killer, adds brokenhearted victims, mixes in cutting-edge crime fighting, and whips it all into a sexy and spell-binding soufflé. Bon appétit!" **—Dawna Kaufmann**, coauthor of *A Question of Murder*

"Rule guides the reader down a slippery slope, with twists and turns of text messaging and online dating, ultimately revealing just how cagey are the deeds of the devious perpetrator." **—Cathy Scott**, author of the *Los Angeles Times* bestseller *The Killing of Tupac Shakur*

Also by LESLIE RULE

NOVELS

Whispers from the Grave

Kill Me Again

NONFICTION

*Coast to Coast Ghosts: True Stories of
Hauntings Across America*

*Ghosts Among Us: True Stories
of Spirit Encounters*

*When the Ghost Screams: True Stories
of Victims Who Haunt*

*Ghost in the Mirror: Real Cases
of Spirit Encounters*

*Where Angels Tread: Real Stories of
Miracles and Angelic Intervention*

A TANGLED WEB

A Cyberstalker, a Deadly Obsession, and
the Twisted Path to Justice

LESLIE RULE

CITADEL PRESS
Kensington Publishing Corp.
www.kensingtonbooks.com

CITADEL PRESS BOOKS are published by

Kensington Publishing Corp.
119 West 40th Street
New York, NY 10018

All Kensington titles, imprints, and distributed lines are available at special quantity discounts for bulk purchases for sales promotions, premiums, fund-raising, educational, or institutional use.

Special book excerpts or customized printings can also be created to fit specific needs. For details, write or phone the office of the Kensington sales manager: Kensington Publishing Corp., 119 West 40th Street, New York, NY 10018, attn: Sales Department; phone 1-800-221-2647.

ISBN-13: 978-0-8065-3998-0
ISBN-10: 0-8065-3998-4

First Citadel hardcover printing: May 2020
First trade paperback printing: April 2021

10 9 8 7 6 5 4 3 2

Printed in the United States of America

Electronic edition:

ISBN-13: 978-0-8065-3999-7 (e-book)
ISBN-10: 0-8065-3999-2 (e-book)

The best of friends stick with us through the darkest of times,
and laugh with us when the sun comes out.
I dedicate this book to my friend, Anne Bradley Jaeger,
who laughed with me in the sunshine
and walked beside me when the shadows grew long and cold.

PREFACE

I will never forget the first time I felt a killer's eyes burning into me. Yes, the *first* time. It happened more than once, because it was my job to photograph murderers on trial, and they were not always pleased when I walked up to them and boldly aimed my camera. I was true crime author Ann Rule's photographer and research assistant. I'm also her daughter.

I was seventeen when my mom started bringing me to trials to take photos for the articles she published in the pulpy-paged detective magazines sold in supermarkets. Throughout the 1960s and 1970s, she saw over a thousand of her articles appear in *True Detective* and its sister publications—articles she typed on an old-style typewriter in the middle of the rec room with the TV blaring and four noisy kids playing around her. She wrote under male pen names because her editor told her, "No one will believe a woman knows anything about crime." When I started working with her, I was studying photography at a vocational school where I spent half of my high school day, and my teachers tried to discourage me from pursuing a career in a male dominated field. Female professional photographers were rare at the time.

There may not have been many women working as crime reporters and photographers, but, *unfortunately*, there were plenty of murderesses. While the majority of killers are male, cases of females who kill go back as far as history can reach. Cynthia Marler was the first murderess I met. She looked more like a movie star than the hit woman she was. The twenty-eight-year-old Hayward,

California, mother of three stood 5′0″, weighed ninety-five pounds, and her thick waves of dark hair spilled past her shoulders.

On August 10, 1980, Marler boarded a Seattle-bound plane under an assumed name and prepared to earn the $3,000 and the 1976 Chevy pickup truck she'd been promised for putting an end to an ugly divorce dispute.

The petite killer disguised herself in a blonde wig and stalked Wanda Touchstone, following the thirty-four-year-old University of Washington student to a parking lot where she fatally shot her in the neck and head.

Witnesses saw Marler fleeing the scene and later picked her out of a police lineup. Testifying in court, one witness remarked that she "was very, very small and had a hard stare." I found myself the recipient of that hard stare soon after I approached her during a trial break in a stuffy Seattle courtroom and asked if I could photograph her. "Yes," Marler replied, "but don't take a picture of me when I'm smoking." I took a few shots and was so nervous I forgot her stipulation. I snapped a photo just as she held a Camel cigarette near her face after exhaling a cloud of smoke. Marler reprimanded me, her voice chilled and unforgiving. "I told you not to take a picture of me smoking!" Her dark eyes bore into me, and I squirmed as I felt the uncomfortable prickle of a killer's wrath.

Ann wrote Cynthia Marler's story twice, once for a magazine and then years later as a case included in her book, *A Rose for Her Grave—Ann Rule's Crime Files: Volume One.* The photo I shot of the petite killer with cigarette in hand appeared in the book. She's smiling brightly in the image, but an instant later, she was angry. I wish I had captured *that* on film!

It might seem odd that my mother exposed her teenage daughter to killers, but she herself met a murderess when she was only nine years old. In fact, the woman taught her to crotchet! Viola was a prisoner in the "Mom and Pop jail" run by my mother's grandparents in Stanton, Michigan. My great-grandfather, Chris Hansen, was the sheriff, and Anna, my great-grandmother, cooked for the residents. When little Ann spent her summers there, it was her job to carry trays of food to the female prisoners.

In addition to the crochet lessons, Viola gave her advice, warning, "never trust those women who pluck their eyebrows into itty-bitty lines."

Young Ann wondered why such a nice lady was behind bars awaiting trial for murder. It was "justifiable homicide" the prisoner explained. Yes, she *had* shot and killed her husband, but she'd caught him in the arms of her best friend in the truck she'd bought for him with tips she made waitressing.

The explanation didn't satisfy Ann's curiosity. How could someone take the life of another? The question intrigued her, and she'd one day explore it in the three dozen true crime books she authored. She was also fascinated by the methods her family used to solve crimes. Not only was her grandfather the Montcalm County sheriff, an uncle was the undersheriff, another uncle was the medical examiner, and her aunt worked in the juvenile court.

How do they do it? little Ann wondered as she watched her grandfather and uncles solve crimes. *How do they take a button and trace it back to the killer?* Sometimes she was allowed to watch them work, and sometimes she *helped*. She was about eleven when her grandfather and uncle recovered the remains of a John Doe. The man had apparently gone missing a long time before and had been reduced to a pile of bones by the time he was discovered. Ann helped spread the bones out on a table as they attempted to identify him.

While forensic science has changed tremendously since my great-grandfather's day, evil has not. It still comes in all shapes and sizes, and he saw his share of it when he hosted some of the Midwest's most dangerous criminals at his jailhouse. He treated them all with respect, and that might be one of the reasons he was legendary for his uncanny ability to coax confessions from killers. He was also famous for the fact he'd never fired a gun in the line of duty in his twenty-four-year career, a distinction so unusual that the story was picked up by wire services in November 1939 and published in dozens of newspapers, along with the caveat, "he still is mighty quick on the draw and a tolerably good marksman."

One of Sheriff Hansen's most widely publicized cases occurred on a cold January night in 1941. It was a little after 6 P.M. when seventy-three-year-old farmer Benjamin Perrien bent over a washbasin in his kitchen in his Clearlake, Michigan, home. He splashed water on his face, unaware of the gun pointed at him. Had he known of the rage building in his killer, he probably wouldn't have turned his back on him. The blast from the 16-gauge shotgun ended Ben's life.

Sheriff Hansen and his deputies drove to the crime scene, forty miles west of their Stanton headquarters. They were greeted by thirteen-year-old Robert Eberhardt and the victim's wife, Sylvia, sixty-three, who'd been milking the cow in the barn at the time of the attack. Partially deaf, she was unaware of the trouble until she found her husband crumpled on the kitchen floor.

Young Robert, however, had seen everything. A sixth-grader at a rural schoolhouse, he was small for his age. He'd moved in with the Perriens two years earlier because his poverty-stricken family had too many children to feed. Robert did chores to earn his keep. Now, he said he'd witnessed the shooting and gave a detailed description of the intruders.

The bullet had entered the back of Ben's head, just as Robert had indicated, but Sheriff Hansen doubted the story—especially when it kept changing. His suspicions were confirmed when the Perriens' dog retrieved evidence from a snowdrift, carrying it gingerly in his mouth as he trotted back to the house. The killer was none other than the small boy with the wild story. His four-footed friend had watched him throw the shotgun shell into the snowbank. Whether the pooch thought they were playing a game of fetch or somehow understood that Robert had harmed Ben, the evidence was undeniable.

When the dog dropped the shell on the floor, Robert hastily hid it beneath his bed, but deputies soon found it, along with the boy's gun. Confronted with the proof, he claimed intruders had placed the shotgun in his hands and forced him to kill Ben. Eventually Hansen persuaded him to reveal the truth and sign a confession. While Robert admitted to the murder, he was later quoted saying he felt only a little sorry about what he'd done. In the kid's mind, it was justified. He told Sheriff Hansen that Ben had been "mean" to him, refusing to give him a vacation and had once thumped him on the head with a pail.

The Perrien case was one of many shocking crimes that Hansen helped to solve. Inspired by her grandfather, Ann dreamed of becoming a police woman, a dream she achieved at age twenty-two when she was hired by the Seattle Police Department. Her beat was the city's Pioneer Square area. In a skirt and high heels—part of the required uniform for female cops in the 1950s—she was not allowed to carry a gun. That was a privilege reserved for male officers. Still, she loved her job and was heartbroken when her career in law enforcement was cut short. She'd been on the force about eight months when the annual physical rolled around, and she flunked the eye exam. The sympathetic examiner allowed her to step up close to the chart, but she still couldn't see the big E. Legally blind without her glasses, she'd be helpless if they were knocked off during a struggle. She was asked to surrender her badge. Devastated, she couldn't bear to drive past Seattle PD and took detours for years.

She got married at twenty-three and had four kids by the time she was thirty-two. My father was stricken with what would turn out to be a fatal skin cancer and couldn't contribute much to support the family, so my mother became a freelance writer, publishing a dozen articles each month in detective magazines. Her old friends at the Seattle PD welcomed her back and gave her access to confidential files. To enrich her reporting, she went back to school to study police science, enrolling in classes such as Crime Scene Investigation and Arrest, Search and Seizure. (I took these same classes in 1978, *not* because I was planning on going into the field, but because I found them interesting and chose them as electives.)

In 1971, Ann was not only a busy mother, she was a full-time writer and part-time student. I took it for granted then, but now I wonder how she found time to volunteer. She would later say it was something she felt she *had* to do. She was partly motivated by her guilt over the fact she'd been unable to rescue her only sibling. At age twenty-one, Don was overcome with a depression his family couldn't help him shake. News of his fate appeared on the front page of the December 31, 1954, edition of the *San Mateo Times*, beneath the headline: *"Wiz" Student Can't Face Life, Dies Suicide*. He was discovered in his carbon monoxide–filled car, parked with the engine running. In his last note, Don Rex Stackhouse apologized, said he loved his family, and asked for his body to be given to Stanford Medical School where he was an honor student.

While Ann couldn't help her brother, she hoped to help other suicidal people and saw an opportunity to do that at the Crisis Clinic, a nonprofit telephone hotline for troubled people. She signed up to volunteer and went through the training program. Teams worked in pairs, answering phones around the clock at the Crisis Clinic headquarters, a somewhat creepy and otherwise empty Victorian house on Seattle's Capitol Hill.

Ann was given the Tuesday-night shift, and her hotline partner was a work-study law student, paid an hourly wage. He was twenty years her junior and reminded her of the brother she'd lost. She developed a sisterly affection toward the man who sat beside her and was so gentle with callers. Together they saved many lives. If one partner discovered they had a suicide in progress, they'd signal the other to alert authorities to trace the call, a process that could take over an hour in the 1970s.

I remember my mom fixing sandwiches to bring to her Crisis Clinic partner because she worried Ted Bundy was too skinny. *Yes, Ted Bundy!* Today his name is almost synonymous with the term "serial killer," but he wasn't infamous back then. Ann considered him a good friend, and they had long conversations about their personal lives on slow nights when the phones didn't light up.

Eventually their time together on the hotlines ended, but they kept in touch and saw each other at the Crisis Clinic's 1973 Christmas party. Soon after, Seattle was on high alert because of the sudden and inexplicable disappearances of several local teen girls and young women. Everyone was mystified because the victims weren't the type to take risks and had vanished from populated areas, often in the light of day. Detectives suspected a cult was sacrificing maidens. Ann submitted a proposal about the disappearances to a publisher and got her first book contract. There was, however, a condition. If the case was not solved, the book would not be published.

The case, of course, *was* solved, and the bizarre coincidence would have been too contrived to be believable in fiction. *What are the chances a writer would contract to write a book about an unknown killer only to learn that the culprit was her friend?* After he was arrested, charged, convicted and sent to death row to await execution for homicides in Florida, Ted confessed to some of the Washington murders. Ann's editor balked, unsure if her book was worth publishing. "No one has ever heard of Ted Bundy," he told her, but he saw the project through. *The Stranger Beside Me* was published in 1980.

Several bestselling books later, she'd learned so much about killers she was invited to serve on the FBI panel that developed the Violent Criminal Apprehension Program (ViCAP). Created in 1985, it was the first computer system to link unsolved violent crimes from police departments nationwide. Prior to that, serial killers and rapists could attack in various counties and states to avoid detection. For the first time, detectives became aware of crimes committed in other jurisdictions, detected patterns, and worked together to make swift arrests.

While I'm proud of my mom's accomplishments, I'm most proud that she remained a kind and down-to-earth person. She never let fame go to her head, preferred costume jewelry to diamond rings and loved to shop at Goodwill. I inherited my mom's fondness for thrift shops *and* her fascination for dark mysteries. But true crime was *her* thing. I wanted to carve out my own niche and sought out mysteries of another sort.

After writing dozens of articles for national magazines in the early 1990s, I published a number of bestselling books with paranormal themes. When my mom and I traveled together, I accompanied her to trials to photograph the cops and killers for her books, and afterward I investigated haunted places for my books. Sometimes she went with me. She, too, had a fascination for ghosts and possessed a strong sixth sense. I had no desire to move into her territory, though I did come close with one book. *When the Ghost Screams— True Stories of Victims Who Haunt* covered cases of haunted locations where the earthbound spirits of victims have been seen wandering.

It must be a combination of DNA and osmosis that has finally compelled me to embrace my mother's genre and write *A Tangled Web*. I was also influenced by hundreds of emails from my mom's readers, some who've practically begged me to write a true crime book. Ann had authored two books each year for the last two decades of her career. She has been gone since the summer of 2015, and her readers desperately miss her books. I won't pretend to have my mother's expertise on crime or expect to replace her in her readers' hearts, but she was a wonderful mentor to me, and I've tried to honor her with a carefully researched story that I hope will help me to carry on the family tradition of saving lives. Sheriff Hansen did it first as he protected his community from criminals, and Ann did it with her books that warned about the dangerous people who walk among us. Nothing made her happier than the letters from readers, thanking her for saving their lives. Because of her books, they recognized danger when they saw it headed their way.

With this story, I hope to warn readers about crimes my great-grandfather could not have imagined as he embarked upon his police career over a century ago. In his pre-computer world, cyber stalkers did not yet exist. Murderers have not changed since the 1920s when he began arresting them. They remain as cold-hearted as they were in the 1960s when my mother first began to write about them. Killers have not changed, but their methods have. They now have an arsenal of electronic devices they can use to dupe us, but we can outsmart them by learning their tricks.

INTRODUCTION

Oh, what a tangled web we weave,
when first we practice to deceive.
—SIR WALTER SCOTT (1771–1832),
SCOTTISH NOVELIST, PLAYWRIGHT,
AND POET

A SPIDER, SOME BELIEVE, cannot be trapped in its own web. While rare, a careless spider *can* be caught in the net it constructed to capture prey. The fact it happens so seldom is a mystery that scientists have yet to solve. One theory suggests that the nimble creatures avoid becoming tangled in their webs by dancing lightly across the sticky strands with only the hairs on the tips of their legs making contact with their clever traps.

While *A Tangled Web* is *not* the story of an actual spider's web, it does follow the wicked journey of a predator who showed no more compassion for victims than a spider shows for the hapless fly caught in its web. The predator in this account used a *different* kind of web to commit cruel crimes. *The World Wide Web!* The majority of us using the Web today are still in awe of the fact that billions of people around the globe have the ability to connect instantaneously with a soft tap of a finger on a computer keyboard—that we can access an electronic system interlinking *millions* of information venues sooner than we can inhale our next breath.

Invented in 1989, the Web has become an integral part of most Americans' lives in only the last two decades. As of this writing, it is still so new that most of us are too naïve to realize the extent of the myriad ways it can be used to set traps designed to deceive us. We often fail to recognize the predators that prowl there, intent upon stealing our money and sometimes our lives. The killer in *A Tangled Web* developed an expertise in the electronic world and used it to assist in not only *committing* crimes, but in the concealment of them. Like the rare spider caught in its own web, the human counterpart in this tragedy spun deceptions so complex that they eventually became trapped in a web of their own making. Unfortunately, it was not before blood was shed and many hearts were broken.

CHAPTER ONE

WHEN CHEROKEE MONTOYA HEARD that her friend had been shot, she was stunned. The violence occurred on December 5, 2015. The 911 operator took the call at 6:41 P.M., and she soon dispatched emergency vehicles to the scene, Big Lake Park in Council Bluffs, Iowa.

Most people called Shanna Elizabeth Golyar by her nickname, Liz, but to Cherokee she had always been Shanna. Cherokee was not surprised to hear that Shanna had gone alone to a deserted park after dark. "She was trying to clear her head—trying to gather herself together. It's what she usually did, quite often. She would just go somewhere silent, so she could think."

Cherokee is still unclear about what occurred that night. "I don't have all the facts," she admits, and there is a hint of bitterness in her voice as she describes what happened, exactly as it was told to her. "She saw the shadow first. They told her to get on the ground. If she didn't do it, they were going to shoot her," she explains, adding that Shanna got down on the cold ground as instructed. "They shot her anyway."

Cherokee and Shanna had met while working in a distribution warehouse about a year earlier in Omaha, Nebraska, and had hit it off immediately. Though Shanna was about a decade older than Cherokee, they seemed to have a lot in common. Both were mothers, and she noted that Shanna appeared to work as hard as she did. "We met, and we bonded really quickly. We just started hanging out. She'd come over and watch my kids, and I'd watch her kids."

She has no problem recalling the good times, but Cherokee is still bewildered by the shooting and the craziness that led up to it. "I don't watch the news," she confides. No one can blame her for being confused about the dark sequence of events that led to crimes so complex that they confounded seasoned detectives. And no one can blame her for turning away from the news. Friends had told her bits and pieces, and that was upsetting enough, especially because Cherokee blames herself. "I didn't stop it. I didn't see it. I could have *said* something . . ." Her voice trails off, as she shakes her head.

In reality, there was nothing she could have done to prevent the horror that tiptoed so quietly into the lives it ruined that no one saw it coming. It, in fact, began long before Cherokee entered the picture.

Dave Kroupa liked women. He made no secret about that, and he made no apologies. He was upfront with every woman he met. He was *not* looking for a commitment, and he made no promises to the contrary.

He had, after all, recently ended a twelve-year relationship with Amy Flora, the mother of his two children, and he was just getting used to being on his own again. Both Dave and Amy had tried very hard to make it work, to hold their family together for the kids' sake. In the end, they came to the painful realization that they just weren't meant to be together. They agreed to remain friends and to work together to make the transition as easy as possible on the children.

The summer of 2012, Dave was still smarting from the breakup and a little bit lonely. He was glad to have regular visits with his kids, but he was otherwise alone. He lived in a barebones Omaha apartment in a huge complex near Hyatt Tire, the shop he managed. At age thirty-four, he was healthy, attractive, and faced years of empty nights if he didn't make an effort to socialize. He realized very quickly that it wasn't hard to meet women. They were as close as his laptop computer, and with the press of a key, he could bring up the profiles of hundreds of attractive females who were hoping for friendship and romance.

Most computer-savvy singles looking for companionship are aware of the many dating websites they can join. Match.com, Coffee Meets Bagel, OKCupid, eHarmony, Tinder, and Plenty of Fish, are among the more popular sites where those seeking romance can view the profiles of thousands of others looking for the same.

Dave was drawn to Plenty of Fish, a website claiming to be the largest dating venue in the world. Founded in 2003, the site boasts 80 million members, with 14 million daily visitors, 60,000 new people joining each day, and over a billion messages exchanged between singles each month. A basic membership is free, and visitors to the site can search for new friends by gender, age, ethnicity, and location, and then scroll through the results like a kid leafing through a toy catalogue, though no one is for sale, of course, and the interest must be mutual before arrangements for dates are made.

Each profile features a photograph, a nickname, and whatever general information the poster is willing to share such as: *Nonsmoker with average body type, born under the sign of Gemini, Caucasian, no kids, works in the service industry* or *Curvy single mother, loves to dance and eat chocolate, just looking to have some fun on Friday nights when the ex has the kids.*

As with any dating website, there are risks. There is no guarantee that the poster's information is accurate. There is no guarantee that the attractive, seemingly charming individual with the enticing description is not a dangerous felon. While the majority of people seeking dates are harmless, not everyone is truthful. Most of the fibs are benign—a few years or pounds shaved off or a photo that was taken last century represented as recent. Sometimes those trolling for romance are married, pretending to be unattached.

One dissatisfied member of Plenty of Fish recently lashed out online, complaining, "I was guaranteed a *single* man. The company did not screen this person well! I am very angry! This site needs to do better!" The grumbler clearly felt betrayed, but she was naïve to think that website managers had the capability to screen out liars. It is simply not possible to vet 60,000 new members each day. Even if *thousands* of website employees worked around the clock to try to verify information supplied by members, they would fall short. It is far too easy to create fake profiles in online venues.

Females are particularly vulnerable when it comes to dating strangers met online. Many women refuse to meet a first date anywhere but a public place, and some even snap photos of the license plates on the cars of their new beaus, sending the images via text to friends, a somewhat morbid precaution should they go missing. Dave Kroupa understood why women were cautious. He couldn't really blame them. He had heard the news stories about women attacked by men they met online. He didn't argue when the women he was interested in suggested coffee in a public place for their first dates.

It did not occur to Dave that online dating could be hazardous for *him*. A former member of the National Guard, he could take care of himself. "I don't think of myself as really bad ass. But I'm not going to hide under a rock. You do what you do, and hopefully it turns out alright."

Dave knew some of the ladies he chatted with had jealous ex-boyfriends. Were any of these men so possessive that they would resort to violence to eliminate the competition? It was not something he worried about. He saw nothing risky about online flirting.

For every online dating horror story, there are thousands of romantic connections so successful they result in marriage. According to a June 2013 article in the New York *Daily News*, a study by researchers working with Proceedings of the National Academy of Sciences (PNAS) found that more than one-third of marriages in the U.S. began with online dating. But marriage was the furthest thing from Dave's mind. "I wanted to have a little fun," he confides. "I did my thirteen, fourteen years. I was never married, but it was as good as. We had the house, and the two kids, and the white picket fence."

Few breakups are *not* painful, and Dave had barely begun to process the end of his relationship when he made the decision to start dating. He wanted to cut loose and enjoy the company of like-minded women. He found lots of profiles for attractive women on the Plenty of Fish website, and he dated his share of them. *Sue. Pam. Joanne. Kelly . . .*

Not in his worst nightmares could Dave have imagined there would come a day when an attorney in a murder trial would rattle off the names of the women he had met that summer of 2012.

Mary. Cathy. Joyce. Beth. Margaret. Sandra . . .

If the chemistry was there, and the woman was willing, Dave was more than happy to explore a sexual relationship, but he had standards. "I wouldn't say I have exceptionally high morals. I'm not against hooking up or booty calls, but I like to *know* the woman." Not everyone subscribing to online dating sites has manners, he notes. "A couple of times I responded to somebody I met online, went over to her house, and immediately she was jumping on me.

That's a little off-putting for me. I'm crazy. I'm kinky. But I'm not that wild."

Jenna. Diane. Megan. June. Lori. Tracy . . .

When the names are read from a list, it seems like Dave has had a lot of dates, but it was not as if he had sex with *all* of them. In fact, in most cases it was only a coffee date. The chemistry just wasn't there, and they quickly parted.

Females are drawn to Dave. He exudes the kind of masculine confidence that comes with humility. At his core—even if he does not consciously recognize it—he is so sure of who he is that he has no need for arrogance, and the self-effacing comments come easily. He is attractive with or without the beard he sometimes allows to grow. With his intense blue eyes and the kind of wavy, blond hair that women are tempted to rake their fingers through, he gets his share of looks from the ladies, but it may be his laugh that is most endearing. He likes to have fun, and his laugh is rich and warm and frequent.

While Dave had a healthy sex drive, he wasn't seeking casual sex with a large number of women *or* a monogamous relationship. He was looking for something somewhere in between. Ideally, he would date several women he enjoyed spending time with, and none of them would put demands on him. They, too, would be as free as he was, and it would be none of his business what they did when they weren't with him. Unfortunately, few women seemed to be seeking this type of arrangement.

Dave did not want to hurt anyone, and he made it clear to the females he met that he was not looking for a commitment. Despite the fact he tried to be careful not to hurt the ladies' feelings, sometimes they got hurt anyway. He hated it when they cried. He was upfront about his desire to maintain his bachelor status, and most of the women had nodded and smiled, seeming to understand when he laid down the rules. But when he pulled away after a few dates, they were too often offended. Did they think he was playing hard to get when he insisted he wasn't looking for a commitment? Did they think he was playing a game? Dave was *not* playing a game. But someone else was.

A very dangerous game, indeed.

CHAPTER TWO

DAVID ALEXANDER KROUPA was born on October 9, 1976, in Sioux Falls, South Dakota, the first child of Tom and Trish Kroupa. As he gulped in his first breath of air, news of Jimmy Carter and Gerald Ford's debates was dominating headlines. The presidential candidates accused each other of "telling untruths," in what by today's standards would be considered gentlemanly allegations but were seen as controversial enough to be newsworthy at the time. Headlines were also buzzing with the U.S. Supreme Court's decision to reinstate the death penalty after a nine-year nationwide ban. Gary Mark Gilmore, convicted of killing motel manager Ben Bushnell in Provo, Utah, was the first death row inmate to trudge to his doom after the moratorium was lifted. He faced a firing squad in Provo twelve weeks later.

But none of the controversies or evils in the world touched young David's life. He was the eldest of three boys. Brother Adam was born in 1978, followed by Max in 1983. "We had a *Leave it to Beaver* family," Dave remarks, referencing the Cleavers, the fictitious squeaky-clean family in the popular television drama that debuted in 1957. The Kroupa family, however, was not only formed a whole generation after the Cleavers, they were also far more devoted to their religion than the TV family who were vague about their beliefs. "We grew up going to church. Southern Baptist. We went three times a week, once on Wednesday and twice on Sunday."

The Southern Baptist Church is considered to be much more strict than the Baptist Church, and followers believe that each word in the

Bible is the truth, while Baptists allow for looser interpretations. Their many differences include their stance on female clergy. The Baptists allow it, but Southern Baptists forbid it. Leaders of both denominations encourage old-fashioned family values, and neither is a fan of divorce or promiscuity. Southern Baptist ministers often preach the virtues of marriage and monogamy, but despite the indoctrination in their formative years, neither Dave nor his brothers embraced it. "My brothers never married, and I'm the only one who had kids."

Their parents, however, have been happily married for over forty-five years. Tom and Trish worked hard to give their boys everything they needed. "My father worked at a printing company for forty years, and my mother was a county veteran-service officer for thirty-seven years," says Dave, explaining that she processed documents to help veterans obtain their benefits.

The Kroupa home was inviting with its shuttered windows, peaked roof, and a big backyard for the boys to play in. It sat on a quiet, gently curving street where the sidewalks were shaded by American elms, hackberry, and sycamore trees. Yards were kept up in the family-oriented neighborhood where gardens bloomed in the summertime with bright red and yellow daylilies. Jack-o'-lanterns grinned from the porches in October, and nearly every house on the block wore strands of twinkling lights in December. Neighbors knew each other's names, and they smiled and waved to each other.

It was an innocent era in Dave's life, one that seems almost surreal when he looks back on it from the perspective of someone exposed to an evil he could not have imagined as a kid. The biggest crime to touch his life had been the theft of his father's fishing tackle. Back then the Kroupa family looked forward to warm days when they could take their sixteen-foot boat out on one of the area's many lakes. Between fishing trips, the boat was parked in front of their home. As the family slept one night, someone climbed onto their boat and stole the fishing tackle. It certainly wasn't a violent crime, and it wasn't even a mystery. The thief was a kid from down the street "who was always in trouble."

"I grew up in the perfect household." Dave is grateful for the good times and his idyllic childhood. His parents had a harmonious marriage, and the brothers usually got along pretty well with each other, too. His parents not only made their sons feel secure, they also encouraged their interests.

Dave gravitated toward sports, playing football on a City League team. "I was a football jock up until my freshman year of high school. I was good enough, but I wasn't the fastest or the biggest or the smartest. I got plenty of trophies, but they hand out trophies to everybody. One year we won the championship. We beat the hell out of a team from Minneapolis. Some fancy team. Must have been seventh grade."

The next year he fractured his leg the night before the first game of the season. "I broke my leg in three places during practice. It was the last time I ever played." It was around that time that Dave started to rebel. "I grew my hair out long, I hung out with the wrong people, and I smoked. I even sported a Mohawk for a while." It was the typical teenage rebellion, but Dave never got into real trouble.

After high school he moved to Denver and joined the National Guard, but after two years, "They stopped paying me. So, I asked them about it. Nothing happened. So, I asked them about it *again*. Nothing happened. So, I just didn't go to drill. A lieutenant called me up one day and said, 'You have to come to drill. We own you. If you don't come, we'll send MPs after you.' I told him, 'It's a job. I get paid. I'll come when I get paid.' I never heard from them again. I got my discharge papers, and that was it. It was around the time they were scaling back, and they were pushing people out left and right."

While living in Denver, he went to college and earned his associate's degree in automotive engineering. "I came back to Sioux Falls for a girl," he confesses. He enrolled in a college there and pursued his bachelor's degree. "It must have been three or four months into the year when we all showed up at school one day, but the doors were padlocked shut. We found out that the owner of the school had gambled away everyone's tuition in Vegas. The feds were there, confiscating everything, and she was going away in cuffs."

The students were told that the government would forgive their student loans, or they could transfer their credits to a new school. "I just said, 'I'm done. I'm out.'" He was barely twenty years old and wasn't sure what to do with his life. Twice burned by administrations mishandling funds, he decided to stick with what he knew best, fixing cars. "That's why I'm still doing this for a living. I never did figure out what I wanted to do."

A couple of years after the school closed its doors, Dave was working at a truck stop's gas station in Council Bluffs, Iowa, when a cute young woman caught his eye. Amy Flora, petite and sweet natured, also worked at the truck stop. She said yes when Dave asked her out. They ended up staying together for over a decade, and they had two children, Calista, born in 2001, and Trey, in 2003. The little family moved to Wisconsin when Dave was promoted. They started out in Madison, later relocating to Oshkosh.

Almost all relationships have conflicts, and Dave and Amy's was no exception. Perhaps their biggest issue was their stance on marriage. "I wanted to get married, and he didn't want to," Amy explains. She needed the security of a forever commitment, but Dave saw marriage as a trap. For all practical purposes, they *were* married. They were monogamous and lived together, raising their two kids, but Amy wondered why the father of her children was reluctant to make it legal. The conflict over the marriage question created an undercurrent of resentment, and their smaller disagreements escalated because of that.

In addition, finances were tight, and it was a stressful time. "We didn't get to do fun things together," Amy emphasizes. "We were working hard to make ends meet, and we worked opposite shifts." They arranged their schedules so that one of them would always be with the children, but it left little time for the couple to spend time with each other.

Wisconsin had never felt like home to Amy. Born and raised in Council Bluffs, she missed her family and friends there. "I lived in Wisconsin for twelve years, and I didn't have too many friends there. I was just lonely. I said, 'If we aren't going to go forward, and we're just going to sit still, I want to go home.'" In the fall of 2011, the family moved into an apartment in Council Bluffs. Amy was glad to be near her friends again, but she and Dave weren't getting along. They made an effort to be civil to each other for the sake of the children, but tensions were high. As painful as it was, they decided they could not stay together.

CHAPTER THREE

THE SUMMER OF 2012 did not start out well for Dave. "I moved into my apartment with a pile of clothes and a computer." He had left the furniture for Amy and his kids. "I had nothing else. Not even a bowl." The new apartment was in Omaha, about twenty minutes from Amy's place across the Missouri River.

When locals claim Omaha "invented hospitality," and encourage tourists to "talk to strangers," they might be joking but visitors agree it's a downright friendly place. Neighbor helps neighbor, and when folks pass on the street, they smile and nod. It's an attitude bred out of necessity because people here *need* each other to survive.

Crippling blizzards can bear down with little warning, while warmer months beckon the deadly gusts that roar through the Midwest's "Tornado Alley," with Omaha smack in the middle. Nebraska averages fifty-seven tornadoes yearly, the most deadly to hit Omaha on Easter Sunday of 1913. With a lethal, quarter-mile girth, it cut a diagonal path through the city, flattening entire neighborhoods, injuring over 350 people and killing 103. The twister ripped open gas lines, igniting the rubble, but citizens toiled through the night to rescue neighbors trapped beneath their collapsed homes.

Despite their own injuries, Omaha's switchboard operators worked in blood-drenched dresses to keep the city's communication lines open so others could survive. The altruistic grit displayed a century ago shaped an attitude of helpfulness that still prevails.

While its natural disasters are remarkable, Omahaians would rather talk about the city's notable contributions. Omaha is the birthplace of thirty-eighth president Gerald Ford, civil rights activist Malcolm X, *and* the TV dinner—the frozen single-serving suppers in aluminum trays created by Swanson in 1954. It's also movie star dancer Fred Astaire's hometown, and the place where Johnny Carson launched his broadcasting career in 1950.

The city's number one tourist attraction, the Henry Doorly Zoo and Aquarium, covers 130 acres, is home to 962 species, and was crowned "the best zoo in the world," by reviewers of a leading travel website.

Omaha may stand alone as a city, but as a region, its "metropolitan statistical area" includes Council Bluffs. While the Missouri River separates Nebraska from Iowa, Omaha and Council Bluffs are linked by bridges. The two cities have little in common other than capricious weather and incredible sunsets, burning brilliant shades of crimson in the endless sky. Council Bluffs, founded in 1804, a half century before Omaha, is much smaller and home to 62,316 people versus Omaha's 466,893.

A Council Bluffs–born resident who now makes her home in Omaha, notes that while both cities have "hardworking people willing to help their neighbor," an unspoken feud exists between them, running deeper than their obvious choices for football teams. (Omaha roots for the Huskers, of course, while Council Bluffs cheers for the Hawkeyes.) Cross the river and political views shift—as do speed limits, slightly higher in Nebraska. Median income is higher in Omaha, but so are taxes and the cost of housing! The median value of homes in Council Bluffs is about 25 percent lower than its counterpart.

Apartments in Council Bluffs might have been cheaper, but Dave chose to live in Omaha to avoid long commutes to work. He rented a place in a huge complex with over a dozen brick buildings, each holding three floors of apartments. The grounds had a park-like feel with lots of grassy spaces and big shade trees. It was affordable, close to his work, and he knew his kids would like the clubhouse and swimming pool. It was fun when they visited, but most of the time it was too quiet.

As Dave settled into his new place, it was summertime, uncomfortably warm with temperatures creeping into the nineties, and his apartment was a stifling and lonely place. "I'd work all day, then see my kids, and then there was nothing else to do. I was lonely at first because I didn't know anybody. The people I did know around here were all Amy's friends." He decided to check out some online dating sites and discovered Plenty of Fish. It was free to create a profile and sign up for a basic membership. He figured there was nothing to lose, so he typed in the requested information and was soon scrolling through photos of dozens of attractive females who lived in the area.

Before long, Dave was chatting online with Liz, a lady about his age, and they made a date to meet in person. She was the first woman he met online. Attractive with dark hair almost to her shoulders, Liz had a nice figure. She was slender but large breasted, and he was a little bit intimidated by her when they met at the agreed-upon place, Perkins, a twenty-four-hour restaurant, in Omaha.

"I was nervous," he admits. "I was fresh out of the thing with Amy, and I didn't even know how to date at that point. I was out of the groove." Dave had been only 22 the last time he was single. Just a kid. Nearly everyone else in his age group had also been unattached, and there were lots of casual get-togethers. Hooking up had been easy, and no one stood on ceremony. Now, a dozen years later, he was not only rusty, he was uncertain how to interact with a mature woman on an official date.

They chose a booth and sat across from each other, making small talk and drinking coffee. Dave added lots of sugar to his. Not only did he like his coffee sweet, it gave him something to do during the awkward pauses. He ripped open packet after packet, poured the sugar in and then stirred vigorously, his spoon clinking loudly against the cup, as he tried to think of what to say next.

He looked across the table into Liz's brown eyes as she stared intently back at him. With a nose slightly too large for her face, she was not classically pretty, but there was something appealing about her. Her heavy-lidded eyes were sexy, and her teeth appeared perfect. Straight and almost too white, they were most likely veneers.

Their kids were about the same ages, and they each had two, a boy and a girl. That was good. They had something in common they could talk about. Dave explained his last relationship had recently ended and that he was not looking for anything serious. Liz nodded. She understood. Frankly, she was very busy with her kids and pets

and her own cleaning business, "Liz's Housekeeping," she explained. She had way too much going on to add more commitments.

"We had four or five similar coffee dates," Dave remembers. Liz
stayed on her side of the table, and he stayed on his. He couldn't tell
if she was attracted to him or if they were destined to be nothing
more than platonic friends. "She might have been giving me signals,
but I wasn't catching any of them." Finally, on the fifth date, as they
left the restaurant, he got up his nerve to kiss her for the first time.

"Why did it take you so long?" she asked him.

"'Cause I don't know what the fuck I'm doing," he confessed.
Whatever he had forgotten came back to him very quickly. They had
sex that night, and on nearly every date after that. "I would have to
credit Liz with helping me get my confidence back. I was feeling
pretty low, pretty worthless, after my breakup with Amy."

Liz obviously liked him. She was an enthusiastic lover, and they
saw each other regularly over the next two weeks, but it didn't take
him long to get restless. He found her attractive, and she was easy to
be with, but there was no deep connection. She was always up for
sex, and that was fine with Dave, but he needed more than that.
"One of the reasons I would never be with Liz is that she was not
well read. I couldn't have a conversation with her about the news."

Though self-deprecating and the last to acknowledge his strengths,
Dave is highly intelligent. If he ever *were* to commit again, he would
need a woman who challenged him intellectually. Liz was definitely
not that woman. He continued to scroll through the profiles of
women on the Plenty of Fish website. "I really kind of started hitting
the books, as it were, and seeing what was out there."

Liz wanted more from Dave than he was willing to give her, and
that became apparent just weeks after he had met her. "She got really clingy. She wanted all of my time." He didn't want to be a jerk
about it, but he wished she would back off and give him room to
breathe.

"What did you do last night?" she often asked with more than a
casual interest when he had not spent the evening before with her.
"That's my business," Dave replied. "I do what I want to do. I told
you that when we met."

He went on a few dates, usually meeting the women in a coffee-house. Most of the time it was obvious within the first minute that there was absolutely no attraction. Sometimes there was a spark, and a second and third date followed. Sometimes the connections resulted in sex. Always he made it clear that he was not looking to commit. His reason for avoiding commitment changed over time. "Initially, my reason for not wanting anything serious was because I had just got out of a long relationship. And then once I got my confidence back, and I was meeting women, I thought, 'Okay, I'm not doing this whole monogamous thing!'"

He told Liz, "You can be here or not. Your call, but I'm going to do what I'm going to do." He had no objection to sex with Liz, but she had to understand that that's *all* it was. He was going to see other women. He was not Liz's boyfriend and never would be. He looked her in the eye and said, "We're not going to ever be together."

Though Dave didn't volunteer details about the other women he saw, he didn't hesitate to tell Liz the reason he was unavailable if she tried to arrange to get together on a night he had other plans. "I can't tonight," he'd tell her. "I've got a date."

The first time Liz popped into Dave's place just before he was about to leave to meet someone, he didn't think much of it. She wanted sex, and he obliged. It took a while for him to notice a pattern. "She'd call and ask me, 'What are you doing tonight?' and I'd say, 'I'm going on a date. This is my night. *Good-bye.*' And then I'd come home from work, and she'd be waiting for me, just to get it on with me before I went on a date. It took me about three times to catch on, and then I thought, 'Wait a minute! She's trying to wear me out!' Afterward she'd say, 'Okay, bye,' like now she thought I wasn't motivated to go out and chase anybody else. It didn't slow me down. She was trying, but I'm not that old," he says, explaining that by the time he wined and dined his date that enough time had passed to revive him.

While Dave continued to remind Liz that he was not committed to her, she made it clear that she wasn't seeing anyone else. "I'm not all there is," he told her. "I'm just a guy. Go on some dates! Go get laid!"

"I'm not like that," she insisted, stressing that her morals were too high to do as he suggested. "I'm not going to do what you're doing!"

"Don't expect me to change," he warned her. "You're wasting

your time if you're waiting around for me to change. I'm going to date, and you should, too."

Liz shook her head, adamant that she didn't plan to see anyone else. She told him that she had deleted her profile from the Plenty of Fish website.

"I'll help you make a new profile," he suggested, but she demurred, saying she wouldn't feel comfortable dating more than one man at a time. If Liz wanted to hang around hoping he'd change his mind, that was her choice. Short of telling her to get lost, he didn't know how to make his position more clear. He never deliberately hurt anyone's feelings, and he didn't want to crush Liz. Maybe she would move on once she realized he wasn't going to change. He continued to see other ladies, but there was no one who knocked his socks off, no one who made him rethink his vow to remain a bachelor.

Not only did Liz try to fulfill Dave sexually before he left for dates, she made their nights together sizzle. "Liz was very kinky." She wasn't shy about trying new things and trying them in new places, including public places. Smack in the middle of a bright, sunny day, the two were visiting a park, and they set out on one of the many well-traveled nature trails. Suddenly, Liz grabbed Dave's arm and pulled him off the path, making her intentions clear as her hands traveled over his body and tugged at his jeans. They sunk into the grass, just out of view of people walking by. "There I was with the sun shining on my bare butt!" he recalls.

Though no one could see them, they were well aware of the passersby just a few feet away, and the risk of getting caught made the sex all the more thrilling. Dave had come a long way from the days he sat on the hard pew in the Southern Baptist Church and listened to the preacher's warnings about sinning and Hell. He'd long since shed the religion and did not believe sex outside of marriage was a sin, but he certainly didn't want to be arrested for public indecency. No one caught them, and they pulled their clothes back on quickly, giggling as they slipped back onto the trail.

Dave had to admit that Liz had it going on when she dressed up for nights on the town. "I remember a group of guys hooting when we walked down the street together," he says, recalling how Liz turned heads in a short skirt. The guys gave Dave the thumbs up as they hollered their approval.

Liz was a lot of fun, *most of the time*. But there was a "real issue. She resented the amount of time that I spent with my kids." She was worried he was hanging out with Amy when he went to Council Bluffs. While Dave and Amy eventually got over their disagreements, they went through a rough period when they split. Their breakup was so contentious that they tolerated each other only for their children in the first months after their relationship had disintegrated.

"Amy and I got along like two pieces of sandpaper, so I didn't hang out at her place. I'd just pull up, pick up my kids and leave. I was living in Omaha, a twenty-minute drive, so we'd find a place to sit down and eat and drink coffee." Glancing around the casual restaurant where he met with this author, he adds, "My kids know this place way too well. We spent a lot of time here early on."

Liz, however, regularly dropped by and made snide comments when he returned from visits with his children. "Oh," she'd say pointedly. "I see you spent a lot of time with *Amy*."

"I wasn't with Amy. I saw my kids," Dave would retort. "But it's none of your damn business what I do with my time."

Liz's approach was passive aggressive, often so subtle her resentment was barely noticeable as she quietly fumed, but before too long, it began to sound like nagging. "As time went on, it would get worse and worse and worse, until I'd say, 'You know what? That's it. I don't need this bullshit. Goodbye.' And then she'd go away for a week or two. Then she'd call and say, 'Oh, can you help me out with this or that?'"

Once Dave had helped Liz with whatever thing she needed help with, she'd get back in his good graces by initiating sex, and the cycle would start all over again. Liz was an expert seductress, and she knew exactly what Dave liked. He was too nice of a guy to tell her to take a hike right afterward, so she would spend the night, the blowup all but forgotten.

All humans are influenced by biology whether we're aware of it or not, and studies have shown that a hormone released by the hypothalamus during sex can create such a physical high that both males and females are often confused by their feelings. Are those warm, fuzzy feelings a genuine indication of caring or are they a temporary rush of "feel good" chemicals? The answer is not always simple. Oxytocin, dubbed "the love hormone" and "the cuddle hormone," fosters bonding in couples, and the natural high can be so powerful that it overrides common sense.

Research continues on the sometimes controversial and debatable effects of human-generated chemicals and how they affect social interaction, but there is no denying the fact that sexual connections make it much more difficult to sever relationships. Dave *did* feel more fondly toward Liz because of their physical involvement. Sex relaxed him, numbing his concerns about her possessiveness. After their reunions, things would be peaceful for a couple of weeks, and then Liz would once again begin to pout and insinuate he had slept with Amy.

Neither Amy nor Dave had any inclination to rekindle their romantic relationship, but Liz refused to believe that. It was exasperating, he recalls. "It was just nag, nag, nag, nag when I'd already told her a thousand times, 'It's none of your damn business. If I get back with Amy tomorrow, that's none of your damn business.'"

The longer he knew Liz, the less inclined she was to back down when he told her off. With each passing week, she kept count of the time she had "invested" in him since their first meeting, as if she were counting dollars deposited in the bank.

"I would think you would give me a little more consideration with three months invested in this relationship," she said in the middle of one of her snits over her suspicions that he was hooking up with Amy. Even the weeks they had spent apart counted as "time invested," as far as Liz was concerned.

Sometimes it was easier to ignore her than argue. As long as he steered clear of the subject of Amy, Dave and Liz got along fine. Sex between them continued to be good, and he didn't mind falling asleep next to her. "I sleep like a brick." Once he closed his eyes for the night, he was almost instantly in too deep of a sleep to be affected by whoever was resting next to him. Liz spent the night often.

When she wasn't obsessing over Amy, Liz was docile and agreeable. While she didn't possess a quick wit or the ability to engage in fascinating conversation, she was okay company for those nights that would have been otherwise lonely. As long as she understood that he would *never* commit to her, he figured he could keep from breaking her heart, so he reminded her often that he wasn't in love with her and never would be. His plan did not work. Liz didn't get the hint, and she continued to push him to give her more. She sought him out constantly, often dropping by without warning. What was he supposed to do? Shut the door in her face? Shove her off when she climbed onto his lap and kissed him?

Two things betrayed him: his body, too easily aroused when an attractive and sexually aggressive woman was insistent upon having him. And his conscience. "I didn't want to be a dick. I'd already been a jerk on numerous occasions because she would push at me until I had to be. And I don't want to be that guy, but sometimes you have to be."

Kindhearted people have a particularly tough time ending relationships, and though David wished Liz would quietly go away, he hoped that would happen without him having to be cruel. He doesn't remember when Paul Simon's sensation "50 Ways to Leave Your Lover" first hit the airwaves in late 1975, because he wasn't born yet. In January 1976, right around the time he was conceived and just before his mother probably sensed the new life stirring within her, the song climbed to the top of the charts. The catchy tune with rhyming suggestions such as "Get on the bus, Gus," and "Drop off the key, Lee," listed various ways to dump a lover and "Get yourself free."

The song makes rejecting someone sound easy, but in reality, it can be just as painful for the dumper with a conscience as it is for the "dumpee." Dave didn't want to see Liz's tears or feel the burden of her broken heart. People have been known to go so far as to fake their own deaths rather than see the pain of rejection in the eyes of their jilted lovers. The more common brush off, however, is used so often it has become a cliché.

"It's not you, it's me."

In theory, the deserted partner is supposed to feel better about themselves when the one severing the ties takes responsibility for the failure of the relationship. Do those five monosyllable words *really* help rejected people salvage their egos? Perhaps in some cases, but most of the time the brokenhearted recognize a platitude when they hear one and end up feeling insulted *and* rejected.

In September 2012, as the nights grew cold, and the deciduous trees were afire with autumn hues, Liz insisted on having serious talks with Dave about the direction of their relationship. He bristled, but she read that as a sign that he was afraid to show his feelings. She had so many questions for him. *How did he really feel about her?*

Backed into a corner, he told her she was attractive and a great gal, and sure, he cared about her. Yeah, they had fun together. "But I'm never going to commit to you," he added. How many times did they have to have this discussion? Dave was irritated.

Liz, however, plucked out the parts of his response she liked the best and discarded the rest. *Dave cared about her!* She decided he might be more comfortable relaying his feelings in writing, and she began to send him long texts and emails, all built around a brilliant idea that had occurred to her. What if Dave committed to her for just four weeks? It would be "a fresh start" for them, and maybe it would "move their relationship forward."

He grimaced when he saw the text she'd sent him outlining her proposal. Why was she suggesting *any* kind of commitment when she knew he wanted his freedom? "I ignored it the first time," he says. "Like it didn't happen."

In another email she asked if he would rather that she just go away. Trying to soften the rejection, he repeated what he had told her from the beginning. As long as she didn't expect anything from him, he didn't mind hanging out with her.

In one of the following emails she wrote, *I know you have things to think over. Do you really not want to try? Stop overanalyzing everything. What did you feel? I got you to say a little bit today, which was nice to hear. That's all I want, really, is for you to tell me how you feel honestly, and I know it's hard for you. You're very vague about things, and I wish you would open up.*

Dave didn't think he was vague. Maybe he was a *little* vague when she put him on the spot and insisted that he tell her exactly what he thought of her. He had hemmed and hawed and tried to change the subject, so he wouldn't say something mean. But he did not think he was vague when it came to where he stood on their future. *There wasn't one!*

He had once made the mistake of telling Liz about his past disappointments in failed romances. Almost everyone has had their heart broken at least once, and he was no exception. Liz concluded that his past pain was the main obstacle they had to overcome to find bliss. *I know your past isn't very good, and I'm sorry for that,* she wrote. *You're a wonderful man and deserve someone who will respect you. I don't want to be full of myself, but I am very good to the man I am seeing. Sorry, but I deserve someone like you, finally.*

The onslaught of words continued, and he responded with about one word for every hundred she expressed. In that September's exhaustive email exchange, Liz continued to ask him for answers to questions he had already answered. *Either you want me to stay, or you want me to go,* she wrote, adding that she would not stop wanting more from Dave. *I understand your position at the moment,* she stated. She ended that email saying he could expect her to continue to ask for a commitment from him in the following months.

Liz was trying to pin Dave down, and it made him extremely uncomfortable. How could he make it clear that he absolutely did not want to be in a monogamous, permanent relationship with her? He didn't want to hurt her feelings, and he wished she would drop the subject.

Dave took a deep breath and typed a reply that he hoped would make her back off but not completely crush her. He wrote that he'd thought he'd made his position clear and added, "I'm prepared to understand that you want more and will ask again. That's cool. Are you prepared to hear 'no' again?" *How much more-blunt could he be?* he wondered as he hit the send button.

Maybe, Liz responded and pointed out that they'd been seeing each other for months, as if that gave her the right to demand more from him. She ended that email asking, *What do I need to do to get you to take a chance?* Seven minutes later, before he could respond, she sent another email. *I guess hearing "no" isn't that big of a deal. It does make me wonder what is wrong with me. Wonder if I'm just a rebound. I guess with almost four months invested, I figured I'd get more from you.*

Dave felt bad that Liz felt bad. Why couldn't she grasp that the fact that he wanted his freedom wasn't a rejection of her? There was so much that she didn't seem to get. When he read her next words, he realized how true that was. Liz wrote, *I always feel we take a small step forward, then you go to Amy, then we take ten steps backward. Am I really always going to have to play this tug of war for you to drop the damn past?*

Once again, he tried to explain that the mother of his children wasn't the issue. *Well, I hardly talk to Amy, and I never see her, so it's not that.* He hit send, and a reply appeared almost immediately.

Are you scared of me? Liz asked. *Do you think I will cheat on you? Do you think you're not good enough?*

He'd rather put the blame on himself than hurt her feelings and was glad she'd steered the discussion in that direction. Elaborating on the standard rejection, "It's not you, it's me," he typed, *I'm not good enough for you. Just because you have low standards, obviously, since you like me, doesn't mean I'm good for you.*

A flurry of emails flew back and forth, and then Liz got right to the point. *Answer the stupid question. Do you want to keep going with us or not? Not that hard, stay or go.* There it was again. The ultimatum.

If she would just stop nagging him to commit and give him room to breathe, they could hang out, but if she vanished from his life forever, he would not shed any tears. "I didn't care if she came or went," he admits, but he was trying hard to be tactful. He typed, *I said "stay" 27 emails ago. But maybe we should back off again. Emotions getting high and all*

Oh my fucking God! Liz shot back. *Whatever. As always, I bring something up, and Dave runs for the hills! You're the only one that has a problem here. It's always easier to run.* She was needling him, calling him a coward for refusing to face a love she was certain he'd see if he weren't so afraid. He did not take the bait.

The most irritating part of their exchanges was her persistence about the four-week commitment. He could hardly believe she'd suggest such a thing, and he was frustrated when he read, *I guess at the end of four weeks this is what I'm hoping for. Maybe persuade you to move a little forward with us. LOL.* Laughing out loud? She obviously wasn't joking, and the use of the Internet abbreviation for laughter ironically came off like a nervous giggle. Dave wished she *were* joking, because the suggestion was truly laughable to him.

Liz stressed in that email, *I'd like a guy who was kind of like mine, someone I could go out with, have fun with, or sit at home with and enjoy playing PS3, cards or whatever.* She added that she was as afraid of a commitment as he was, but a few sentences later she wrote that she was "asking for constants." She rattled on, basically repeating what she had already said, and then ended with, *Does that make sense, or did I just make it worse?*

What did Liz think a one-month commitment would accomplish? Did she believe he'd realize he was hopelessly in love with her after thirty days of an exclusive arrangement? "She was dumb to think that would be the case." He shakes his head. The first time she'd suggested the four-week commitment, he ignored her, hoping she'd drop it, but she asked again. "I just shut her down. And then she asked *again*, and I shut her down. She just *wouldn't* let it go. Finally, I'm like, 'okay, whatever.' By then I was already talking to Cari."

Cari. Incredibly smart, funny, *and sexy*, she was the only woman he had met organically since his breakup with Amy. While all the others had stepped into his world through his computer screen, Cari was the only one he had met the old-fashioned way, face-to-face in a chance encounter. "She was a customer, and it was purely professional," Dave stresses, recalling the day the vivacious Cari Farver brought her Ford Explorer into Hyatt Tire for a minor repair.

He was instantly attracted to the tall, slender lady with the smiling hazel eyes. A powerful energy crackled between them as they met each other's gaze, and Dave sensed she felt it, too. *Should he ask her out?* No. He was at work, and she was a client. Asking her for a date would be inappropriate, he told himself. Besides, he couldn't be certain she'd be receptive. Her eyes seemed to say she was interested, but maybe he had misread her. If she said no, it would be embarrassing and awkward.

About two weeks later while perusing the Plenty of Fish dating site, Dave was pleasantly surprised to see Cari's profile pop up on the screen. He sent her a message: *Hi! I know you!* "It was a chance to say hello without being too creepy."

Cari wrote back, and the exchange was friendly but brief. About two weeks later, she came back to the shop with her Explorer. Dave went with her to the parking lot to check out one of the vehicle's windows that had been sticking. This time they were both acutely aware that the other was single and looking to date. "Sparks kind of flew," Dave remembers. "We weren't making out in the parking lot, but right then and there we exchanged phone numbers and expressed our interest in each other."

He hadn't dated anyone but Liz in the past month, the month she had insisted should belong exclusively to the two of them. While Liz seemed to be desperately holding onto the idea that the monogamous month would seal them as a couple, he didn't pay much attention to it. He'd gotten very tired of Liz nagging him about it, and had half-heartedly agreed to shut her up.

No, he had not dated anyone else in the last weeks, but not because of a sense of obligation. He'd been busy. Between work, his kids, and the hours Liz gobbled up, there wasn't time for much else. Their exclusive month was almost up, and if she thought he was going to drop to one knee and profess his undying devotion toward her, she was about to be very disappointed.

Dave was excited about Cari and was looking forward to seeing her, but he did have an obligation to Liz. It was not a commitment to a lifetime together but a promise of a date Liz had made with him weeks earlier when she got tickets to the Freaker's Ball. Hosted by Z-92s *Todd N Tyler Radio Empire,* the Freaker's Ball was a big Halloween bash at Harrah's Council Bluffs Casino and Hotel. The doors opened at 7:30 P.M. on Friday, October 26, 2012, and partygoers danced to music played by the band, The Vybe, "bobbed for bullets," and competed for best costume in a contest sponsored by Coors Light Beer. The generous prizes included a thousand-dollar award for the best costumed pair.

Liz fashioned their costumes, togas made partly from white sheets. Dave wore a gold armband, gold sash, and incongruous blue tennis shoes that peeked out beneath his floor-length getup in a snapshot. "We handed our cell phones to someone and asked them to take pictures of us," Dave remembers. The pair, with Liz cuddled close to Dave, are forever frozen in that instant. Liz's chest looks so huge she's top heavy, and her toga is strategically draped to show off her high heels with the long, gold straps crisscrossing up her shapely calves.

The costumes weren't authentic, and they didn't win any prizes, but if Liz's goal was to present herself and Dave as a couple, she succeeded. The Roman themed outfits left no question that they were a matched set. At least for the night of the Freaker's Ball, Liz got what she wanted. But just as Cinderella's magic night at the ball

ended when her magnificent coach morphed back into a pumpkin,
Liz's ball, too, came to a disappointing end. As the night wound
down, Dave did not exactly behave like a besotted Prince Charming.
Sure, he was as into the sex as he always was. She knew just how to
touch him to drive him wild, and at the end of their date, she made
sure he was satiated. But afterward he seemed more distracted than
usual. If Liz suspected he had another woman on his mind, she was
right.

CHAPTER FOUR

MONDAY NIGHT, three nights after The Freaker's Ball, Dave and Cari had their first date. They met at Applebee's Bar & Grill at Omaha's Oak View Mall. It was fun from the moment Dave sat down across the table from Cari. She was witty, and she not only made him laugh, she laughed at his quips, too. They ordered drinks, and as they sipped, conversation flowed naturally.

He learned that she was a computer programmer with an expertise in coding. She worked for West Corporation, a developer of technology-enabled communication, with offices less than half a mile from his apartment. She had been hired in May, so it was still relatively new to her. She was twice divorced, thirty-seven, and lived with her teenage son, Maxwell, in Macedonia, Iowa, a small country town where she had grown up, about thirty miles east of Omaha. It was a long commute to work, she told him, but she enjoyed her job.

They had an excellent rapport, and the more Dave got to know Cari, the better he liked her. "Then my phone started blowing up with texts and phone calls." He tried to ignore the distraction, but in a ten-minute period, he received about twenty texts and calls. He glanced at his phone and saw Liz's number. He wasn't going to answer her in the middle of a date. "That would have been rude! I was giving Cari my attention. But it continued until I assumed something very serious was going on, and I excused myself and went to the bathroom." Dave called Liz and asked her what she wanted.

"I left some things at your apartment that I need to get."

"Can't it wait?"

"I really need to get my things now."

The situation was exasperating. Liz was suddenly worried about a couple of T-shirts, a toothbrush, and some pans, items she had left at his place weeks ago and had gotten along fine without until now. "She wanted me to immediately drop what I was doing and go get her stuff. I told her I was on a date and to leave me alone. I went back to my date. We got done eating, hung out for a little longer talking, and then I invited her over to my place to play cards, watch TV, or whatever.

"We met at my place, we went inside, and we didn't even get to sit down before my phone was blowing up again, and the security doorbell was ringing. That was Liz trying to get my attention." Dave could ignore his phone but not the obnoxious buzzer on the security door. It was loud and grating, and there was no way he and Cari could have a conversation with all that noise. His intercom was broken, so he had to go to the building's vestibule, where Liz stood on the other side of the locked glass door. "I need my stuff!" she insisted. "I want it right now!"

"You don't need to come in right now!" Dave said. "I have a date in here."

Red faced, with tears drifting down her cheeks, she stood her ground. "I need my stuff right now! I'm coming in!"

"I'll bring it to you later."

"I want it *now!*"

Defeated, Dave went back inside. "I've got a situation here," he told Cari, explaining that a woman he'd been dating was nearly hysterical, refusing to leave. Later, he would remember what a good sport Cari had been about the whole thing. "She laughed it off. She said something like, 'Okay! We've all been there! Call me when you get it straightened out!' It didn't bother her one bit."

He walked Cari to the security door where a pouting Liz waited. He didn't bother to introduce the women, and they didn't acknowledge each other as he played gatekeeper. He let Cari out, and Liz rushed in. "Liz comes into the apartment and gathers up her stuff, and we have kind of a heated conversation. She's upset, and when she finally gets her stuff, she doesn't want to leave anymore. She wants to talk about it, argue, cry. She wasn't happy with me at the moment. I asked her to leave. I wasn't up to dealing with her. I was very irritated. Here my first date with Cari is ruined, and now I got Liz upset! At that point I just wanted to shut my door and call it a night! Not long after that, maybe ten minutes or so, I called Cari. She was on her way to her house, and she invited me out to her place."

It was barely 9 P.M., and he did not hesitate to take her up on her invitation. He made the forty-minute drive to Macedonia and found her in her charming little house, smiling her beautiful smile at him as she brewed coffee. The two-bedroom house, built in 1870, had belonged to Cari's grandparents, and they had sold it to her at a fraction of its value to keep it in the family. It was warm and welcoming, and Cari had decorated it in an eclectic style of antiques mixed with newer furniture. They had the place to themselves. Cari's son, fourteen-year-old Maxwell, was staying the night with his grandparents in their nearby home.

Cari was *perfect*! Easygoing, beautiful, funny, and brainy! "She was exceptionally smart," he emphasizes, confessing that he thought she was far more intelligent than he was, and he found that to be very attractive. "She had her shit together. That was at least as attractive as her being a very pretty woman."

Cari handed Dave a steaming mug of coffee, and they sat down on the couch. This was the first time they had been alone together. The two minutes they had spent at his apartment didn't count, because Liz had burst in on them almost immediately. There was no denying the powerful attraction between them. Within minutes they were kissing passionately. Before things went too far, Cari had something to tell him. She wasn't looking to commit, she explained. She, too, had had relationships that had soured, and she wasn't ready to be tied down again.

In addition to her divorces, there had been serious romances that had fizzled. Though Cari didn't mention it to Dave, in one case an ex had been reluctant to let go and had become so aggressive that she had been compelled to file a restraining order against him. She hadn't seen Alec in at least two years, but his bad behavior had made her wary. The last thing she wanted was more drama, and she told

Dave that she was open to having a physical relationship, but he shouldn't read too much into that. She was not ready to give up her freedom.

"I felt like I hit the jackpot," he remembers. She wanted the same things he did, fun and excitement without expectations. After months of Liz badgering him, Cari's freewheeling approach to love and life was a welcome relief. "It was all laughs and giggles from there." He stayed the night, and though they were both busy over the next couple of weeks with their jobs and their kids, they made time for each other and saw each other about every other day. Their chemistry was incredible, and between dates he looked forward to seeing her again.

Liz, however, would not let go. On November 1, at 7:38 A.M. she sent Dave a rambling email: *I know you don't know what will happen down the road, and you don't really want to think about it. Are you asking for the long break, so you can forget everything? I'm going to give it to you, so don't worry. I was just wondering, sorry. I guess I need closure. Do I forget everything about us? I'm going to date others, but if no one catches my eye, do I get to hope time makes the heart go fonder? Or do you want me to go and never come back? I'm not saying we will ever get back together. I'm just asking, do I go and never look back? I guess I hope even if you're dating others that you'll look back and smile when you think of me, that someday you'll let me back in, no matter what it be, a friend or whatever.*

The email went on, with Liz urging him to tell her what he was thinking, apparently oblivious to the fact he had told her multiple times that he liked her, but she didn't mean all that much to him and that she should never *ever* expect him to stop seeing other women or to commit to her. She ended the email telling him she hoped he had a great day and that she would understand if he wanted to stop talking to her. A few minutes later she wrote again, explaining that she hadn't hugged him the last time she'd seen him because it would have felt like "a goodbye." It was not as if Dave were sitting around fretting about why Liz had not hugged him. He was pretty annoyed with her after she'd barged in on his date, and all he had wanted that night was to get her out of his hair. He didn't care, and frankly didn't *notice*, that she hadn't hugged him.

Twenty-four hours later, at about eight in the morning, Liz sent

Dave another email, sarcastic and abrupt. Apparently, she had not meant it when she said she would understand if he wanted to cease communicating with her. She was obviously offended that a full day had passed, and he had failed to reply to her heartfelt emails. *Well thank you for no response to email,* she wrote. *I get the answer. That's it. Later.* While she was stewing because he was ignoring her emails, he probably hadn't even read them. He didn't check his email every day, and his focus was on Cari. She was spending a lot of time at his place, and he wished he'd fixed it up nicer. He was the first to admit his apartment was not exactly luxury quarters.

He could not afford to buy new things after his split with Amy, and he had furnished his place with garage-sale finds and castoffs. "I had an ugly couch that Liz had given me. Supposedly from her grandparents' house. It would be something you'd expect to find in your grandmother's *grandmother's* house. It had a wood frame and a floral pattern on horrible, scratchy corduroy."

Cari teased Dave about his ugly couch, and it became a standing joke between them. She had impeccable taste, and he had been impressed when he saw how beautifully she'd decorated her home. When he said that he wasn't about to spend money on new furniture, she told him he could find great deals on used stuff on Craigslist, a free online website of classified ads. She made it her mission to find him a nice couch, and she sent him links to sofas she found, but they ended up going to Goodwill where Cari spotted a loveseat in a soft shade of silver at a bargain price. Dave bought it, and they loaded it into her SUV. Back at his apartment, they rearranged his furniture to make room for Cari's find.

While Cari shared her expertise on interior design, he advised her on cars. They had been seeing each other for about a week when she found a car she thought her son would like. Max would begin driving soon, so she bought it for him, though it wasn't yet roadworthy. "It was an old Volkswagen," says Dave. "Some kind of fancy sports model. She wanted to fix it up, so she brought it to the shop. We did quite a bit of work on it."

He and Cari were having a great time together, but when Liz called to say she realized she hadn't gotten everything she'd left at his place and was wondering about some pans she'd left behind, he offered to bring them to her. Later, he would not be able to recall the exact date but estimates he went to Liz's home sometime between November 6 and 8. He had planned to just drop off the pans, but she had something else in mind. He was barely in the door when she brushed her body provocatively against his. "We ended up getting naked right there," he recalls. "We had sex in the entryway. We didn't even get past the couch."

Liz had managed to make him forget about his new girlfriend for the duration of the sex act. But she didn't change his mind. He continued to see Cari. He didn't mention his encounter with Liz to Cari. It wasn't as if he were cheating on her, because they were not exclusive. Still, he wouldn't have sought Liz out for sex. In his mind, his relationship with Liz "was over," but when she threw herself at him, he figured it was "one last fling." He admits that it was fun, but that his attitude about their parting could be summed up in a few short words: "Whatever. Goodbye. Here're your pots and pans!"

Liz saw things differently, though she tried not to seem desperate. On the afternoon of November 10, she emailed him and asked: *If sometime, not saying right now, but if I felt like it, would you be comfortable as friends grabbing a drink or dinner or both sometime? Like I said, not sure when, kind of busy next few weeks, just seeing if you'd be comfortable with it.*

Even as she attempted to set up a date with Dave, Liz was trying to make it appear that it would happen only if *she* felt like it, and that *she* might be too busy for *him*. There would come a day when a prosecutor would ask Dave if he went out for that drink with Liz, and he would testify that he was certain that he had, and that while it *was* during the time that he had been seeing Cari, he did not recall the exact day.

Only one person in Dave's world was aware that something horrific was about to happen that November 2012. None of the others would realize until much, much later that the sequence of ordinary events would one day be scrutinized. He had no way of knowing he'd be asked to recollect times and dates of seemingly trivial things, or that they would hold any more significance than any other myriad occurrences in the thousands of mundane days of his life.

Dave Kroupa would wish mightily that he could step back in time and change those events, that he could relive those days but do so with a superhuman ability to recognize evil.

CHAPTER FIVE

WHEN SAM CARTER ASKED to be her friend, Cari Farver wasn't sure what to think. She didn't recognize him, but he seemed to know her. He didn't accost her on the street, but through a popular venue in cyberspace. Facebook. Sixty-eight percent of adult Americans use the online social network, according to the Pew Research Center, an established "Fact Tank," that gathers data via polls and demographic research. While two thirds of us use Facebook, most of the remaining one-third have at least heard of it, though they are often confused by talk of "walls," "likes," "shares," and "friending."

The walls on Facebook are simply pages that fill our computer screens when we click on prompters. Each Facebook user has their own wall where they can post things such as photographs, opinions, jokes, and videos. Facebook friends are users whose pages connect to each other. They become friends when one user sends another a "friend request," and it's accepted, but requests can also be rejected. Most Facebook friendships stem from relationships outside of the cyberworld. They know each other most often because they are family, real-life friends or have met in school or at jobs, past or present, though many connect on the site because they are on the friends' list of mutual Facebook friends.

"Likes" are thumbs up icons that users click on to indicate they approve of a post. "Shares" are posts that friends copy and add to their own Facebook walls by clicking the share icon. They can also type comments beneath their friends' posts and send each other private messages.

While some users rarely log on, others spend hours interacting each day, sometimes so compulsively they post photographs of their meals. Facebook can be a friendly place where cute pet photos receive many "likes" and kind comments. It can also be an aggravating place where offensive or political posts incite verbal wars with users snarking at each other in the comments section. This often results in "unfriending."

Facebook, which boasted a billion active users in the fall of 2012, can be a convenient place for people to connect with each other, but it can also be dangerous. Scammers go phishing there, taking on fake identities in order to steal, or in some cases molest or kill. While no one can be physically harmed *in* cyberspace, criminals lie in wait there, constantly contriving new ways to lure victims out into the real world where they can prey upon them.

Did Cari feel a ripple of warning when Sam requested her friendship? There was nothing overtly sinister about him. His photo showed an attractive fortyish guy with thick black hair. He wore a dark suit with a bright red tie, and he leaned toward the camera with a friendly smile of straight, white teeth. He appeared respectable enough, but it was odd that his profile said he was from Cari's hometown. Macedonia had a population of just 240, and she knew everyone there, but she didn't recognize him. Odder still was the fact he spelled the name of his alleged hometown wrong. Mecedonia with an "e," rather than Macedonia with an "a."

Most people would have hit the ignore button and rejected the guy. Cari, however, never wanted to hurt anyone's feelings. She glanced at Sam's wall and saw that he'd posted several photographs of familiar places in Macedonia. She didn't reject Sam's friend request but didn't accept it either. What if she *did* know Sam, maybe from a forgotten encounter years earlier? She would give him a chance to refresh her memory rather than reject him outright. Early in the morning on November 13, she sent him private message. *Do I know you?* She had spent the night with Dave.

In fact, she was spending several days with him because she was in the midst of a time-consuming project at work. West Corporation was so close to Dave's apartment that Cari could have walked there

if she had chosen to. By skipping the commute to and from Macedonia, she was able to shave nearly two hours off her day. Meanwhile Maxwell was happy to stay with his grandmother.

Cari's mom and stepfather, Nancy and Mark Raney, also lived in
Macedonia. They were very close to Max and promised Cari they'd
make sure he got to school. She was relieved to know he was in
good hands but a little bit frustrated that the work project demanded
such long hours because she would have to miss his football game
that week.

Max was an active kid, and his mother not only attended all of his
football games, she was also there for his track tournaments, basket-
ball and baseball games. Her supervisor had assured her she wouldn't
miss too many games. The hours would let up when the project was
completed.

At least it had worked out well that Dave lived close to West Corp
and had invited her to stay with him. The relationship was still fresh
and exciting, and in the two weeks since their first date, they'd spent
a lot of hours together and hadn't had a disagreement. Though Dave
had yet to find flaws in Cari, he realized people are on their best behavior at the start of relationships. Obviously, she was brilliant and
gorgeous, and he could tell by the way her eyes shined when she
spoke about her son that she was a dedicated mom. But only the passage of time can reveal true character.

If he *had* known Cari better, he would have been even more impressed. She was tenderhearted and loyal, and one of her most ad-
mirable traits was her tolerance for all types of people, no matter
how strange their idiosyncrasies. A defender of the underdog from
the time she was a little girl, she stood up to bullies on the play-
ground when they picked on other kids.

Cari's mom recalls that as a child she was naturally fastidious and
always kept her room neat, but she never criticized others' sloppi-
ness. When Cari was eleven years old and babysitting for a family
they didn't know well, "She called me and said, 'Mom, there's not
much to eat here, and the kids are hungry!'"

Nancy rushed over with cookies for the children, and when she
walked into the house, she was shocked. It was the filthiest home

she had ever seen. "I walked into the place, and it was just awful," she says, remembering the garbage piled up in the corners and the sink stacked high with dirty dishes.

Cari must have noticed the mess, but she did not say one word about it to her mother. She was too nice of a girl to speak badly about anyone, even when they were out of earshot. Almost anyone else would have made a snide comment, but not Cari. She didn't say mean things about people because she thought kindly of everyone. Her nonjudgmental attitude was one of the things that made her many friends love her so much. They knew they could tell her anything, and she wouldn't criticize them or raise her eyebrows. She listened, and she offered advice only if they asked for it.

It is a tragic irony that the kindest people are most easily manipulated by those with dark intentions. Cari had probably never thought about that and what it might mean for her. She was certainly not worrying about it on the morning of Tuesday, November 13. She got up very early with Dave because he had to be at work by 6:30, and she immediately fired up her computer and started working on the coding that her bosses expected her to complete soon.

Six years later, Dave still remembers his last glimpse of Cari that morning. "She was on the couch in her pajamas, with her laptop out. She had all of her work-related stuff surrounding her on the couch." Cari was focused on something on her computer screen. "She showed it to me, but I didn't understand it," he says, remembering how impressed he was by her ability to grasp the complexities of computer coding.

Dave went out the door, headed to Hyatt Tire, at around 6:25, telling Cari he'd see her that night. She seemed as happy and carefree as always, and he was looking forward to the end of his workday, so they could spend the evening together. If anyone had told him right then and there that he would soon come to detest her, he wouldn't have believed it. And neither would those who loved her.

When Cari Farver didn't show up for work on November 13, her supervisor, Colleen Whitner, was puzzled. Cari was one of West Corp's most reliable employees, and she always alerted them if she was going to be delayed. Colleen discovered that Cari had called in at 6:15 A.M. with an update on the coding she was writing. Cari was to verify the accuracy of her work upon her arrival, and her coworkers were counting on her. Her input was crucial if they were to make the deadline for the next step of production.

Cari had not made an appearance by mid-morning, so Colleen called her but got her voice mail. Where was she? Had she fallen back to sleep after making the early morning call? Had she gotten sick? If so, why hadn't she called? Colleen left a message and continued to phone her throughout the day, but there was no response.

Cari's devices left a trail of digital footprints that morning. Her laptop logged onto Facebook early and logged off at 6:42 A.M. At 9:54, her phone logged onto Facebook, and an odd action was taken. David Kroupa was unfriended. In other words, he was deleted from Cari's Facebook friends' list.

About twenty minutes later, he received a text. He recognized Cari's number and was startled by the message. "She was asking if we should move in with each other. She already knew I didn't want that! I said, 'No.' Within twenty seconds, I got a text back that said, 'Fine. Fuck you. I'm seeing somebody else. Don't contact me again. I hate you. Go away.' That sort of thing. I had no idea how to feel about it at the time. It was out of left field, and I was very busy at work, so I didn't have time to contemplate it. I put my phone down."

When Dave returned to his apartment that night, he was apprehensive. Would Cari be there? He glanced around. It was so quiet. The only sound was the faint hum of the refrigerator, and the rooms felt emptier than ever. There was no trace of her. It was almost as if she had never been there, almost as if she had been nothing more than a pleasant daydream.

He wasn't really surprised to find no sign of her because she wasn't in the habit of leaving things behind even when she planned to return. Unlike Liz who left her toothbrush next to his, her clothes hanging in his closet, and her pots and pans in his cupboards, Cari always carefully packed everything up and took it away with her in her rolling luggage. "When she left, everything went with her. She didn't leave a bobby pin."

Cari's abrupt breakup with him was disturbing. How could she have changed so completely? How could she be so mellow, so reasonable, and so optimistic when he went out the door that morning and then turn so crazy and hostile four hours later? Determined not to let it bring him down, he decided to be philosophical about it. "I thought, 'Whew! I dodged a bullet. I exchanged stories with guys at work about similar situations that they've had. So, I was just happy it didn't drag on any longer."

"Happy" was probably too cheerful of a word for how he felt. More accurately, he was *relieved* that he hadn't been swept up into unwelcome drama. The fact that this promising relationship had imploded so quickly proved to him that he had been right to swear off commitment and the big stinking mess that often came with it. Though he tried not to show it, the breakup stung. He forced himself to consider the bright side. It was over, and it kind of hurt, but he would never have to think about her again.

If only it were that simple.

Someone else was becoming increasingly concerned about Cari's seemingly erratic behavior. Her mother. Nancy Raney knew her better than anyone in the world. Though she normally talked to her every day, two days had gone by with no word from her except for a puzzling text. On the same day that Cari's supervisor was bewildered by her absence and Dave had received the weird breakup message, Nancy also got a text. She glanced at her phone and saw it had come from Cari's number. "It said she was going to take a new job. That shocked me, because I thought she was happy with the job she had." When Cari had last discussed her job with her mother, she'd told her she loved it but was extremely busy with a work project she was racing to finish, so she could enjoy her brother John's wedding in the upcoming weekend.

John was actually Cari's half-brother, the son of Nancy's first husband, Dennis Farver, but none of them thought in terms of half or full. They were all family. Even Dennis and Nancy, both remarried, got along splendidly and sometimes celebrated holidays together. Everyone was looking forward to the wedding. Maxwell had been invited to be an usher, and Cari was so proud her handsome son was going to be in his uncle's wedding. But she knew it would be bittersweet. Her father was dying of stomach cancer, and Dennis was declining so rapidly that the wedding date had been moved, so he could be there. John and Hillary had wanted a summertime wedding, but it was more important to them to have John's father there. Dennis was in hospice and not expected to live long.

Cari and her father were very close, and it hurt her to see him so sick. She took Max to see his grandfather as often as possible, and they put on cheerful faces to make the visits pleasant for the dying man. Everyone knew that this wedding could be the last time the family was together.

After the Tuesday text announcement about Cari changing jobs, there was no more word from her. Nancy repeatedly tried to call her. "We needed to know when she was going to pick up Max." Cari and Max had planned to drive to Des Moines, Iowa, for the wedding. They were to go to the rehearsal dinner Friday, spend the night in the hotel Cari had reserved, and attend the wedding on Saturday. "I was getting really concerned," Nancy says. "Friday came, and we hadn't heard from her."

While Cari's father made it to the rehearsal dinner, he was too sick to attend the wedding. Both Dennis and Cari's absences were disturbing to the family. Dennis's absence they understood, but Cari's made no sense. Where was she? Had she been in an accident? Max was especially troubled, and throughout the wedding and reception, he found himself repeatedly turning to look at the door, willing his mother to walk through with a reasonable explanation as to why she was so late and why she hadn't been in touch.

Not only did Cari miss the wedding, she didn't show up for a baby shower she was expected to host and failed to alert the expectant mother, her close friend, Amber Jones. She'd said nothing to Amber about postponing or canceling the shower. All that week, Nancy waited near her phone. Surely, she would hear from Cari any minute. But the minutes dragged on, melting into hours and then days. "I had feelings all that week that something was terribly wrong. By Friday, I decided something was definitely wrong, and we reported her missing."

An officer from the Pottawattamie County Sheriff's Office came to Nancy's house and took down the information, but it was obvious he didn't share her sense of urgency. The fact Cari had missed a baby shower and wedding and hadn't talked to her mother for a few days didn't register as serious as far as he was concerned. He pointed out she was a grown woman and didn't need to check in with her mother. If Cari chose to take a trip without telling anyone, then that was her choice. Nancy told him that of course she knew Cari had a *right* to take off, but she hadn't done that. "It was really frustrating," Nancy stresses. "I *knew* something had happened to my daughter, but the police wouldn't believe me."

While maternal instinct is the most powerful of intuitions, it's not unusual for a mother's concerns to be ignored. Cari's mother was not the first woman in the throes of panic to be politely dismissed by those in a position to help. Nancy could tell by the way the officer's eyes glazed over that he thought she was paranoid, and maybe a bit of a nut. She wished it were true. She would have given anything to be proven wrong.

CHAPTER SIX

IT WOULD BE A VERY LONG TIME before investigators seriously considered Nancy's fears, and a very long time before they scrutinized Cari's Facebook activity and became aware of the significance of the message exchange between the missing woman and Sam Carter's pages. In the interim, the conversation might as well have taken place in a vacuum. It unfolded in private mailboxes and couldn't be viewed by Facebook "friends."

At first glance, it appeared so ordinary it sounded like a million other Facebook exchanges. In answer to Cari's November 12 question asking if she knew him, Sam Carter's message two days later explained they'd attended Iowa Western Community College together. The response from Cari's page said simply, *I remember you.* Despite his alleged college education, Sam's reply contained a blatant grammar error: *You still as pretty.*

His spelling was as bad as his grammar, investigators would note when they saw the misspelling of Macedonia. Detectives would also notice that Cari had rejected a friend request from someone named Amber Mildo, just a week before Sam's request was accepted. Amber's profile photo depicted a slender blonde, about age thirty, with her eyes hidden behind oversized shades.

Why had Sam's request been accepted but Amber's rejected? According to their Facebook pages, both had ties to Macedonia, and oddly *both* had spelled it wrong. Mecedonia instead of Macedonia. The misspelling of the town's name wasn't the only thing that made the interaction with Amber suspect. One hour after Cari Farver rejected her, Amber posted that she "was partying it up in Mecedonia [sic]." Residents would laugh at that, but not because of the spelling error. "Party and Macedonia" is an oxymoron, for Macedonia is "small-town family life" at its tamest.

Macedonians are proud of their Main Street of tenderly cared-for historic buildings that house a few shops, a restaurant, a community theater, a museum, the Post Office, and City Hall. Everybody in Macedonia knows everybody else, and nobody there knew Amber Mildo or saw her "partying it up" on November 7 or any other day. While Amber Mildo was unknown, everyone in Macedonia was familiar with Cari. Her roots in the town wend back generations, most notably through the Bisbee line. Nancy, a Bisbee by birth, grew up in Macedonia, and so did her parents, her grandparents, *and* some of her *great*-grandparents.

The blood of those who came before us flows through our veins, and in Cari's case, we can look at family history and see certain traits passed on, generation after generation. While intelligence and physical attractiveness are among the family's obvious traits, their compassion is the most endearing. Kind hearts run in the Bisbee family.

Is kindness inherited?

Apparently so, according to the findings of a recent study. In November 2011, *The Huffington Post* reported on an international study conducted by researchers from a number of colleges, including the University of California at Berkeley. The results of the intense genetic analysis revealed that a gene variation does indeed appear to be linked to caring. Whether or not empathy is inherited or learned, the genesis of Cari's kind heart can be traced back to her great-great grandmother, Anna Sophia Meyer Reichstein. Anna, born in October 1871 in Strawberry Point, Iowa, was known for her generosity.

Anna's German born uncle, Henry Meyer, was only nine when he became ill and developed a fever so high it caused permanent brain damage. His intellect stunted, Henry never learned to speak English or to read or write. Uncle Henry was childlike, and Anna felt protective of him. He couldn't live on his own, so when his parents died, she took him in. He was thirty-six years older than his niece, but he called her Mama.

Anna and her husband, Frank Reichstein, married in 1891 and

lived on a big farm in Grove Township, Iowa. They had eight children—nine counting Uncle Henry! Three babies were born within their first four years of marriage: Lillie, Amiel, and Lonnie. The rest of the children arrived with at least three years between them: Gail, Henry "Scoop," Mabel, Etta, and Beulah.

The sixth child, Mabel Marie Reichstein Bisbee, was Nancy's grandmother. Many years ago, Mabel shared her memories via tape recorder and marveled at how devoted her mother had been to all of the people she cared for. Mabel recalled that Uncle Henry liked to sit by the stove as "Mama" worked in the kitchen. Uncle Henry "always carried the wood, and we always had plenty. But the trouble was that he always sat right there by the stove, and when Mama was baking, she had to watch him like a hawk. He'd put in too much fuel and burn it up."

Mabel, too, was fond of the elderly man, and she remembered how he'd sing the babies to sleep, crooning in German, as he held them and swayed in the old wicker rocking chair. He continued with the tradition long after Mabel felt she was too old for it, but she went along with it, so she wouldn't hurt his feelings. Everyone could see that Henry wanted to be helpful, but it was difficult for him to communicate, so "Mama was about the only one who could talk to him."

Kind-hearted Anna also welcomed a homeless man—an out-of-work carpenter who Frank had hired to run the threshing machine. When the harvest season was over, he asked Frank if he could stay. "Well Gee-whiz," Mabel recalled, "Mama had a house full of kids! Papa said, 'You'll have to go ask my wife.' He went in and asked Mama, and she wouldn't turn him out." The man stayed for seventeen years, and though it felt crowded at times, the Reichsteins were good to him and treated him like family.

Mabel inherited her parents' compassion, and she, too, developed a reputation for her generosity. She fell in love with Bret Beem Bisbee, a man every bit as kind as she was. They married in February 1923 when she was twenty and Bret was twenty-one. They were living on the south side of Macedonia near the railroad tracks when The Great Depression hit. Hobos rode the rails, stowaways in empty boxcars, and a steady stream of them hopped off on the south side of Macedonia. From there, they walked to town where they could spend a night in jail and get a free meal.

Word soon got out that a nice lady who lived near the railroad tracks never turned away a hungry person who knocked on her door. It was Mabel, of course. She and Bret had their own cows, and they were happy to share the milk. Mabel handed each man a thick slice of home-baked bread with sugar and a glass of milk. So many vagrants showed up that sometimes it seemed there wouldn't be enough food to go around, but Mabel somehow always managed to feed everyone.

Mabel and Bret had four children, including Nancy's father, Max. They eventually moved away from the house by the tracks and bought a home closer to town. The new Bisbee house would stay in the family for decades. It would one day be Cari's house, and she loved the fact that Mabel's old dresser held a place of honor in her bedroom.

Nancy wished that Cari could have met her Great-Grandpa Bret. He died at age seventy before Cari was born. "Grandpa had rheumatic fever when he was a kid and had an enlarged heart. I don't believe his childhood was as loving and caring as my grandmother's. As he was getting better, his father made him work on the farm, even though he probably shouldn't have been working so hard. It affected his health for the rest of his life."

Mabel, however, lived till she was ninety-six, nearly three decades without Bret. Cari had twenty-four years to bond with her great-grandmother Mabel, and the two were close. Mabel could expertly twist Cari's fine blond hair into a magnificent French braid, something Nancy admits that she could never master. "Grandma had a way with all of her grandkids. In all of my life, I never heard her say anything cross or bad about anyone. She never raised her voice. She was a very special lady."

Though Cari had not met Great-Grandpa Bret, she heard lots of stories about him from her mother. Nancy looked up to him and was so proud to share a Fourth of July birthday with her grandfather. "My grandpa loved kids. He was a bus driver the entire time I was in school here. All the kids loved riding on his bus," she says, emphasizing it was easy for him to keep the peace because the kids respected him too much to misbehave.

While Cari inherited the Bisbee heart of gold, she got her musical talent from her Grandma Ella Luanne Clark, who always went by Luanne and became a Bisbee when she married Max. Not only

could Luanne sing, she played the piano. She studied vocal performance at Simpson College in Indianola, Iowa, and mesmerized au-
diences with her beautiful soprano voice. While she sometimes
performed in public arenas, her stage was most often Macedonia's
Methodist Church where she was frequently called upon to sing at
special events.

Her talent was actually passed down daughter to daughter—from
Luanne to Nancy to Cari. From the time Cari was a tiny girl, she and
her mom would sing along with tapes of their favorite musicians,
Billy Joel, Emmylou Harris, and Ricky Lee Jones. "We would dance
around the house singing, and when we listened to music in the car,
we sang at the top of our lungs!" They harmonized beautifully and
knew they sounded good. They were talented singers and actresses,
and though neither pursued careers in the arts, they were active in
their community theater. Nancy performed there recently, playing a
nun in *Sister Act*, and Cari also performed there over the years. A
framed 1985 photograph hanging in the theater shows Cari, at age
eleven, among the costumed cast members of *The Miracle Worker.*
"She played one of Helen Keller's friends," Nancy recalls. "When
she was in fifth or sixth grade, she played the wicked stepmother in
Cinderella. She was a really good wicked stepmother!"

Both Cari and Nancy loved Macedonia and The Grist Mill Theater, a creative venue that thrives because of community effort. The
residents who aren't acting in, directing, or designing costumes and
sets for the plays can be counted on to fill the audience seats. Some
out-of-towners show up to watch the plays, and though they're welcomed, it's apparent that they don't live there. With a population
under 250, with many second and third generation residents, Macedonians notice outsiders. Yet a stranger with malice on the mind
slipped into town unseen on a cold night in November 2012. Most
likely it was too late at night or *too early in the morning* for potential witnesses to be awake and watching.

Just as it would be years before detectives became aware of the
Facebook interactions with Sam Carter and Amber Mildo, it would
also be years before they realized that the damage the stranger did
that night held special significance. The troublemaker went to Cari's
house, the very house that had once belonged to Bret and Mabel Bisbee, and targeted her Ford Explorer. The black SUV had been in

pristine condition, but after the defacing "had silver spray paint scribbles, all over the hood, down the side of the front fender, and a long key scratch down the side," her son recollects.

Maxwell Farver isn't sure which night the vandal struck, but it was Sunday, November 11, when he and his mother worked together for six hours, wiping the paint off of the car. They used WD-40 and managed to get all but a bit of the paint off. Nancy stopped by their house that day and saw them working. She noted her daughter wore her signature do-rag tied around her head as she scrubbed. "She was happy. She was upset that the car had been painted," but was otherwise cheerful.

Cari posted about the vandalism on Facebook. A couple of days later, around the time that Dave Kroupa was deleted from her friend list and Sam Carter was accepted, Cari appeared to make a brief comment beneath her own earlier post about the destruction: *It turned out to be just kids.*

There were no other details—nothing said about *which* kids had damaged her car, how they were caught, or if they'd been ordered to make restitution. Neither Nancy nor Max knew how this Facebook revelation had come about. Cari had said nothing to them about learning kids were responsible. But the vandalism of the Explorer was not something Cari's family dwelled upon. It had been a mean "prank" and very annoying, but they would not connect it to her disappearance for some time to come.

With virtually no evidence Cari was in danger, her case was not a priority for Pottawattamie County law enforcement. They processed her report, and she officially became a missing person, with her information entered into the database for the National Crime Information Center (NCIC). Now, if a cop anywhere in the U.S. should encounter her and run her driver's license info, she would instantly pop up in the search results as a missing person.

Cari Lea Farver was one of 661,593 people reported missing in the United States in 2012. By the end of the year, all but 2,079 would be accounted for. It was an average year, as far as missing person cases go. As usual, many of the absent adults had not met with danger, but had taken off for their own reasons. Once located, many were surprised to learn anyone had been worried.

Law officers are aware of the statistics and can't be faulted for playing the odds when it comes to the level of priority they place upon the cases of missing, able-bodied adults. They will search *immediately* for missing children. And if an adult disappears under suspicious circumstances, they act quickly. Though police had yet to grasp it, those close to Cari realized her absence *was* suspicious. Even so, her relatives were confused. They had no actual proof she wasn't the one texting them.

In the middle of that bleak winter, only one thing was certain. People were afraid. While Cari's family was afraid *for* her, David Kroupa was growing afraid *of* her. As it turned out, the nutty texts he'd received at work on Tuesday, November 13, did not signal the end of the drama. Within a few days after the hostile breakup text, he began to receive more nonsensical, angry texts, all from Cari's number. The messages were riddled with blatant grammar and spelling errors and focused on Liz, calling her a "fat, ugly whore."

The first time one of the vulgar texts popped up, Dave blinked, unsure if he was reading it right. Cari had appeared unaffected when Liz interrupted their first date. Had it been an act? Was she in reality obsessed with him and psychotically jealous of Liz? Had she been only pretending when she expressed a desire to remain free? If so, how had she managed to appear so confident and strong while harboring such a dark and unpredictable side to her character?

David was not the only one with questions. When Liz called to inform him that his "crazy ex" was harassing her, she wanted to know how in the world the nut had gotten her phone number. How had she gotten her email address? And how did she know where she *lived*? He was shocked when Liz told him that not only had she been getting threatening emails and texts, but that the troublemaker had apparently broken into her garage and painted the words "Whore from Dave" on the wall.

He hadn't really expected to see Liz again, but now he was compelled to meet with her to discuss the alarming situation. He sheepishly apologized when she told him how upsetting it was to be dragged into his mess. He couldn't fault her for being miffed, and he was grateful she didn't drop the blame entirely upon him. The world was filled with nuts, she acknowledged, and it was their bad luck to encounter one—though if he'd just been satisfied with what he had then they wouldn't be in such a horrible situation.

He listened quietly as Liz described the vandalism she had come home to. In addition to the graffiti on the garage wall, some old checks had been taken from the garage. She reported the vandalism and theft to the Omaha Police Department.

If Dave had any doubt about the identity of the perpetrator of the crimes, those vanished when they both received an email, allegedly from Cari, gloating over her handiwork in Liz's garage. Liz's missing checks were tied to a now-defunct account, but she said it bothered her someone could write bad checks in her name, even if they were invalid. One of the checks in question surfaced, or rather an *image* of it did. It was nearing midnight on Saturday, November 17, when a photo of a signed check for $5,000 was sent to Nancy's phone, along with another text message. The check was made out to Cari, signed in Liz's legal name, Shanna Golyar, and the notation indicated it was for the purchase of Cari's bedroom set. The accompanying text, allegedly from Cari, explained she'd sold her bedroom set and instructed Nancy to allow the buyer in to pick up her purchase. Apparently, the picture of the check was "proof" the furniture was paid for.

Cari's bedroom furniture was not an actual set, though it looked as if it could be because she'd selected pieces that complemented each other. Great-Grandma Mabel's antique dresser was so cherished that it was hard to believe Cari would willingly let it go. Nancy sent a return text: *I need to hear your voice first, so I know it's really you.* She wasn't about to let a stranger into Cari's home to take her possessions. Not only did she doubt that Cari had sold her furniture, she was almost certain she wasn't the one texting her. Nevertheless, Nancy was shocked when the texter got so mad at her refusal that they lashed out, accusing her of being a bad mother and too controlling.

"It got really nasty. At that point, I got a little angry." She felt a flash of annoyance at Cari as she pictured her daughter tapping out the hostile words, but her irritation was immediately washed away by guilt. "This *can't* be Cari!" Nancy reminded herself. The daughter she knew would never treat her like this. "I couldn't find her, and I couldn't talk to her, and I had all of these feelings bouncing around. I was not in a good place."

The messages, laced with rage, sounded nothing like Cari. But it was not the hostile attitude that spooked Nancy the most. Nor was it the claim she had sold the furniture she was so fond of. Nancy was most alarmed by the *grammar.* "Cari was meticulous with her grammar and spelling. Texts and emails had to be perfect, or she'd correct them." The sloppy texts were practically proof that someone had commandeered her daughter's phone.

Though it was very late, Nancy didn't hesitate to call the Pottawattamie Sheriff's Office again. Deputy Karl Rhyster was working the graveyard shift and arrived quickly. He appeared unmoved when she showed him the odd texts. He didn't seem concerned when Nancy stressed that her daughter's grammar was impeccable and that she'd never send such sloppy texts.

While he was courteous, it was obvious he doubted missing commas and misspelled words warranted immediate action. Considering the limited information available to him, his response was appropriate. Deputy Rhyster took down the information and asked Nancy to forward the image of the check so investigators could look into it.

At some point in her exchanges with police, Nancy mentioned that Cari suffered from anxiety and had been diagnosed with bipolar disorder, a mental illness marked by extreme mood swings, formerly known as manic depression. While some suffering from the disorder display outrageous behavior, that had never been the case with Cari. Nancy wasn't so sure the doctor had gotten it right.

As of this writing, there are no definitive physical tests to diagnosis bipolar disorder. Cari's diagnosis was based upon symptoms she'd described to her doctor, not on the results of blood tests or brain scans. Cari had seen more than one doctor, and none of the others had labeled her bipolar.

As for Cari's anxiety, Nancy remembers times when Cari suffered terribly. According to the Anxiety and Depression Association of America (ADAA), over forty million Americans over the age of eighteen are affected by anxiety. Cari's bouts were severe but not unusual, considering that about one in five people struggle with the disorder. But when police learned about Cari's bipolar diagnosis, they latched onto it, certain they understood what had transpired. They were very familiar with the scenario, they told Nancy. Her daughter had flipped out. They saw it all the time, especially when someone with a mental illness stopped taking their meds.

Could they be right? Had Cari lost her marbles? It was hard for Nancy to picture, because Cari had never before behaved in an irrational fashion, but she *had* left her medication behind. The bottle of pills still sat on a shelf in Cari's bathroom medicine cabinet. The term "mental illness" technically covers a wide range of issues, including depression and anxiety, but it seemed too extreme of a label to attach to somebody as reasonable as her daughter.

Though she realized that chemical imbalances resulting in mental illness are nothing to be ashamed of, Nancy doubted her daughter had had a breakdown. But if she *had*, then at least there was hope. It meant she was still alive. She could recover and come home. The idea of a mental breakdown was easier to accept than the grimmer alternatives. The possibilities swirled around, making Nancy dizzy with confusion. Each scenario was devastating, yet some were worse than others. What if someone was holding Cari against her will, forcing her to send the odd texts? If that was the case, was she deliberately making grammar and spelling errors to signal something was wrong? Had Cari been abducted by human traffickers? Nancy shuddered and tried not to imagine it. The moment the worried mother dismissed one frightening idea, another horrendous possibility took its place.

Had Alec, the unstable ex from Cari's past, kidnapped her? That didn't seem likely, because he hadn't been around for years—not since 2008 when Cari suspected he'd broken into her garage. He had settled down after being served with a restraining order. Nancy doubted that Alec had anything to do with what was going on now, but it was not out of the realm of possibilities. If Alec or anyone else *were* holding her hostage, were they feeding her? Seeing to her basic needs? Were they hurting her?

She also wondered about the guy Cari had been staying with in Omaha. *Dave.* Could he be behind her disappearance? Nancy didn't know that he, too, was troubled by hostile text messages sent from Cari's phone. While aware of each other's existence, neither Nancy nor Dave knew each other's last name or phone numbers. Nancy would have been shocked to learn that he believed her kind and gentle daughter had sent threatening texts and vandalized property. And Dave was not about to track down Cari's mother to tattle on her as if she were a child who had misbehaved. He expected Omaha police to handle the criminal complaints, though Liz's report of vandalism and theft had yet to result in an arrest.

Two separate law enforcement agencies in two different states were conducting two entirely different types of investigations, and neither agency was aware of the other's case. Iowa had Cari's missing person case, while Nebraska was investigating the vandalism and theft of checks. Neither Iowa nor Nebraska investigators had reason to believe they were dealing with serious matters. Police in Iowa suspected Cari had left on her own accord. As for the Nebraska police, they figured Liz's complaint about the break-in was an isolated incident. It wasn't yet clear that the two cases were connected and that they involved a devastating crime. The cases were as muddled as two jigsaw puzzles jumbled together with half of the pieces lost. Neither police agency should be blamed for failing to piece the mess together quickly.

CHAPTER SEVEN

ON MONDAY, NOVEMBER 19, three days after Nancy reported Cari missing, the case was assigned to Pottawattamie County Deputy Sheriff Randal Phyllips. By 2012, he'd worked in law enforcement for a dozen years and had handled his share of missing persons reports. "A lot of the missing persons cases we get are going to involve kids that are a little defiant, got grounded for something, got the Xbox taken away, and they just don't want to be home," he notes, adding that those cases are usually resolved quickly.

But Cari was no runaway teen. She was a grown woman and devoted mother with a promising career. Had she met with foul play? Phyllips hoped it was a simple case of miscommunication and that they could locate her quickly. He left her a phone message and also sent texts. She did not respond.

Teaming up with Corporal Rob Ambrose, Phyllips reviewed Cari's thin file and then interviewed her supervisor at West Corp. Coworkers had last seen her exactly one week earlier on Monday, the twelfth. Several people had left the building at the same time as Cari that night, and they'd chatted as they walked to their cars. She gave no indication anything was wrong. She'd smiled and said she'd see them in the morning but had not shown up for work the next day.

A couple of days later, the supervisor had received a resignation text, allegedly from Cari, informing her she was moving away and had a new job in Kansas. Cari had lived in Iowa and worked in Nebraska. Had she now moved to yet another state? Investigators hoped that technology would provide the answers. If she was still in possession of her phone, she could possibly be located via cellular tower triangulation. At the time she disappeared, approximately 300,000 cellular towers across the United States were interacting with over 300 million cell phones. All cell phones in use regularly interface with the closest towers, sending signals known as pings. With the cooperation of carriers such as Verizon and Sprint, investigators can track those pings, following them like trails of breadcrumbs.

Though Nancy felt Deputy Rhyster dismissed her concerns, he had made an effort to find her daughter through her cell phone. He'd set the wheels in motion for Verizon to grant permission to the Pottawattamie County Sheriff's Office to access the pertinent files, and the pings revealed that Cari's phone was still in Omaha. On Sunday, November 18, police had reviewed the information and zeroed in on an area a few blocks north of the intersection of West Center Road and 114th Street. The surrounding territory included residential neighborhoods and a busy business district. Police searched the area but saw no sign of Cari or her black Ford Explorer.

By the time Deputy Phyllips had taken over the case on Monday, the pinging revealed that though the phone was still in the same general area, it had traveled about half a mile to the west. The investigator noted that thirteen texts had been sent in the last twenty-four hours. The last one was at 11:00 that very morning, and at that time Cari's phone's pings pointed to a location north of West Center Road, near "the start of a residential area." The pinging still did not pinpoint an address but indicated a neighborhood.

Deputy Phyllips knew Cari was most likely using her Explorer for transportation. "We drove around a lot of the residential streets looking for the vehicle. We also drove through all the parking lots of any apartment complexes and businesses that were in that general area." They didn't find Cari's car, but had been somewhat reassured after learning her employer had received a resignation text. While Phyllips expected to wrap up the case quickly, he was thorough, and he continued to study the clues Nancy Raney had shared with them. He scrutinized the image of the $5,000 check that had been sent to her phone. "It appeared to be a starter check," Deputy Phyllips explains, adding that no name or address was printed on the check itself, though the signature was legible.

The signee was Shanna Golyar. Deputy Phyllips had no idea who she was. At this point, he was still unaware that she'd been dating the same man as the missing woman or that Shanna had reported to Omaha police that checks had been stolen from her garage. When the deputy searched records, he found an address for a Shanna Elizabeth Golyar in Omaha. It was in the vicinity of the cellphone pings, though Cari's phone had pinged north of West Center Street while Shanna lived *south* of West Center Street.

Ambrose and Phyllips went to Shanna's listed address, a split-level rental with a big shade tree in the tiny front yard. As a single mother with a low income, she qualified for the government's Section 8 program and paid a reduced rent. Built in 1966, the house had a floor plan that was popular that decade and nearly identical to the layout of the other homes in the long row on the quiet street. They knocked, but no one came to the door. The deputy left a message, and Shanna called him the following day. "I explained to her that we were conducting a follow-up on a missing person report and told her we were looking for Cari Farver." He soon learned that Shanna and Cari were two corners of a love triangle. They both dated David Kroupa, and Phyllips figured he must be the guy Cari had been planning to stay with when she'd last spoken to her mother.

Liz told him that Cari blamed her for her breakup up with Dave and had been harassing her. As for the $5,000 check, allegedly signed by Shanna, she had a reasonable explanation for that. A checkbook had been stolen from her garage. There was vandalism, too, she added. The intruder had painted "Whore from Dave" on her garage wall. The break-in had left her rattled, Liz told Deputy Phyllips as she gave him Dave's contact info. Dave lived and worked about three miles north of Liz's place. When the investigators stopped by to see him at Hyatt Tire the next day, Dave mentioned that he, too, had been receiving intrusive texts.

The behavior described by Liz and Dave sounded like the actions of a stalker. If Cari was stalking the pair, that would explain why her phone had pinged near Liz's neighborhood. Had the missing woman been lurking near her rival's home, waiting for a chance to pounce? It was possible, of course, that Cari was no longer in possession of her phone, but it seemed unlikely that someone would go to the trouble of impersonating her. If someone had stolen her phone, why in the world would the thief then spend days pestering Dave and Liz,

pretending all the while to be Cari? Police figured that only someone with a personal vendetta would go to that extreme. Detectives
came to the logical conclusion that Cari was jealous and behaving
like the proverbial woman scorned.

Dave was surprised to hear that she had been reported missing,
and he promised to phone Phyllips if she showed up. Dave was disturbed by the avalanche of messages filled with crazy rantings and
wished he could confront her. But his tormentor was in hiding, and
he never so much as glimpsed her.

Shortly after he left the tire store, Deputy Phyllips finally got a
text message from Cari's number: *I don't care about this missing
person report, but I would really appreciate it if you leave Dave
Kroupa out of it. I will be leaving the state. My mother overreacted.
I have been to my house a few times.*

The deputy texted a warning: *If you get stopped even in another
state, you will still be held until this matter is settled.* He was referring to the fact that Cari's missing person file was in the NCIC database and wouldn't be removed until investigators could speak to her
to verify she was okay.

"Cari" responded: *Dave texted me and said you had the sheriff at
his work. Please stop talking to people. I have nothing to say to anyone. I want one person to go away for destroying everything for me.*

That sounded like a threat! It confirmed what Shanna had told
Phyllips about the harassment. "I contacted Shanna and informed
her of the text message and told her she might want to contact the
Omaha Police Department and have a report placed on file."

She seemed grateful for the advice and was quick to tell Dave that
police were worried his ex could harm her. Shanna showed Phyllips
a text Dave had forwarded to her. It had originated from Cari's
phone and referenced the stolen checks: *Well, I've been talking to
my mom on and off, but when I was at Liz's house a few nights ago,
she had some stuff in her garage. I stole a checkbook from her. I
wrote a check for $5,000, and because I haven't gone home in a few
days [my mom] made a missing persons report. LOL. I think she
thinks Liz is involved. [My mom] told me today to go talk to police,
[to inform them] that I am okay, but I don't think so. I hope she is arrested. Then you can't be with her.*

If the text, allegedly from Cari, was to be believed, it was obvious she'd left on her own steam. It also indicated she'd stolen Liz's checks in an effort to frame her. The texter was jealous of Liz's relationship with Dave, and frankly, sounded like she had a screw loose. That fit investigators' theory she'd had a breakdown. From the cops' perspective, it sure seemed that the lady was not in danger as her mother feared but had shirked her responsibilities and was now whiling away her days playing head games.

The games were wearing Dave down. As November wound to a close, he was bombarded with over sixty texts and emails per day. He remembers watching television as he tried to relax after work. Suddenly he got a text: *I see you in the chair with your feet propped up. You're wearing your blue t-shirt.*

Dave was startled. His feet *were* propped up. He glanced down at his shirt and realized with horror that his shirt *was* blue. "That kind of thing happened quite a bit. I'd run outside and look for her." The wooded setting was appealing in the daytime but eerie at night. The grounds were unlit, and the lights on the street did little more than cast shadows. The trees provided too many hiding places. It didn't matter how quickly Dave reacted. The watcher seemed to melt into the darkness, always beyond his reach.

He began to shut the blinds at night, but if someone crept close to the window, they could see him in whatever tiny gap he failed to close. They seemed to delight in reporting this to him. *You're in your robe! You just got out of the shower! I see you!* The stalker was constantly observing him, aware of his every action. Though he would not have been afraid to face Cari, the idea of being spied on was downright creepy.

Every corner of Dave's life was invaded. He was nearly fired when someone called his work phone, only to hang up and call back and hang up again. It went on for an entire day, and his boss was not pleased. The incessant calls tied up the line, making it impossible for customers to get through. Dave also worried about his kids and their mom. Amy was receiving multiple intimidating messages daily, often dozens in a twenty-four-hour period, all from someone claiming to be Cari. Amy was called unflattering names, sworn at and warned to: *Leave Dave alone!* She was uneasy, and somewhat resentful of her ex for inviting a madwoman into their lives.

When his kids visited, Dave watched them closely. Calista was twelve, and Trey, ten, old enough to walk across the grounds to the apartment's clubhouse without supervision. Now he wouldn't let them out of his sight. There was no telling what the bully might do.

Dave went to every nearby shop, restaurant, bar and business, and asked managers and employees to be on the lookout for the lady who was making his life so miserable. He showed them her photo, and they listened, astonished, as he told his story. They all shook their heads. No one had seen her.

Dave and Liz began to date again, seeking each other out for comfort whenever their nemesis struck. Compared to the stress of being stalked, the conflicts he'd once had with Liz seemed trivial. Their tormentor, as usual, was aware when they were together. "Sometimes Liz and I would be hanging out, watching a movie together, and we'd both receive an email." Caught up in the movie, their troubles momentarily forgotten, the sudden alert from their phones was jarring. Liz's phone was usually tucked in her purse across the room when this happened. Only one person contacted them simultaneously. *The stalker.* As their phones chimed in unison, they would stare at each other for a moment, delaying the inevitable. Dave remembers Liz sighing in exasperation as she retrieved her phone. He felt a flash of guilt when her eyes widened in fear as she read the latest threat. As usual, the texter vowed to harm Liz while professing devotion for Dave.

Despite the fact that he hadn't been the one to end his relationship with Cari, the notes he received now expressed romantic feelings for him and didn't acknowledge that there had even been a breakup. She seemed to be in her very own odd realm where reality had been churned inside out. After the garage incident, the texter had written: *So how did Liz like having her life destroyed while she was with you? That's what will happen to everyone else who comes into your life . . .* As usual, the writer pointed out in that message that Liz was a "whore," but ended on a cheerful note: *I hope we can see each other soon.*

Meanwhile, Cari appeared to remain active on Facebook. On November 21, her family was shocked to see a new post. *Moving to Kansas for a great job. Will miss family and great friends.* On November 26, another appeared. *Hey, got a great guy, David Kroupa. Moving down to Kansas. Now if I can get my son to move with me, I'd be so happy.*

Dave had not seen Cari since the day he'd gotten the break-up text, so the reference to them as a couple was another sign the stalker lived in her own warped world. Most alarming to Cari's family was the idea that someone could be planning to take Max. Nancy had also received texts from "Cari," insisting that Maxwell go away with her. She didn't believe that Cari was the one posting on Facebook and texting her, but she couldn't be certain, especially after Max verified that his mother had once mentioned the possibility of moving to Kansas.

Maxwell's life was in Macedonia. He was involved in school activities, and he had friends and a girlfriend. His mother understood that and had always put him first. Even if Cari had toyed with the idea of moving, it couldn't have been an immediate plan because she'd never mentioned it to her mother. It would be very unlike Cari to uproot her son. Either someone was impersonating her or she'd truly lost her mind. Both scenarios could be dangerous for Max. The teen was spooked. He and his mom were extremely close, and he had never *ever* had a reason to be afraid of her, but if this really was his mother doing all of these strange things, she was *not* herself.

The situation was perplexing, but Nancy was sure of one thing. Cari loved her son more than anything. If Cari was no longer among the living, Nancy was certain that her last thought would have been for her child. If her daughter *had* flipped out, Nancy knew that deep down, Cari would want Max protected. The one thing Nancy could do for her was step in and become Max's fiercest protector. Even so, she was overwhelmed with guilt as she and Mark took legal action to become Maxwell's guardians. What if things were not as bad as they seemed, and Cari came home to find she had taken away her rights to her son? Would her daughter ever forgive her for such a betrayal? Nancy's attorney told her not to worry. The guardianship didn't have to be permanent. They could undo it if Cari returned in her right mind.

CHAPTER EIGHT

MARK AND NANCY RANEY became their grandson's guardians on November 29, 2012. The next day was Cari's thirty-eighth birthday. Nancy vividly remembers November 30 in 1974 when she welcomed her baby girl into the world via natural childbirth. The infant was amazingly calm, *so* calm that she woke up only once during her first night home. By her second day on Earth, Cari was sleeping through the night, and she never again interrupted her parents' sleep.

Nancy's first child, Adam, was born about two and a half years before Cari. "He was a beautiful baby—a mama's boy until he was about three." But his temperament was the opposite of his sister's. Nancy loved him every bit as much as she loved Cari, but he was colicky and cried incessantly. "I had postpartum depression after Adam was born." The fact she was sleep deprived didn't help. She laughs as she recalls that she didn't get a single good night's rest the first year of his life. "He would sleep for a couple of hours and then be awake for three or four. When he *did* sleep six hours, I felt like I'd died and gone to Heaven."

Nancy had steeled herself for more sleepless nights with the new baby and was relieved to see how easily Cari slid into a peaceful slumber. The infant was not only relaxed, she seemed surprisingly aware of her surroundings. When friends and family gathered to see the baby for the first time, they commented on her intense gaze. The infant's knowing blue eyes seemed to hold a thousand years of wisdom. Cari looked around, assessing her new environment as if it were familiar to her. She was, some remarked, "An old soul." Nancy didn't argue with them, for she, too, was in awe of the newborn's serene demeanor, and she noted that the baby seemed to be thinking, "Okay, here I am again."

Because she was her second child, Nancy was more aware of Cari's uniqueness. She was the exact opposite of her big brother in many ways. While Adam had been a typical infant and had clung to his mother when he was tiny, Cari was surprisingly independent and adventuresome, but very quiet. "It took Cari a while to start talking," Nancy remembers, adding that her daughter was age three before she talked, and when she did, it was in complete sentences. "It was as if she was waiting until she had everything right before she spoke."

By kindergarten it was apparent that she was brilliant. Her teacher told Nancy it was a challenge to find things to keep the little girl's mind busy, adding "She's so advanced. She's the only one in the class who can read." It was somewhat of a luxury for her to count her among her pupils, because it was almost like having an assistant. At age six, Cari sat down with her classmates, reading books to them as they listened, enthralled. In elementary school, Cari was enrolled in the talented and gifted program. Even among the smartest of the smart, she always rose to the head of the class.

While she had been the dream baby who slept through the night and the brilliant child who kept her room neat, she was no Goody Two-Shoes. She had her rebellious moments when she became a teen. She ruined her mother's thirty-ninth birthday, on the Fourth of July 1990. She can laugh about it now, but Nancy was livid on that sultry summer day when teenage Cari and her friend went out drinking with some boys. Nancy and the other girl's mother were worried sick when their daughters didn't come home that night. The next morning when Cari nonchalantly walked through the front door, Nancy was waiting and said firmly, "You aren't going anywhere for two months!"

Grounded for the rest of the summer, Cari apparently learned her lesson. It was the last time she missed her curfew. She was a spirited teen, and she and her mother had their share of arguments, but they always made up. When Cari went away to college at the University of Kansas, she indulged in the normal amount of partying and was not that excited by her classes, but she did well and never got into trouble.

Overall, Cari had been a pleasure to raise, and her mother and both fathers could attest to that. While she was close to her father, she lived more years with her stepfather, Mark Raney, and she couldn't have loved him more if he *had* been her biological father. While Mark is Nancy's second husband, he was her first love and one of her very first *friends*. "We've known each other since we could communicate." They first played together as toddlers when their parents met at the Methodist church. Mark's parents, Charles and Betty Jane Raney, were a little older than Nancy's parents, but they had a lot in common. The Raneys' four kids were in the same age range as the Bisbees' three.

Charles and Betty built floats for the Macedonia's annual summertime festival, Donia Day, and spearheaded the creation of The Grist Mill Theater. They not only produced, directed, and acted in the theater's plays, they were among the group who helped to *create* the theater. Housed in the building once occupied by the old John Deere Implement store, inside it looks as if it has always been a theater with its heavy stage curtains and rows of plush, red-velvet seats. The seats had been an exciting find. When one of Omaha's grand theaters was remodeled, their old seats were discarded, and Macedonians were thrilled to discover them.

Betty was also among the group credited with rescuing the rock quarry, just north of town. Tucked into a forest of old oaks and cottonwood trees, the quarry's spring-fed lake has been a favorite place for swimmers and picnickers for generations. Many years ago, the owner of the quarry had planned to close it down and fill it but generously agreed to give it to the community when Betty approached him.

Whenever the Raney and Bisbee parents worked together on various causes for their church and community, their kids played together. If it was raining or too cold to be outside, they played checkers or Monopoly or gathered on the floor to watch television—George Reeves in *Superman* or *The Huckleberry Hound Show* and *Yogi Bear* cartoons, all in shades of gray on a small black-and-white TV set.

"I didn't pay much attention to Mark until junior high school," Nancy admits. They had no classes together because he was a year older, but when they hit their teens, they became very aware of each other as they passed in the school corridors. They made a point to linger in the halls in the spots where they knew they would run into each other, and at first tried to make their encounters seem accidental, but it soon became apparent they shared a mutual attraction.

Nancy was bashful, unaware of how pretty she was. Dark haired with a creamy complexion and bright blue eyes, she melted Mark's heart when she smiled—and he knew just how to make her smile! He was the class clown, a daredevil and as outgoing as Nancy was shy. Mark challenged authority and was a mischief-maker, but so charming that the teachers quickly forgave him. He was also an athlete and competed in both wrestling and football, though he was smaller in stature than his teammates. "He was very good looking," Nancy remembers, "but I fell in love with his personality. He doesn't know a stranger, and he can take hold of most any situation."

They went steady from the time she was fourteen through high school. It was the 1960s, and they were drawn to two popular Iowa bands with Beatlesque sounds, The Green Giants and The Rumbles. The Rumbles had started in Council Bluffs as a garage band, and the members of The Green Giants hailed from small towns around Iowa and Missouri. Mark and Nancy's song, however, was the Righteous Brothers' incredibly romantic "Unchained Melody." They often double-dated with other couples, driving long distances to the dances where their favorite bands performed.

After high school, the couple drifted apart when they attended different colleges. Mark studied art in Maryville, Missouri, and Nancy went to business school in Des Moines, Iowa, where she met Dennis "Denny" Farver. "I became infatuated," she recalls. He was charismatic, quick witted, and handsome. "He always looked put together, no matter the situation or event." He put his sense of style to work when employed by a clothing store while going to school. Denny's meticulous grooming was a lifelong habit, and that didn't change when he became terminally ill decades later. "Even when he got sick, he still dressed immaculately."

Nancy was only nineteen, and Denny, twenty-one, when they were swept up in the thrill of the kind of love that comes only to the young and starry-eyed, and they married in the misty autumn of 1970. Soon they had two children, Adam born in the summer of

1972 and Cari in the winter of 1974. Cari was named by her father. He chose the name after watching ten-year-old singer, Carrie Mc- Dowell, debut on Johnny Carson's *Tonight Show* in October 1974 with her extraordinary performance of "Somewhere Over the Rain- bow." Carrie McDowell was adorable, talented and from Iowa—all factors that inspired Denny to select the name for his baby girl, born a few weeks after that Carson episode aired.

Nancy had named Adam, so she bowed to her husband's choice for their daughter. "I wanted her to be a Kelly," she admits. "I let him spell it, too, otherwise it would have been Carrie." The uncom- mon spelling was occasionally frustrating for Cari. When she was a young girl, she was somewhat "upset when she couldn't find her name on a barrette or a bracelet in a store. When she started working and had to wear a nametag, her name always looked like Carl, be- cause it would be spelled out in caps. She even got a letter once ad- dressed to Carl Farvere! She really wasn't pleased with that!" Despite the unusual spelling, Cari liked being named after a famous singer. The singing Carrie was from Des Moines, Iowa, the same city where the young Farver family lived for a while before relocat- ing to Lincoln, Nebraska.

Denny would eventually earn a good living as an insurance actu- ary, but finances were tight early on. "Dennis worked two jobs, and I went back to work when Cari was nine months old." Nancy was an excellent secretary, detail oriented, efficient, and always cheerful. Denny was a little old-fashioned and didn't like the fact his wife worked, but she enjoyed her job, and they needed her income. "Other- wise we couldn't make ends meet."

With the shine of the romance worn off, they realized that they had little in common, and neither was happy in the marriage. Adam was almost four, and Cari eighteen months old when their parents divorced in the spring of 1976. Though it wasn't always easy be- cause sometimes they lived in different cities, Denny and Nancy worked together to make sure their kids felt loved and spent quality time with each of them. Little Adam craved time with his father, and Nancy missed her son terribly during the long periods she lived apart from him, but it was only fair that Denny, a dedicated dad, got an equal role as a parent. Cari was so young when her parents split that she naturally gravitated more toward her mother, but when she got older, she visited her father often, and they formed a strong bond. Nancy was glad about that. "Denny was a very good father," she remarks. "He was great with kids, and his kids looked up to him. He always had time for them."

By the summer of 1979, Nancy had been a single mother for three years, and it had been almost a decade since she and Mark had split up. When they discovered they had both been invited to a friend's wedding in Macedonia, they were excited about seeing each other. Though Mark had had his share of girlfriends, he'd never forgotten his first love and was pleased to learn she was unattached. Nancy took extra care getting ready for the wedding and looked stunning in a white skirt with a sleeveless brown blouse. "It was August, so I had a good tan," she remembers, adding that both she and Cari had always tanned easily. When Nancy's gaze locked with Mark's at the reception, it was immediately clear the attraction was still strong. He asked her out, and the next evening they went to the quarry. It was a hot night, with a bright moon reflected in the calm, black lake. The water was deliciously cool after a scorching day, and they slipped in for a swim. It was romantic and also fun. The first friends and first loves were thrilled to be back together, and it felt right. Mark could still make Nancy laugh, and he was even funnier than she remembered.

Neither of their mothers, however, was enthusiastic about their reunion. Nancy suspects that Betty felt she was too shy for her gregarious son. As for Luanne, she was worried that her divorced daughter was moving too fast. Both mothers were glad to be proven wrong when they saw how happy their kids were. Nancy and Mark were married in a magical outdoor ceremony in the quarry in 1981, at the tail end of the "hippie" era. Cari made an adorable flower girl, in a summer dress trimmed with gingham. Nancy was lovely in a gauzy, off-white ensemble with a flowing skirt as she and Mark faced each other and exchanged vows. Nearly forty years have passed since that summer swim in the moonlight, and they have been together ever since.

Mark was a teacher and good with kids, and Nancy's children took to him instantly. He taught drama and art but realized that his days in that field were numbered when the school lost its funding for their art programs. He ended up working as a salesman for thirty years, selling filters for the engines of diesel trucks, and he was so likeable that he thrived at that job, too. Even as he pedaled filters, the artist in him could not be squelched, and Nancy loved the way he doodled elaborate masterpieces on the paper tablecloths whenever they had to attend boring banquets.

Nothing delighted Mark more than seeing kids happy, and he was so excited about the Barbie House that he got Cari for her ninth Christmas that he roused her hours before she was ready to wake up. She was eleven when she started serving as his chauffeur—but only when it wasn't a school night! He played on a volleyball team, and after the games, the teammates got together at a local bar. Cari often went along, and while the kids ran around playing, their parents drank beer and played cards. "Mark likes his beer," Nancy notes. But he was not about to drink and drive, so Cari drove home. The roads in their little town were long and lonesome and surrounded by cornfields. Very rarely did they encounter another vehicle on the two-mile drive. Cari was a good driver, even as a child, and she got them home safe.

The girl was fearless, always up for any challenge. That didn't change when she grew up, and she didn't hesitate when one of her boyfriends invited her to go skydiving. She bravely leapt from the plane and found the experience thrilling. As is often the case with intelligent people, she grew restless without variety in her life. When she was a teen, she had many boys interested in her, and they would "go together" until she broke up with them. She was always the one who did the breaking up and tended to tire of them quickly, but "she always managed to stay friends with them."

Cari met Max's father, Frank, at the University of Kansas, and while it was at first romantic and wonderful, the relationship fizzled when the excitement did. Cari discovered she was pregnant just as they were breaking up, so they attempted to stay together. Despite their best efforts, it didn't work out. Nancy was worried about how her young daughter would cope with single motherhood. At the time, Cari was working as a secretary, and Nancy advised her to find something more lucrative. "She'd always had a good aptitude for computers" and had a chance to take a special, six-month course but didn't have the five-thousand-dollar tuition. Grandpa Max and Grandma Luanne stepped up and paid for it. Cari gave birth in December 1997, and about ten weeks later, she graduated and "got a tremendous job because of that computer course."

Cari announced that she planned to name her baby after her Grandpa. While Max Bisbee appreciated the sentiment, he was not so certain it was the best thing for the boy. With only three letters, it sounded more like a nickname, and he admitted he had never really liked his own name.

"How do you feel about Maxwell?" Cari asked him.

"Dad was okay with that," says Nancy. "He is so very proud of Maxwell, and now he tells people he is his namesake."

The baby was officially Maxwell but also called Max. When Cari and Maxwell moved in with the Raneys, he became more like a son than a grandson to Mark, who had never had his own biological children. Maxwell's father lived too far away to play an active role in his life, but there was no lack of love and attention from father-figures. His Great-Grandpa Max, Grandpa Denny and Grandpa Mark were thrilled to welcome a new baby, and Cari was pleased her son had a trio of positive male role models.

The instant Cari held her son for the first time it was obvious she would protect him with the ferocity of a lioness guarding her cub. Any qualms Nancy had about how twenty-three-year-old Cari would cope instantly vanished when she watched her with Maxwell. He was her number one concern, and motherhood made her stronger. There were still struggles ahead, but now Cari had a sense of purpose that would never waiver. Over the next years, she would marry and divorce twice, and change occupations several times. When Maxwell was very young, he and Cari moved to Topeka for a couple years, and "It broke our hearts," Nancy remembers. But they moved back to Macedonia, and life finally seemed to be going well for Cari in the months before she disappeared. Her position at West Corp had been a good fit, but some of her earlier choices had baffled her mother. Once, Cari had accepted a job doing office work for a construction company, and Nancy was certain she'd be bored. She was right, and Cari did not stay long there.

At one point, she studied to become a surgical nurse. She got through the classes "with flying colors." Cari had a strong stomach and had never been one to get weak in the knees at the sight of blood. Her training required her to be present during surgeries, and she didn't flinch when the surgeon's scalpel cut into flesh. But there was a problem. Whenever the surgeon *cauterized* flesh, Cari fainted.

Nancy remembers Cari's bewilderment as she confided, "Mom, I don't know what's wrong. I'm not squeamish. That smell just made me pass out. All of the sudden I was waking up on the floor." It was not a one-time thing. *Four times* Cari fainted when she smelled burning flesh. The last time she woke up on the operating-room floor, she looked up into the worried face of her supervisor who was peering down at her. The woman gently suggested, "This might not be the right career for you."

She was right, but Cari was annoyed. Her plans were thwarted by her own inexplicable and peculiar reaction. After she got past her irritation over the wasted hours studying for a profession that could never be, she found humor in the situation and poked fun at herself. Everyone who heard the story laughed along with her. It crossed no one's mind that there was a dark reason for her reaction. Had Cari had a premonition—one she sensed on a visceral level? We'll never know for certain, but considering what came to be, the fainting spells could have been a harbinger of the tragedy to come.

CHAPTER NINE

WHEN THEY RECEIVED A MESSAGE from the maniacal texter telling them the car was missing, the Raneys reported it stolen. The 2005 Ford Explorer was in their names, and they also paid for the insurance. "If it was in an accident, we'd be liable," Nancy explains. That, of course, was the least of their concerns. The car could lead them to Cari. Maybe the police would find it, rolling along the highway with their daughter at the wheel. On Monday, December 3, 2012, they filed a stolen car report. Dave, too, was looking for the Explorer. From his perspective, it was his stalker's car, and if he could find it, he could confront the crazy person who was making his life so miserable. He regularly cruised the neighborhood on the lookout for the black SUV but saw no sign of Cari or her car. If he'd known her better, he'd realize that it was completely out of character for her to turn her back on those she loved, especially at such a crucial time. Her father was nearing the end.

Nancy couldn't bring herself to tell Denny that their daughter was missing. She knew she'd see the pain in her own eyes reflected back at her in his. How would a father, ravaged with cancer, deal with the news his daughter was missing? No one wanted to add another burden to the man's thinning shoulders, but Cari's absence was devastatingly apparent. Denny knew his daughter would never purposely abandon him when he was so ill. He would know something was wrong. He had to be told. Another family member broke the news to him as gently as they could.

On December 7, 2012, Dennis Farver slipped away. Three days

later, Maxwell turned fifteen. His birthday passed with no word from his mom. With both his mother and his grandfather gone, it was a time of great loss for him. How could so much have changed in a year? Only twelve months earlier he had celebrated his fourteenth birthday. His family had been complete then—happy and healthy and excited about the holidays.

Services for Dennis were held on December 12 at the Lutheran Church in Newton, Iowa. Mourners gathered at 1 P.M. Many took their seats, only to find themselves glancing anxiously at the entryway, hopeful that Cari would appear. She did not. It was a horrendous December for Cari's relatives. While most of the families around them were caught up in the spirit of the season, enjoying the holiday lights and cheery Christmas music, it seemed hollow and pointless to Nancy. How could they celebrate without Cari? Nancy and Mark pushed through for Max. They put on brave faces for their grandson, and he did the same for them. They bought Christmas presents for each other and some for Cari, too. They prayed she would be home to open them.

On December 20, the skies opened, releasing an avalanche of white over the Midwest in a snowstorm so powerful that one CNN news reporter wryly noted that the timing was right for the anticipated eve of destruction. December 21, 2012, was the predicted Mayan doomsday, the writer pointed out, and while the furious storm was not exactly the end of the world, it zapped the electricity in nearly half a million homes in thirteen states. Some areas got over a foot of snow, and thousands of holiday travelers found themselves grounded when flights were delayed or cancelled. Iowa's Interstate 35 suffered a thirty-vehicle pileup with fatalities, near Fort Dodge, about a hundred miles north of Des Moines. Drivers' vision was obscured by the blizzard, and they had little control on the icy road, creating a snarled nightmare of crunched metal and human suffering for the Iowa State Patrol to sort out.

In her Macedonia home, Nancy stood at the window, staring out at what might have been a wondrous, white world under different circumstances. Now she worried about the fact that Cari had left her winter coat behind, and she thought, *She could be out there. Is she freezing?* It was hard for Nancy to enjoy the feeling of wrapping her hands around a hot mug of coffee or snuggling under a warm blanket. How could she take pleasure in the warmth when she didn't know if her daughter could do the same?

Dave Kroupa was hunkered down in his apartment. He didn't worry about whether or not Cari was cold. She seemed to be doing just dandy from where he was standing. The snow hadn't slowed his stalker down. He continued to receive dozens of antagonistic emails and texts each day, all from someone claiming to be Cari. What had he done to make her hate him so much? In the space of a couple of hours, she had gone from being what seemed like the perfect woman to a spiteful fouled-mouthed nut. The behavior was so outrageous that Dave surely could not have expected a logical explanation. And yet, he asked for one. Maybe he was hoping that the wonderful woman he had known would shed the craziness and become herself again—if only for a moment—and explain why she had thrown everything away. Dave texted: *Why did you start acting that way? It frankly blows my mind. It all came out of leftfield.*

But there were no explanations, only more ugly words.

It didn't help to block the calls. They came from multiple untraceable numbers. Someone had also gone to a lot of trouble to create numerous email accounts, most with addresses that were variations of Cari's name, some with Dave's name mixed in. The addresses registered with Google included DavesgirlCari, KroupaCari76, JustCari29, and leakroupa. Many times, Dave deleted the emails without opening them. Changing his phone number didn't help. His stalker managed to almost magically find his new number, though he gave it to a short list of people. Liz and Amy told him that they were having the same problem.

It was as if the tormentor were invisible, peering over his shoulder as she obsessed over his every move. Liz dubbed her "Crazy Cari," and they often vented to each other. "We'd both become victims," Dave stresses. "We had something in common that we didn't have with anyone else. We knew each other, and it was easy to talk to each other about the situation." Some of the messages were more disturbing than others. In late December, an email, allegedly from Cari, was sent to Dave. *I really am pregnant. I'm seeing Dr. Michael Woods. I love you, and we need to figure things out for this baby, so please talk to me.*

If Cari *were* pregnant, he was not responsible. "I got fixed a long time ago," he confides. Cari had had a hysterectomy before she met Dave, so the claim was ludicrous, clearly a fantasy of someone out of touch with reality. Liz complained that she, too, had been dragged into the baby drama. She showed Dave an email exchange that started with a message, apparently from Cari: *Dave and I want to provide a happy home for this baby, so I am kindly asking you to please back off and leave Dave alone.*

Liz had responded with a desperate plea: *Listen. Just leave me alone. If you want David that bad, have him. I am so sick of all this drama. I don't want to be in the middle of it anymore. You are terrorizing me, and I don't need it. I like David, but this is way too much. Just leave me alone. Please, I am asking, go away. If seeing David is the problem, then I will stop. I just want you and your craziness to go away. I can't take it anymore.* Liz's email made it clear that "David" was not worth the terror she was forced to endure. Even so, she stuck by him, and he had to give her credit for that. She was proving to be a loyal friend.

Not long after Cari's father passed away, Nancy dreamed of him. Her ex-husband no longer appeared sick. Denny stood before her, strong and vibrant. "Nancy, she's with me," he said gently. She both heard and felt his words, spoken with such intensity that she was yanked from her slumber. Mark was asleep next to her, and she listened to the steady rhythm of his breathing as she realized something wondrous had happened. She had seen Denny, and though he had appeared in a dream, it was *more* than a dream. "It was very vivid," too vivid to be a story her subconscious had created. It was as real as anything she had ever seen or heard in her waking hours. The ache in her heart was soothed by a sudden certainty that Cari was okay. Not here among the living, but in the Afterlife. *Heaven.*

Cari was with her father and Grandma Luanne, her great-grandparents Bret and Mabel Bisbee, and all of those she loved who were no longer here. They were taking care of her, and she could never be harmed again. The "dream" was a gift—not an outright cure for her grief, but a balm that numbed the edges of horror. In many a quiet moment, when she allowed herself to relax, Nancy recalled the love in Denny's voice and again felt that certainty that Cari's soul had survived whatever evil had been done to her.

As much as it helped, the dream was not absolute proof. It didn't banish all of her doubts and fears. She was still plagued with confusion and worry and frustration. Her remaining doubts were amplified by the fact that Nancy did not *want* to believe the dream, for she still possessed a whisper of hope that her daughter walked among the living. The devastated mother still needed answers.

The families of the missing are rooted in place, unable to move forward without knowing the fate of their loved ones. While it hurts to learn someone we care about has died, it hurts more to *not* know what became of them. When we can grieve a death, most of us eventually recover enough to live fulfilling lives and maybe even discover joy again, but if even a slight possibility exists that the absent person is alive, then healing is impossible. The mystery is akin to an open wound incessantly picked at, never allowed to heal.

Is the victim suffering? Waiting to be rescued? Or did they leave voluntarily, not caring about those they left behind? Each of these questions is painful to ponder, and each haunts the relatives of the missing. The unanswered questions would have been agonizing for Cari's family even without the tortuous teasing of the stalker who continually picked at the scab. They were at it again on Sunday, January 6, 2013. Nancy logged onto her Facebook page and felt a rush of adrenaline when she saw the message from "Cari." It was not sent from her daughter's usual page, but from a new page created in her name. Nancy noted it featured actual photos of Cari, and she couldn't help her racing heart.

Mom, why are you not talking anymore?

Nancy typed: *Is this really you?*

Yes, Mom. The other account was hacked. I'm sorry I missed the funeral.

Nancy wrote: *The only way I'll know it's you, is if you call me, and I hear your voice.* She waited, hopeful, but when the response came it was defensive, filled with grammar errors, and sounded nothing like her thoughtful daughter. *Everything is about phone calls. I was just heading to bed. Who else would know about Dad? Fine, I will call you sometime. I just wanted you to know I'm okay. I am happy. I may not be the greatest person in the world right now, but I am talking. Fine, I will call you, but I'm done after that. You have Max, and I am grateful, but after the cop stuff from before, I am done. I am not ten years old, Mom. I can leave him and move on with someone new.*

Move on with someone new? It was an odd way for a mother to speak of her son, and Nancy felt sure that her daughter had not written the message. "I don't care what man is out there." Nancy shakes her head. "She would have *never* left Max!" A startling post soon popped up on the new page. It was a photo of a hand with a sparkling engagement ring, and the caption read: *Dave and I got engaged.*

"It was absolutely not my daughter's hand." Nancy emphasizes that Cari's fingers were long and slender, and the photograph depicted a squat hand with short fingers. This new Facebook page in Cari's name was obviously the work of an impostor. Impostor or not, the owner of the new page had managed to friend a few people associated with Cari's original page. Some who did not know her well assumed that the posts were genuine, and they clicked "like" and commented enthusiastically over the news of her engagement.

Nancy alerted Deputy Phyllips, and he contacted Dave, who was still single and intended to stay that way. He was certainly *not* anyone's fiancé, but he had something even more bizarre than a fake engagement to share. At 12:30 A.M. on January 6, Dave had received an unsettling email from someone claiming to be Cari. *You will do exactly as I say, and then I will let her go,* the letter began. The attached photo showed a woman in a car trunk with duct tape covering her mouth, her hands tied behind her back. The email stated that the victim was Liz, but her face was turned at such an angle her features were not discernable. She looked a bit like Liz, but she could have just as easily been some other dark-haired woman.

The instructions were clear and to the point: *You will dump Liz, and you will start seeing me again.* He was to call Liz and break up with her via voice mail. Kidnapped Liz would then play that message for her abductor to verify that he had followed orders. If he did not comply, Liz would die, locked in a trunk where no one could find her. In a phrase that sounded like it was plucked straight from a low-budget late-night TV movie, the stalker added: *So, tick tock.*

Tick tock? The implication was that Dave had better hurry or he would never see Liz again! If the email was meant to frighten him, it didn't work. "I called B.S. on it right away." More words popped up: *I am sick of her getting what belongs to me. You can't play with my feelings, understand? Do it, or say good-bye to her.*

Though Dave doubted that Cari had kidnapped Liz, he had to admit that the woman in the photo certainly looked like Liz. Just to be sure, he texted her. "She's potentially in a trunk, tied up. It was the least I could do." But Liz didn't respond.

It was late, and she was probably sound asleep. It would be ridiculous to take this seriously, Dave told himself. She texted him the next morning and asked why he had been trying to reach her in the middle of the night.

He tapped out a reply: *Psycho was playing games. Was just checking on you.* Pleased that he cared enough to be concerned, Liz texted: *So sweet. What's up today, handsome?*

The stalker was especially active that second week of January, and Dave was drawn into numerous text conversations. When a female friend, Lisa, left his apartment after visiting on January 7, the tormentor immediately sent him a message threatening to follow her, but nothing came of that. Apparently, she realized that Lisa was not her competition. Dave and Lisa weren't dating, and he received no more warnings about her.

In another text, "Cari" claimed she'd moved into his apartment complex. She toyed with him, first suggesting they meet, then backtracking when he agreed. He pretended to flirt, hoping to lure her out of the shadows, so the cops could nab her, but she wasn't easy to trick.

On the morning of January 8, Dave was driving through his parking lot when he noticed a single vehicle, heaped with snow. The other cars had long since shed signs of the storm, but this vehicle obviously hadn't been driven for days. He took a closer look. It was a black Ford Explorer. *Cari's car!* He was certain it hadn't been there all along. How was Cari getting around without her car? Had she really moved into his apartment complex? Is that why the SUV was here? Dave called police, and they towed the Explorer to the Omaha Police Department impound lot.

While Cari had been reported missing in Iowa, she'd vanished from Nebraska. The mystery overlapped several police jurisdictions from two counties and two states, and that created some confusion. Despite their separate databases, police from the various offices were keeping each other in the loop. Iowa police reviewed Liz's reports of threats and vandalism in Omaha. Liz had accused Cari, and that fit their theory that Cari was in hiding because she'd flipped out. Deputy Phyllips and Omaha Detective Travis Oetter went to see Dave at Hyatt Tire. Dave showed them the text from "Cari," claiming she'd moved into Unit Twelve near him. But that apartment didn't exist. The nut was still playing games.

Both Dave and Liz showed the investigators the hostile texts sent to them by their elusive tormentor. The sheer volume was overwhelming. It would take time to pore over the *thousands* of messages to find clues that might lead to the missing woman. Dave and Liz cooperated, signing waivers to allow investigators to download the contents of their cell phones. The process, known as a "phone dump" is accomplished using a Cellebrite, a small hand-held device that facilitates the transfer of files from cell phones to jump drives through cables. The gadget can be used to accomplish both logical and physical downloads. Logical downloads retrieve data that has not been deleted, while physical downloads recover the entire contents of the memory of the phone, even deleted items.

Worn down by the stalker's hostile rants, the last thing Dave wanted was another email. But Liz probably didn't realize that because she continued to send him long letters. In one email, she invited him to a tattoo show and prattled on about how he didn't have to entertain her and how easy it was for them to just hang out and "chill." She mentioned commitment several times, insisting it was *not* an issue for her. She wrote: *You have to stop thinking that I'm trying to get you to commit to me,* and *stop thinking that I'm mad.*

Liz wanted a day each week, set aside for the two of them. *I guess I feel like that, geez, seven months gets me a few extra privileges, is all.* It was a variation on the one-month commitment she'd asked for in September. Now, instead of a month, she requested one day a week—fifty-two days per year. While she'd had "four months invested" when she asked for the month, now she stressed that she'd put in "seven months."

She pointed out how the "past has been a little challenging," and how happy she was that they weren't "rushing into things." She said

she didn't "want to get in the way of your dating," immediately con-
tradicting herself to say that "parts of me do, LOL," but never in a
"psycho" way. She felt she "wasn't good enough," and that a lot of
men had told her that. The email seesawed between emotions, at
times sounding confident, and in the next sentence, insecure. She insisted she wanted no commitment, but demanded he compromise
and promise her one day each week. Somehow, she managed to
wrangle that day from him. He might have been too overwhelmed to
argue, or maybe he gave in because the stalker had scared off his
other dates. He had to admit he was impressed by Liz's loyalty. She
was the only woman willing to stick by him in the midst of the
nightmare. Even when "Crazy Cari" was vandalizing Liz's home
and threatening to harm her, Liz was steadfast.

She was pissed at him for inviting a lunatic into their lives, but
she was still there. In fact, the stalker had actually brought them
closer. "We bonded over it," Dave explains. Liz was the only one
who understood what he was going through. They spent countless
hours talking about their frightening situation, comparing notes on
the latest threats and trying to figure out how to get out of the horrific mess.

The least Dave could do was give Liz her day.

CHAPTER TEN

ON THURSDAY, JANUARY 10, 2013, Deputy Phyllips asked crime scene technician Katie Pattee to process the recovered vehicle. With degrees in Criminal Justice Administration and Forensic Science, she was also a Certified Crime Scene Analyst with hundreds of hours of training in crime scene processing, photography, and fingerprint identification. Though the Explorer had been found in Douglas County, Nebraska, and towed to the Omaha Police Department impound lot, it had been reported stolen in Iowa, so the theft was under the jurisdiction of Pottawattamie County.

As the sole crime scene technician for the Pottawattamie County Sherriff's Office, Pattee was busy investigating everything from criminal mischief to burglary to homicide. On this day she was *not* investigating a homicide. She was assigned the task of examining a recovered stolen vehicle. She had never heard of Cari Farver nor the worried mother who had reported her missing seven weeks earlier.

As far as law enforcement in Iowa was concerned, Cari was an unbalanced woman who had shirked her responsibilities to take off on a thoughtless adventure, leaving a paranoid mother behind to fret. From the perspective of the *Nebraska* police, Cari was a malicious stalker, obsessed with Dave Kroupa.

It was not Pattee's job to know about any of that. She had more than enough responsibility just examining evidence. She did her job well, and now she meticulously followed the procedural steps to process the recovered car. First, she verified that the Vehicle Identification Number (VIN) matched the one in the theft report. Since

1981, each new on-road vehicle in the United States has been assigned a unique code of seventeen digits used to track ownership and accident history. Just as people have only one Social Security number, vehicles have just one VIN, etched or printed on various parts of a vehicle and also displayed on stickers, usually found inside the car's door jam on the driver's side.

Next, Pattee photographed the exterior, noting a scratch on the side. She dusted the exterior for fingerprints and found none. When she moved to the inside of the car, she was immediately struck by how clean it appeared. The cloth seats had recently been vacuumed and still bore the telltale marks of a vacuum attachment tool. She noticed a faint, pink stain in the middle of the front passenger seat. It looked as if someone had spilled a strawberry-flavored drink. She photographed every inch of the Explorer's interior, including that stain. It was not unusual to find stains from spilled food and beverages in recovered cars.

The floor was not nearly as clean as the seats. There was some light debris, apparently tracked in by shoes, but nothing out of the ordinary. She dusted the car's interior, paying attention to the windows, door handles, and other smooth surfaces that are conducive to retaining fingerprints. The Explorer held very few contents. A parking permit for West Corporation was tucked into the visor on the driver's side, and that, too, was dusted for prints. The glove compartment was empty, but the rear cargo area held jumper cables and empty grocery bags. Pattee painstakingly documented all of it.

Sometimes she found cigarette butts or cups with straws that could be tested for DNA that might lead to the car thieves, but there was nothing like that here. She couldn't find a single fingerprint on the car itself. The Explorer had been wiped clean. She found no fingerprints on any of the contents *except* for an empty mint container left in the cup holder between the front seats. After dusting the tin, she observed fingerprint ridge detail on the top of the container as two fingerprints emerged. She carefully placed lifting tape atop the prints, peeled the tape away, and secured it to lift cards that she labeled with the subject, date, and time.

Pattee later used a magnifier to examine the prints to determine if there was enough ridge detail to warrant running them through the Automated Fingerprint Identification System (AFIS). A national

computerized database of fingerprints maintained by the Criminal
Justice Information Services Division of the FBI, the AFIS contains
the palm and or fingerprints of over fifty million subjects—people
arrested for a variety of crimes but not necessarily convicted. With
their distinctive patterns of arches, loops and whirls, fingerprints are
unique to individuals, and prior to recent discoveries about DNA,
were the most damning of all physical evidence.

She had one viable print. She didn't know the age or gender of the
subject, information that helps narrow results in database searches.
She scanned and entered the print into the system, but there was no
match.

With the processing of the Explorer complete, it was released to
the Raneys. Nancy had never dealt with a stolen vehicle and didn't
know what to expect. "I remember looking inside and thinking,
'Boy, this is clean!' My daughter had a spotless house, but not so
much her car." It didn't cross her mind that there could be a sinister
reason for the car's pristine appearance. She assumed it was standard procedure for county employees to clean recovered vehicles
before returning them. She found it odd, however, that the car was
empty. "There was absolutely nothing in it. There were no papers,
no insurance, no registration, *nothing* in there."

Now that Cari wasn't driving it, the Explorer would be used by
Max who was taking Driver's Ed and would turn sixteen this year. His
mother had been so excited about fixing up the sporty Volkswagen for
him. The 1984 Rabbit GTI now sat abandoned at Hyatt Tire, still far
from roadworthy, but with unpaid bills for the work done.

It's always a shock to realize that life goes on when someone we
love dies, that the Earth keeps spinning as it always has and always
will. Those who grieved for Cari had no choice but to get up in the
morning and face agonizing days, fraught with anxiety and uncer-
tainty. They still had to go to work or school. They still had to be polite and smile at people and try to behave as if nothing had changed.
They still had to pay bills, do housework or homework and then get
up the next day and do it all again. Even *Cari's* responsibilities had
to be seen to. Nancy applied for and was awarded conservatorship
over her daughter's affairs. She took over her bills, managed her
Rolling Hills Bank account, and filed her taxes.

Nancy saw that West Corp had deposited Cari's last paycheck into her checking account, bringing her balance up to about $10,000. There had been no withdrawals, though someone from the bank had left a message about two transactions deemed suspicious because they strayed from Cari's normal habits. Her debit card had been used twice in mid-November, once at Walmart and once at a dollar store, both in Omaha. When Cari didn't respond to the alert, the bank froze her card. Nancy passed the information on to police.

It was painful for Cari's family to go to her house, so empty and cold and quiet. Nancy threw out the spoiled food in the refrigerator, and Maxwell packed up the rest of his clothes. They had the power shut off and made sure that the little house was buttoned up tight against the weather.

Dave continued to be bombarded by texts and emails, and the troublemaker continued to be fixated on Liz. On the twenty-eighth of January, he opened the nut's latest email and read: *You tell Liz to stay away from you, or I will come after her again . . . I don't want to find out you two had sex. I better not find out you two are texting or calling each other, either, or I will go after her. If I find out someone else is around, I will go after them also. I am mainly after Liz. She ruined everything.*

Dave was not about to let the bully tell him what to do. If Liz was brave enough to keep seeing him, she was welcome to come around. The lady had guts, he realized. Twice in the month of February, she filed police reports about vandalism to her vehicle. The vandal struck again on the first of April—April Fool's Day—and apparently used a key to scratch the words "Whore, stop seeing Dave" into the side of her car. Despite the constant threats and damage to her car, Liz didn't abandon him. As promised, he gave Liz her day. He saw his kids on the weekends and on every Tuesday and Thursday. Monday and Friday were Dave's days to do what he pleased after work. Wednesday night belong to Liz.

No matter the day of the week, Dave never had a single day off from the abuse. The threats and weird rantings were endless. There were so many messages that he wondered when the stalker had time to sleep. Sometimes he avoided his computer, so he wouldn't have to see the twisted emails piling up there, but he didn't want to turn off his phone. What if his kids needed him?

Meanwhile, Cari's family still waited for answers. They still received the occasional text or Facebook message from someone claiming to be Cari. None of the notes sounded like her. Nancy repeatedly told skeptical police that someone had stolen her daughter's identity, but no one would listen, and she was discouraged.

Where is my daughter? It was Nancy's first thought when she opened her eyes in the morning. On April 17, 2013, approximately five months after Cari went missing, Nancy received a phone call from a man identifying himself as Dave Kroupa. "Cari called me," he reported. "She's at a homeless shelter in Omaha. She wants you to pick her up." It was the best news Nancy could have imagined, but she began to tremble. After months of believing her daughter was gone forever, she was now learning she had been wrong. *Cari was alive!* Did this mean that Cari really did have a breakdown? Was she okay now? Whatever her state of mind, Nancy would help her heal. They would get through it together.

According to the caller, her daughter waited for her at The Siena/Francis House. "Mark was out of town, and I didn't think I could drive, so I called my brother." Jeff lived nearby, and he rushed over to pick up his sister.

Nancy called Deputy Phyllips, and he told her that he and Detective Oetter would meet them at the shelter. The thirty-minute drive felt like forever as the familiar terrain rolled past the window. She stared at the endless cornfields she'd seen a thousand times, first as a child riding in her parents' car, and later as a mother driving her children. She knew this land so well, but today it felt surreal.

On the last leg of their journey they crossed the Missouri River via the Grenville Dodge Memorial Bridge, eight lanes of traffic connecting Council Bluffs to Omaha. Midway across the bridge westbound travelers are welcomed by a giant, green overhead highway sign announcing, "Nebraska . . . The Good Life. Home of Arbor Day."

Siena/Francis House holds the record for the area's busiest homeless shelter. It is just north of downtown Omaha, about a mile west of Iowa as the goldfinch flies. Surrounded by warehouses, factories, and vacant lots, the facility is well kept, and on the outside resembles an elementary school with its landscaped grounds, wide, clean walkways, and big rack of bicycles near the front entryway. Founded in 1975, the institution has a policy of "unconditional acceptance," and

opens its doors to everyone in need, including the chronically ad-
dicted and mentally ill. As Jeff pulled up in front of the building,
Nancy glanced anxiously around, half expecting to see her daughter
waiting outside.

They had arrived about the same time as the detectives. "They
didn't want us to go in," Nancy recollects. "They had a photo of Cari
and took it in with them." She wasn't sure why the investigators
asked them to wait outside, but she did as they requested. Jeff, too,
had been devastated by his niece's disappearance, and he tried to reassure his anxious sister as they waited. They nervously eyed the
door, eager for a glimpse of Cari.

Any minute now, Nancy's prayers would be answered. Any minute
now, her tall and lovely daughter would walk out that door and into
her arms, and Nancy would hold on tight. But the detectives came out
alone. Phyllips shook his head, and Nancy's heart sank. Cari was not
there and never had been. No one at Siena/Francis House had recognized her picture.

Heartbroken, Jeff and Nancy headed back to Macedonia. The horrific roller-coaster ride of grief and then hope and then loss again left
Nancy nauseous. Remembering the heartless hoax, she says quietly,
"Talk about being kicked in the gut!" She was glad she hadn't told
Maxwell. She had made the wise decision to wait until she had a
grasp on the situation before sharing the news with him. If there was
anything that hurt more than missing her daughter, it was knowing
that Max grieved for her, too. The boy was stoic around his grandparents, trying to spare them the pain of knowing he was in pain, but
he grieved openly at his girlfriend's house.

When Dave Kroupa was questioned about his call to Nancy, he
was surprised. He had not phoned her for any reason and certainly
not to tell her that Cari was at a homeless shelter. Nancy was thoroughly shaken. Had the phone call been nothing more than a twisted
prank? Or had Cari actually planned to meet her at the shelter? Had
she asked a man to call Nancy? If so, why did he say he was Dave?
What if Cari *was* behind the phone call? If that were the case, then
why did she reach out only to dissolve back into the mist?

Someone had gone to a great deal of trouble to make people believe that Cari was at the shelter. As it turned out, not only had they
phoned Nancy, they had also relayed the same message to Deputy

Phyllips. And when Nancy later checked her Facebook page, there was another note, apparently sent before the call from "Dave." It was from impostor Cari: *Mom, I don't have a phone anymore. I need you to come get me at the Sienna House in Omaha, please. I have no money, no car. I need help. I asked Dave to call you, but not sure he will help . . . Mom, please, I need you.*

It was a heartbreaking plea. Nancy's child *did* need her—if she were still alive. If Cari was no longer on this earth, Nancy imagined that there had been a moment near the end when her daughter had made that plea. What kind of a person would type those words and send them to a grieving mother? It seemed the hoaxer had a heart of ice.

Deputy Phyllips wasn't sure what to make of the disturbing wild goose chase. On Monday, April 22, Mark Raney gave him permission to search Cari's home. The Raneys hadn't found anything there that could tell them what had happened to their daughter, and they hoped that Phyllips could find answers.

While most missing adults are quickly located, Cari had not been seen in over five months. "This was a little beyond the norm from somebody being gone for just a few days or weeks, so I wanted to take a look at her residence and see if there was anything that stood out that could help us find out where she may have gone," the detective explains, adding that the text messages allegedly from Cari indicated she'd moved to Kansas. If that were true, he expected to find evidence of Cari's plans in her home.

With the power shut off, it was hard to see, so the deputy pinned back the curtains on all of the windows to allow the sunlight in. To prevent thieves from taking advantage, the Raneys had put some of Cari's valuables into storage. Maxwell had moved most of his things to his grandparents' house. Otherwise, Cari's home was pretty much as she'd left it. Her yellow coat still hung on the back of a dining room chair, and personal items were scattered over her dresser. It looked as if she had stepped out to run an errand and had not planned to be gone long.

The "systematic search" called for each room to be photographed from various angles. Phyllips followed procedure and opened each closet door and every drawer, documenting everything with a camera. He photographed the full wardrobe of clothing, the rows of neatly rolled socks in a drawer, and the toiletries and medications in the bathroom medicine cabinet. In one drawer he found an empty box for a silver Nikon Coolpix S4100 camera, and he photographed it along with an empty box for a tripod.

He didn't know if the images would prove to be useful. He realized that Cari's family feared something horrible had happened to her, but he wasn't ruling out the possibility that she'd left willingly. Still, he was meticulous in his documentation. There was no telling what might turn out to be significant, so he recorded it all, everything from a deck of cards to crossword puzzles to a small, round container of breath mints.

In addition to taking photos, Phyllips collected potential evidence. "I took a checkbook log, a 2012 day-planner, and a resume she had typed out," he says, adding that the resume had handwritten notes that might provide a clue. He also collected receipts from Hyatt Tire, and a plastic bag of medication, prescribed to Cari. "All items were secured in the investigations division at the Sheriff's Office." Despite his careful combing of the home, he'd found nothing to indicate where Cari had gone. His efforts were not in vain, but it would be a long time before he realized that.

CHAPTER ELEVEN

ON THE THIRD OF MAY, 2013, Maxwell mustered up the courage to send a message to his mother's new Facebook page. He knew his grandmother believed that the page belonged to an impostor, and he was inclined to agree with her. *But what if it didn't? What if this was really his mom's page?*

He wasn't sure what to say, so he kept it simple. Two letters. H and I. *Hi.*

He soon received a response that he admits "freaked me out a little bit."

Hey, little man. How are you?

His mother certainly had never referred to him as a "little man." It was demeaning, the kind of endearment someone might use when addressing a small boy—not a robust fifteen-year-old football player. He stared at the breezy greeting, sent by someone he was almost positive had to be a stranger posing as his mom. Thoroughly spooked, he could not bring himself to reply. He waited a week or so before he attempted to get the truth. Then he typed three questions: *What is my middle name? What was the name of our first boxer? Who was my best friend when I was growing up?*

"Anyone could figure out my middle name," Maxwell acknowledges. "But only my mom would know the answers to the other two questions." Max's middle name could be found in an online search, but nothing on the web would reveal the identity of his childhood friend or the name of their boxer dog. If this were really his mom communicating with him, she should be able to easily answer his questions, and there was no reason why she shouldn't.

There was no reply.

Though the stalker didn't answer Max, they were so active that May 2013 it was hard to believe that just one person was creating so much havoc. Threatening emails and texts popped up faster than Dave could read them, and much of the time he didn't. What was the point in reading all of those ugly things? She had favorite words and used them repeatedly. *Whore. Fat. Ugly. Kill.*

At first Dave had scrutinized it all for clues, but his harasser was too clever to give away her location. While she came right out and said she was Cari, she never told him where she was, not until she had moved onto the next place. She was always one step ahead of him. The messages continued to express a peculiar animosity toward Liz and made her the focus of most of the threats. Sometimes Liz's children were mentioned. On one May night, Dave received an email from KroupaCari@gmail with an attached photograph of Liz's kids: *These are the ugliest kids, just like their whore mom. They should die with their whore mom, so I don't have to see their ugliness anymore. No one wants her and her bratty kids around.*

The image showed the kids inside of Liz's home, and the picture was apparently taken by someone outside, shooting through a window. Liz told Dave that it made her very uncomfortable to know that someone was watching her children. How in the world did the maniac manage to photograph her kids? Had she been creeping around in the bushes outside of Liz's home like a paparazzo shooting celebrities for the tabloids? How did she manage to be everywhere, yet never be seen?

While Liz was the favorite victim, the harassment wasn't limited to her. If Dave sent a brief message to a female he met online, it created trouble. That May, he met a pretty woman on the Plenty of Fish dating site. Jessica McCarthy had two young sons, and while not technically single, she was separated and free to date. Jessica was drawn to the photo of the good-looking father of two. Though she was a decade younger than Dave, they had things in common. Both lived in Omaha and were hardworking people and devoted parents.

"My acquaintance with Jessica lasted about two hours," says Dave. "I forget which one of us approached the other, but we com-

municated on the site, messaging back and forth, for about an hour."
Then Jessica suggested that they "friend" each other on Facebook.
Once "friended," they could not only message each other privately,
they could also comment on each other's posts.

All Facebook members can view the contents of the pages of
other members, including their photos and their lists of Facebook
friends unless steps are taken by individual users to make their
pages private. Most people are unaware that clicking on the arrow in
the top righthand corner of their pages reveals a settings option that
opens a page where privacy adjustments can be made. But it didn't
matter what steps Dave took to block the intruder, she always found
a way around it. His stalker was ever present. She knew things about
him that she should have had no way of knowing. She managed to
see and hear so much, yet *she* was never seen or heard.

When Jessica became Facebook friends with Dave, she was
stunned to realize she'd also made a Facebook *enemy*. On Friday,
May 10, at 4:39 P.M., Jessica received a startling Facebook message.
It appeared to be from a woman named C. Lea Farver, and it got
right to the insulting point. *So, you must be Dave's new whore. He
has herpes from the whore he was dating. I would watch out for him,*
the message began, and continued on, sprinkled with crude words
and threats. "C. Lea" vowed to find Jessica and vandalize her car as
she had "the other whore's car."

Jessica asked Dave about "C. Lea Farver." It wasn't his first
choice of topics when he was just getting to know an attractive
woman, but he told her about the crazy person who'd been making
his life miserable for the last six months.

What about the claim Dave had herpes? He had not been diagnosed with herpes, a contagious virus plaguing up to sixty-five percent of American adults, though many are unaware they carry it
because they've never had a blistering outbreak. Most have the less-
severe strain that commonly appears on the mouth and is referred to
as cold sores, but one in six adults are infected with the severe
strain, usually contracted through sexual contact and found on both
the mouth and genitals.

It was obvious to Jessica that "C. Lea Farver" was so obsessed
with Dave she'd say whatever it took to scare away the competition,
even if it meant lying about a sexually transmitted disease. Jessica

tried to shrug off the hostile message, but another arrived two hours later: *So, whore, I'll keep messaging you. He has been with me for five months. I will run off any woman who tries to be with him. He is sleeping with three people I know, and I got rid of one whore.*

At 9:42 P.M., the next message hit her like a fist in the gut. *Guess you're not learning by what I'm telling you,* it began, followed by profanities before delivering the threat: *I will come kill you and your fucking kids. I have killed a dog owned by Dave's last whore he tried to be with . . .*

Jessica was shaken. It was bad enough that she was a target, but when her kids were included in the threat, it both frightened and angered the young mother. Had this person really killed a pet? Jessica had refused her tormentor's friend request and blocked her, but that didn't help. The stalker had created many Facebook accounts, most in some variation of Cari Farver's name, and she continued her attack.

At 11:53 P.M. another message began by noting that Jessica had failed to cut ties with Dave. The bully knew that she and Dave were still Facebook friends. When Jessica read the next line, she felt sick.

I will cut your kids' throats and yours while you sleep.

The thought of someone hurting her sons, Benjamin, age eight, and Christopher, two, was more than she could stand. At 8:29 the next morning, the next threat contained no profanities but was every bit as chilling.

I know where you live. I will be coming for you and your son.

The message at 10:47 A.M. was brief and to the point: *I will kill your whole family.* Two hours later, the stalker's message was chatty: *You divorced now? Or do I tell your husband you're messing with someone else's man? See that picture of the car? I did that to another whore who wouldn't leave Dave alone.* A photograph of a vandalized car was attached to the message. While Jessica certainly didn't want her car damaged, threats to her vehicle were far less disturbing than threats to her children.

The stalker tried every angle she could think of to hit a nerve. She'd tried scaring her with the herpes lie, threatened her car, and then her children. Now, she'd gone back to the vandalism threats *and* was hinting she'd tell Jessica's estranged husband she was cheating on him. Jessica was free to date, but she was *not* dating

Dave. They'd never even *met*. He seemed like a nice-enough guy, but she wanted nothing to do with the drama, and had decided not to meet him. At 11 A.M. a new message popped up: *Well, keep going whore, and you won't have a family any more. I will take everything from you.*

Jessica reported the harassment to the Douglas County Police on May 11. "She was threatening my children. Any good parent will do anything they can to protect their children, and I was terrified that something would happen to them." Now there was a police report, but the cops couldn't stop the threats. The police had tried for months to find the stalker and gotten nowhere.

Another message arrived at 3:41 that afternoon with escalating rage: *You dumb, stupid whore. You're like the rest. I can find whoever I want. If you don't stop talking to Dave, I will kill you, your kids and whoever else. It's not hard to find people. I will kill you. Stay away from Dave, and if you talk to him, stupid whore, I will come for your family and you, just like I did the other whore.*

All that day, the messages continued to pop up. The last one that night came in at 10:45 P.M. . . . *You must be a worthless mom like the whore Dave tried to get with, but I nipped that. I control Dave, and he will leave whoever I tell him to . . . Am I at your place? See, I find everyone.*

The messages the next morning contained more chilling threats: . . . *I will kill your sons. I am not joking. I don't joke around. You better stop talking to him . . . I will know if you talk, smile, or anything with him, and I seriously will kill you and your son . . .*

Jessica sat Benjamin down and had a talk with him about strangers. She'd warned him before, just as all parents do when they teach their children to be careful in a world that is not always safe. Now the danger was real and immediate. Someone had made it clear that they were ready and willing to press a sharp blade to the youngster's throat and end his life.

The concerned mother chose her words carefully. She didn't want to frighten her second-grader but had to make him understand that even *women* strangers could be dangerous. He must not go outside to play without her watching, she stressed, and she had to know where he was at all times. Benjamin nodded and promised his mother he wouldn't let a stranger into their apartment. As for Christopher, he was too young to understand. It was ultimately up to Jessica to protect her sons. The stalker accused her of being a "worthless mother" and caring more about a man than her sons' lives. It was far from true. She'd already decided it was too risky to meet Dave.

At 7 P.M., on May 11, a message arrived with no outright threat and no profanities. It was simply Jessica's address, complete with her apartment number. The stalker knew exactly where Jessica was, but she had no idea where her stalker was. The horrific threats nibbled at her serenity. She double-checked the locks on her doors and windows but couldn't shake the image of a cruel hand holding a knife to her boys' throats. Jessica did not sleep well.

She figured she'd better learn all she could about her new enemy and visited her Facebook page. As she scrolled through "C. Lea's" pictures, she was shocked to find a familiar photo. It was a picture of Jessica with Benjamin. Jessica had posted it on her Facebook page for her friends and family to enjoy, and the stalker had downloaded it, posting it on her own page.

"I felt very, very threatened." Her voice trembles at the memory. She hated the fact her tormentor knew what her sons looked like. She changed her Facebook settings, so her images couldn't be downloaded. It wasn't much of a deterrent. Photos posted on the web can be captured just as easily with screenshots, a feature available on most computers.

Jessica had had enough. She sent a text to Dave: *You're probably a very nice guy, but I don't need this headache.* As soon as she "unfriended" Dave on Facebook, the terrorizing stopped as abruptly as it had begun. Still, it took a while for her to believe that someone was not creeping around in the shadows, knife in hand, ready to leap out and attack her family.

Four days after Jessica's second harassment report, Liz filed another complaint with the Omaha Police Department. Sergeant Brett Schrage was working the front desk at the Southwest precinct that day. He reviewed some of the threats on Liz's phone and advised her to save them and apply for a protective order.

The bully was finding new ways to terrify. On May 11, the same day that the stalker had sent Jessica her own address, and Dave had received the email threatening Liz and her "ugly kids," a memorial for Liz appeared on Remembered.com, a website where grieving families can post photos and bios of their deceased loved ones.

The nut sent Dave a link to the memorial. He was shocked to see a photo of Liz with "June 28th 1975 to May 11th, 2013" printed beneath it. The obituary read: *I didn't know her very well expect [sic] that she was a whore and a man stealer.* It continued with run-on sentences and atrocious grammar and punctuation mistakes: *She kept stealing my man she is unable to get her own man that she has to keep taking everyone else's men. Thank God she is gone you rid dines [sic] to you.* Apparently, the writer had meant to type: *Good riddance to you,* but didn't use her computer's spell-check feature. Either that, or the errors were deliberate.

While Liz was not *dead*, she told Dave she was scared to *death.* According to the obituary, she died on May 11. That's *today,* Dave realized as he studied the memorial. Liz was still alive, but the day was not over. Could someone be planning to end her life that day? Nah! It was a ridiculous idea. He figured the ugly words were empty threats. It was quite a leap from keying a car to murder. A few hours later, at nearly 2 A.M. on May 12, Dave received an email with the subject line: *How do I find a hit man, contract killer?* It began: *I am trying to hire someone to get rid of that whore Liz for us. You told me before you wanted her gone. I can't do it myself because the cops will figure it out.* It went on to ask if they should also have Liz's kids killed, and ended with: *I love you, Dave, and I am glad you're in this with me. I hope to see you soon. Your beautiful Cari.*

It was more nonsense, but Liz appeared frightened. Dave tried to reassure her. It was B.S., he insisted, just like when the stalker had claimed she was locked in a car trunk. "Liz, she's just trying to scare you," he told her. He hoped he was right.

CHAPTER TWELVE

I love you. Don't ignore me, or I will tear out
your whore's eyes and slit her throat . . .
—TEXT FROM STALKER TO DAVE KROUPA,
JUNE 23, 2013

ON MAY 18, 2013, the Facebook impostor uploaded a new profile image, originally posted by Cari on her real page. It was a photo of Cari with her dad about a month before he died. Denny looked sickly and gaunt as his daughter wistfully rested her head upon his shoulder. The accompanying text, riddled with grammar errors, was disturbing to Cari's friends and relatives, and none of them believed she had written it: *I have answered enough questions to prove myself to everyone*, it began before angrily declaring that she was indeed Cari and wanted to be left alone. *I left on my own free will, and I am sick of everyone giving me a hard time for doing what I needed to do.* Particularly painful to Max was the claim he had refused to go with his mother. The post ended with: *I love you all very much, but I need time still to sort things out.*

It wasn't just Cari's family who was going out of their minds with worry, her friends, too, were devastated and lost. They spent countless hours combing the Internet for a sign of Cari. Nancy's heart went out to Cari's friend, Joy Norstrum, when she showed up at her door, so excited she was practically bursting. She thought she had located Cari through a recently posted online video and couldn't wait to show Nancy. They turned the computer on, and Joy accessed the video. It was definitely made by Cari, but while Joy had assumed it was recent, Nancy recognized it as one Cari had filmed before she disappeared. Nancy recalls how she gently broke the news, and all of Joy's excitement drained away. "She put her head down on the table and cried."

Cari Farver's absence tore holes in the serenity of many people. Over six years after her best friend vanished, Amber Jones's eyes are still bright with pain when she talks about her. She met Cari in October 2009. Amber's boyfriend had invited her to attend the wedding of his friend, Phillip Wades, who was marrying Cari. From the instant Cari and Amber first smiled at each other, the connection was undeniable. It was as if they'd been friends forever.

For their first outing, Amber and her fiancé had gone on a double-date with Cari and Phillip, but Amber was apprehensive. After overcoming an addiction, she was clean and sober and avoided situations where others imbibed. Cari was sensitive to Amber's discomfort and quietly reassured her that she would abstain, too. From then on, whenever the group went out together, the ladies remained sober while the guys drank.

Amber and Cari always had so much fun together that they didn't need cocktails to unwind. They shared a sense of humor and laughed so much that sometimes people turned to stare. While they abstained from alcohol, they found something else that was bad for them to indulge in. Amber was lactose intolerant, and Cari was allergic to gluten. "Whenever we went out to eat, we always ordered a brownie with ice cream and split it." The guys looked at them like they were nuts. *Didn't they realize they were going to be sick later?* Of course, they did! And that's what made their choice so decadent. That's what made it so delicious and so *funny*. They giggled as the guys stared at them like they'd lost their minds.

The bond between the two women had been instant, powerful and rare. Amber marveled about the fact that they were so close that they often knew what each other were thinking. She loved that she could tell Cari anything, and her friend would never judge her. They could also count on each other, and it meant a lot to Amber when Cari helped her plan her wedding. As close as they were, sometimes life took them in opposite directions. They hadn't seen each other for months when they got together for lunch the first week of November 2012. There was a lot to catch up on. Amber was very pregnant with her first child, and Cari was thrilled for her.

Cari had some exciting news of her own. She'd been seeing someone for the last week, and it was going very well. She told Amber about her first encounter with the handsome mechanic when she'd brought

her Explorer into Hyatt Tire, and an undeniable energy had ignited between them. Cari said she'd been instantly taken with Dave Kroupa,
and though the attraction had seemed mutual, he hadn't asked her out.
Cari told her friend that she'd sought Dave out, signing up on the
Plenty of Fish dating site because she'd hoped to connect with him.
In the end, Cari had gone back to Hyatt Tire, and they'd arranged for
their first date at Applebee's. Amber was glad to see her friend so
happy.

They ended the lunch with Cari promising to throw Amber a baby
shower, and they set a tentative date. But Amber had been hurt and
confused when Cari failed to follow through with the party plans
and ignored her phone calls. It would be weeks before she learned
that Cari was not being inconsiderate, she was *missing*.

Amber's first months with her new baby should have been the
most joyful of her life, but instead she was sick with worry. Around
the time of the Siena/Francis House hoax, Amber got a text from an
unfamiliar number. Her hopes soared when the texter claimed to be
Cari. But the messages were troubling. "Cari" asked for help but
was vague about her situation. Amber kept her phone near, ready to
hop in her car and drive to her friend the moment she was given an
address. But the story kept changing. Amber's phone was flooded
with texts, some that filled her with absolute horror. "Cari" said she
was being held captive, locked in a room, unable to escape.

How are you able to have a phone? Amber texted.

The explanation made sense. The phone was prepaid, and the
captor didn't know she had it. She claimed the guy had been tortur-
ing her and followed that with a frantic message: *I can hear him!
He's coming!* Then there were no more messages, not for many long
and agonizing days. Amber was left picturing her best friend being
viciously attacked, maybe even killed. She contacted the police and
Nancy, though she spared Cari's mother the frightening details.
Amber was a nervous wreck, and her tiny infant surely sensed her
anxiety and suffered, too. After days of silence, more disturbing
texts appeared. Amber was never given a specific location. The texter never asked about Amber's baby, or mentioned anything that
convinced her that Cari was behind the messages. But Amber was
afraid to cut off the communication. What if it really *was* Cari? If

there was even a small chance that Cari was the one texting her, Amber would not abandon her.

Meanwhile, the stalker continued to harass Dave. He tried to ignore her and continued to meet women online. If he could catch his tormentor lurking outside, he would follow her and find her hideout. Then the cops could arrest her. In the meantime, he planned to keep dating, if she didn't scare away all of his dates!

He was grateful to Liz for having the guts to stick by him, but it didn't mean he wasn't restless. He still got mad when she couldn't contain her jealousy, and he broke up with her regularly because of it. The breakups didn't last long because the stalker would always do something horrendous that would send them scurrying back to each other for comfort. While he was glad that he could talk to Liz about the problems, their conversations got old very fast because they all revolved around the stalker, what the stalker had just done, what the stalker was planning to do, and how they could catch and stop the stalker. Dave estimates that "our conversations were all about that for 99 percent of our relationship." There had to be more to life than being stalked and *talking* about being stalked!

One Friday night in mid-June, Dave was visiting Amy and his kids when he received an email with the subject line, *Now at your place,* and the message read:

I know you're there. Hello. Do I need to break the sliding door to get you to talk?

The sliding door was in his apartment, and the stalker apparently figured out he wasn't home because she emailed him again a couple of minutes later: *I told you I was coming to see you tonight. You weren't there. I took out a window. I hope your whore inside was scared and never comes back . . .*

Dave arrived home that night to find a brick had shattered a bedroom window. He called police to report the damage. Though the stalker had seemed to think he had a female visitor, it wasn't so. The apartment was empty when the window was broken. Multiple emails and texts continued to come in each day, often many an hour. On the twenty-third of June, one email threatened: *I'll kill her. She stole my heart. She broke my dreams. She stole my future when she took you away from me. That whore will die.*

The next day another appeared: *I will remove all your whores. All that will be left is me. You left me for that ugly whore. Now I destroy your life.*

The last week of June, Dave got up one morning to find his car had been keyed. Scratched in giant letters along one side of the car were the words: *Dave loves fat whores.* The stalker took credit in an email: *I keyed your fucking car. Let people know you like fat whores.*

The next day, another email laced with threats popped up: *I will kill that nasty-ass whore Liz for getting in between us and every fat ass that you have been with. Then I will kill that loud-mouth kids' mom of yours for getting in my business. She thinks she knows what's going on. Wait till I cut her throat.*

In addition to being beaten down by the stalker, Dave was also once again feeling stifled by Liz's incessant nagging, and he pulled away. He met a woman online he was very attracted to. Sally was a voluptuous blonde in her late thirties. "She seemed to have her stuff together. She had a job and a couple of Volkswagens because that was her thing."

As always, his harasser seemed to know exactly what was going on in his dating life. One of the emails he received on July 1 made that point clear: *Oh, Loser, I saw you out on another date tonight. I see you gave up on that whore Liz. Thank God. I haven't seen her at your place lately. Well, I'm glad. Everyone told me you can't stand her and that you two aren't even friends, and you two aren't even talking to each other. Thank God you woke up and realized she was no good for you.*

On Wednesday, Sally brought one of her Volkswagens to Hyatt Tire to have Dave look into a problem she was having with the radio. "I put a fuse in it, and I walked her out to her car. I said good-bye, and I gave her a little kiss." He didn't realize someone was watching. Within two hours, Sally was bombarded with calls, texts, and emails from someone claiming to be Cari. Dave also heard from "Cari," boasting about how easy it had been to trace Sally through her license plate number: *So now I found two of your whores. One drives a burgundy car and lives close to downtown. The other I saw at your job through binoculars from Menard's.*

Dave glanced across the busy four-lane highway at Menard's, a huge home-improvement store that was part of a Midwest chain. He realized with a shiver that someone *could* park in the lot and watch him at work. "I was in the Menard's parking lot two minutes" after the text arrived. "Of course, it was well after the fact, and I didn't find anybody."

On July 3, at 6:10 A.M., one of the emails Dave received referred to both Sally and Liz: *So, loser, I told you I watched you, and I saw you with a fat-ass whore at your work. Got that fat-ass whore's license plate number, can get her address, name, telephone number from it. Now I see that ugly whore Liz at your apartment. If you don't want them finding out about each other, break up with ugly whore Liz now, or I will ruin your life like I told you I would. I can see the whore's car.*

"Loser" was apparently the stalker's new pet name for Dave, but she stuck with her old standby for Liz, continuing to refer to her as "a fat-ass whore." In the stalker's mind, the two worst things a woman could be were "a whore" and "fat," and when that fat accumulated around a woman's lower region, the insult was as bad as it could possibly get. "A fat-ass whore" was the ultimate denigration, and the stalker seemed to delight in the slur. It was not reserved just for Liz. Any female who so much as smiled at Dave was a "fat-ass whore" and in danger of being sliced by the sharp blade of the watcher's knife.

Neither Liz nor Cari were fat. The size and shape of a person's body were not something that Cari *ever* would have criticized. She had never judged or mocked anyone for their physical appearance, and had, in fact, been accepting of all manner of idiosyncrasies of her fellow human beings. Dave, however, still knew very little about the woman he had spent two blissful weeks with. Whatever good qualities he had noticed in that short period of time were overshadowed by eight months of foul-mouthed threats.

I would do anything to make you hate her.

The stalker had written that in reference to Liz. But Dave did not hate Liz. If anything, he felt more fondly toward her, more protective of her, *because* of the thousands of threats and ugly words targeting her. It was *Cari* he had come to despise. How ironic that the stalker, so determined to make him hate Liz, had succeeded only in making him hate *her*. Dave was so exhausted by the crazy games that he didn't stop to reflect on this. He never questioned his stalker's identity. He had assumed from the beginning that Cari was behind all of the ugliness. The first disturbing texts had come from her phone, and the troublemaker had claimed to be her, brazenly and gleefully taking credit for every mean deed. Why would the stalker lie? She said she was Cari, so who else could it be?

Dave was not alone in his belief. He was one of many intelligent males, including experienced detectives, who saw exactly what the culprit had wanted them to see and nothing more. Several *females,* however, had suspected the truth. Some tried to speak up but were shushed or laughed at. Others knew that no one would believe them and didn't bother to voice their theories.

When Dave looks back on those dark days, he remembers two inexplicable events, so peculiar that he wasn't sure what to make of them. He had shrugged them off at the time, and it's only in retrospect that he realizes that he should have been paying closer attention. The first occurred in the springtime, though he can't remember exactly when. "It was still cold out. I was coming home from the bar. It was rather late—I would guess about 11:00 or midnight." On foot because he'd been drinking, he was walking across the dimly lit lot toward his unit when something caught his attention. "I heard rustling." He peered into the shadows and witnessed a startling sight. "I saw Liz crawling!" Confused, he watched her "army crawling" with "butt down," in the same fashion that he'd been trained to do when he was in the National Guard. She crept between a car and the building, and she seemed to be hiding. "I was fairly inebriated. I hollered at her a couple of times. She didn't come out, and she didn't answer me." He couldn't figure out what kind of weird game she was playing. Annoyed and too cold to pursue it, he went inside and shut the door. "Then my phone started blowing up. It was Liz. She was calling and texting me. She said, 'I'm sorry! I'm drunk! I was over across the street at the bar with my friends. I don't know what I'm doing.'" Too drunk to realize she had been crawling like a crab across dirty pavement on a freezing night, she had managed to sober up at a record pace and leave Dave a coherent message.

The second event also involved a figure in the shadows. Dave didn't see it, but his daughter did when his kids were staying with him. One night when Calista had stayed up very late, she was certain she had a ghost sighting. "She saw someone creeping down the hallway, and she threw her shoe at it and shouted, 'Go away, ghost!' She was about twelve at the time." The preteen was fascinated with the paranormal, and she assumed that the phantom-like being that had retreated into the darkness was a restless spirit. Did she manage to hit it with her shoe? She didn't know. She was too spooked to investigate.

Dave had dismissed Calista's story at the time. He didn't believe in ghosts, and he figured it was a simple case of a tired kid with an active imagination. But he now realizes that there very well could have been someone sneaking into his apartment, someone who knew he was a deep sleeper but did not realize his daughter was awake. He wishes that he had taken her "ghost sighting," more seriously. Maybe he could have set a trap and caught "the phantom" in action.

Dave was so exhausted by the never-ending deluge of hate that his thinking was uncharacteristically jumbled. If he could have gotten a break from the stalking and been able to live free of the anxiety that comes with knowing that someone with ill intent is constantly watching, he might have been able to see the situation with more clarity. If only he had had a week or two to clear his mind, he might have suspected the truth. But Dave's tormentor relentlessly tortured him and never allowed him a moment of peace. Thousands of texts and emails continued to inundate him that July 2013, including one at 6:40 A.M. on the third day of the month, targeting Sally: *I will ruin your loser life everyday if you do not break up with your ugly whore . . . I have a key to the building. I will just go in then. I will figure out how to get inside, kill the whore in your apartment, get you arrested.*

On July 5, in a 10:30 P.M. email, the bully warned: *I am going to fuck the whore up when she comes out.* A few hours later, Dave received an email focused on Liz. It arrived with an attached photo of Liz's Honda Civic: *Found the slutty whore who took everything from me. I hate her so much . . .*

Shortly after, another email popped up, this time with complaints about Amy who had had a heated email exchange with someone claiming to be Cari: *I am going to the cops for harassment from your kids' mom. I am done with you, sick of her running her whore mouth to me. I feel like stabbing someone."*

Liz. Sally. Amy. The stalker seemed to detest them equally, although Liz was a favorite target. It was a big, tangled mess, and Dave had grown wary of trying to explain it to friends, family, coworkers and the various law officers he called upon to report his tormentor's crimes. Detective Paul Prencer from the Omaha Police Department got involved that July, and Dave once again found himself reciting the long and complex horror story that had become his life.

Prencer had worked for OPD since 1999, and after a decade there, he was assigned to the Special Victims Unit. He mostly investigated crimes against children and vulnerable adults, domestic violence, and sexual assaults. Prencer frequently investigated domestic violence, crimes that include destruction of property, vandalism, harassment, assaults and sometimes burglaries. While initial reports are taken by uniformed officers, they are later assigned to detectives for follow up. Detective Prencer met with Dave that July to follow up on the report of the broken window. There was no question in Dave's mind who had smashed the window. The vandal had contacted him, jubilantly taking credit, just as she always did.

"The victim, Mr. Kroupa, identified a photo of Cari," recounts Detective Prencer, who was eager to talk to the alleged troublemaker. He applied for a misdemeanor warrant for the arrest of Cari Lea Farver. By the end of July 2013, the warrant was active. Now, if an officer pulled her over for speeding or some other traffic infraction, they could see the warrant in their database. Cari Farver was still listed in the NCIC as a missing person, but not a single officer had encountered her in the eight months she had supposedly been running amok, recklessly destroying property, terrifying innocent people, and sometimes flaunting her actions in full view of the public—though no witnesses had actually seen her.

Cari Farver, missing person, had not been found. Cari Farver, alleged criminal, was equally elusive. The warrant for her arrest would never be executed.

CHAPTER THIRTEEN

IN THE SUMMER OF 2013, two things were bothering Dave. There was the stalker, of course. And Liz. Her jealousy was becoming a huge problem. She would not let go of her suspicion that he was sleeping with Amy. While Liz was wildly jealous of her, she had no reason to be. Amy had plenty of interest from men, and she, too, was dating. Dave had become like a pal to her. "I always tell him he is one of my best friends. A lot of people think our friendship is weird, because he comes over here and hangs out with the kids. I don't see anything wrong with it. We chat about the kids or our significant others."

Amy remembers when he met Cari. "Dave talked about her once or twice in the beginning before all of the craziness started. He said, 'I'm dating a girl named Cari.' I said, 'Oh, what does she look like?' I was just curious because if this person was going to be in my kids' life, I wanted to know about her. Dave was at the store where I work one day when he came in to pick up something for the kids, and he showed me her picture."

Amy glanced at the smiling image of Cari and said, "Oh, she's cute!" She'd been relieved to know he had met someone nice. "All I wanted was for him to find someone good for him—someone who wanted the same things he wanted. He talked kindly about her, and I was happy for him. Cari sounded like a good person who would be good to my kids if they got serious."

While Amy had at one time been disappointed that Dave didn't share her desire for commitment, she'd long since gotten over that. Now, she was just grateful that he was such a wonderful father to their children. "Anyone who knows me, knows my kids come first," Amy stresses. She was determined to make her kids happy because, "My own childhood was kind of traumatic."

When Amy was thirteen, her family was split up because her mom had some issues that made it difficult to keep her children with her. Amy and her sister went to live with their aunt, but the aunt had kids of her own, and the place soon felt crowded. "With four teenaged girls in one house, my aunt couldn't really handle it, so we ended up going to a place called Children's Square. It's a home for kids who don't have parents. They either get adopted or go to foster homes."

The sisters made a pact. They would never let anyone separate them. A kind woman was impressed with Amy and invited the quiet, studious teen to live with her. But there was a problem. "She wasn't going to take my sister. I said, 'You can either have us both, or not at all.'" But the lady was unable to accommodate both sisters. "We couldn't let anyone split us up. All we had was each other." The girls had some rough years, but Amy was strong and determined. By the time she was seventeen, she was living on her own and working two jobs to support herself. She never forgot how shattered she'd felt when her family fell apart, and she vowed that when she had kids, they would never go through that. She hoped for a solid marriage and a traditional family where the kids felt loved.

When she and Dave worked together at the truck stop, she admits she didn't exactly imagine him as the father of her future children. At first glance, "I thought he was dorky." But he seemed very nice, so she agreed to go out with him, and they had a lot of fun. Before long, Amy was lost in his intense blue eyes and was surprised to discover she was very attracted to him. Dave's commitment issues soon became apparent, but he didn't bail when she got pregnant. They lived together and were, for all practical purposes, married. It bothered her that it wasn't official, but she was ecstatic when their daughter was born. Moments after Calista entered the world, Amy was so overcome with emotion, she looked Dave in the eye and said, "I love you." Now, when she remembers his response, she laughs, but it stung at the time. "He said, 'Thank you.'" She tried to be understanding. She knew he'd been hurt badly when, "his high school girlfriend cheated on him." By the time their second child was born,

Amy thought Dave should be ready to put a ring on her finger. But it was not to be.

The break-up was hard at first, but Amy set a wonderful example for her kids when she welcomed their father back into her life as her friend. Unfortunately, the fact that they got along so well irked Liz. She sent Amy emails and texts, insinuating that Amy was still sleeping with Dave. Amy politely explained to her that they were simply co-parenting their children and that she had no interest in getting back with Dave. The jealous messages from Liz confirmed Amy's initial impression of her. "I always had a weird feeling about Liz from day one. From the first time I met her."

When Dave met Liz, Amy, too, was seeing someone new. Dave and Amy agreed to get to know the people spending time with their kids. One Sunday night, Amy's boyfriend took her to pick up the kids from Dave's place. Amy phoned from the car to say she was on the way, and when Dave mentioned that Liz was there, "I said, 'Perfect! We can all meet each other!' Dave and my boyfriend hit it off real well." As Dave and Amy's boyfriend made small talk, she reached out to shake Liz's hand, smiling as she said, "Hi, I'm Amy. Nice to meet you."

"Liz wouldn't even shake my hand. She just sat there. She just glared. I asked my boyfriend later, 'Is it just me, or did you get a bad vibe from her?' He said she was not nice at all. She didn't really say anything to him, and he introduced himself to her, too. She was rude to him. Later I told Dave, 'She's not very friendly.' He said, 'Oh, well, it was probably an odd situation for her.'"

Amy didn't think that was a good enough reason to be rude. "I didn't want to say much about her, and how negative she was, because that upset Dave. There was something off about her, but I tried to keep those comments to myself."

The kids didn't like Liz, and they reported that fact to their mother. "She's your dad's girlfriend," Amy told them. "I want you to treat her with respect."

Amy continued to be polite whenever their paths crossed, and Liz continued to be cold and unfriendly. Amy dreaded seeing her, and she did her best to avoid her. She was not the first person to feel uncomfortable around her. A decade earlier, Melissa Strom was encountering Liz for the first time, and she, too, had experienced a prickling anxiety in her presence. While Amy had met Liz because of Dave, Melissa, too, had met Liz because of a man. But in Melissa's case, *Liz* had been the ex—a very jealous ex, determined to get her man back. Amy, of course, didn't want Dave back. "I just wanted him to be happy," she stresses. But that didn't seem to matter. Liz was convinced that Amy was her enemy. David Kroupa was the prize, just as Dirk Rhodes had been Liz's prize a decade earlier.

If not for a memory lapse, Melissa would never have met Dirk. She wasn't old and forgetful. She was a sharp twenty-two-year-old who worked as a pharmacy technician. On a March night in 2003, she and a friend went out to Omaha's Pheasant Bar and Grill. It was not until the next morning that she realized her mistake. "I accidentally forgot to pay the tab, and they had my credit card!" She went back to the bar to pay her bill and retrieve her credit card. Lovely, with a trim figure and shiny blond hair that fell halfway down her back, she was accustomed to the stares of men, and she barely noticed Dirk seated at the bar, watching her.

As the bartender teased Melissa about her slipup with the bill, she chuckled along with him. "Dirk overheard me and the bartender joking about my forgetting to pay the tab, and he made a silly comment that made me laugh." Melissa and Dirk began chatting. "I remember thinking that his hair was overly bleached, and I wasn't sure if he was my type. But he had really nice blue eyes and a funny sense of humor."

She said yes when Dirk asked her out, and soon they were seeing each other exclusively. Dirk worked at a prison, but his passion was art. He created amazing artwork and also wrote poems. Melissa was impressed and found herself drawn to his creativity. He was single, he assured her, but he had a child. That was fine with Melissa. She loved kids, and she didn't mind helping him care for two-year-old Peter. The little boy was adorable, but Melissa was not prepared for Peter's mother.

Dirk shared custody of Peter with Liz Golyar, but he knew her as Shanna. Their breakup was so new that they hadn't yet hammered out the details. He explained to Melissa that he had broken up with his son's mother because of her over-the-top jealousy. When he had met Shanna, she was a single mother of a little girl, Trina, about two years old. Shortly after he began dating Shanna, she got pregnant, and they had stayed together for the baby. After Peter was born, Shanna's jealousy intensified, and she constantly accused Dirk of cheating on her when he had been nothing but loyal to her. He put up with it for as long as he could, but he felt suffocated by her possessiveness.

He met Melissa on the rebound, barely two weeks after he had moved out of Shanna's place. He had not planned for his new girl-friend to meet his ex so soon, but Melissa was visiting him on one of his days with Peter when Shanna popped in. "Dirk was supposed to drop Peter off at her place," Melissa explains. "That was the usual arrangement. But she had gotten the idea that Dirk was seeing some-body, and she showed up at the door."

Shanna made no attempt to hide her displeasure when she saw Melissa. The angry mother marched into the apartment and scooped up her child. Dirk tried to make polite introductions, but Shanna was not interested in meeting his gorgeous new girlfriend. Shanna left abruptly.

Melissa couldn't blame her. "The breakup was very, very fresh. I understood that Shanna was hurting." But Melissa had *not* been the cause of the breakup, and Shanna's hostile energy had left her shaken. "When Shanna got home, she called Dirk. He didn't pick up, so Shanna left a message on his answering machine and said some-thing like, 'I'm not sure I'm comfortable sharing custody of Peter if *she* is going to be around. I want Peter to know that *I'm* his mom.'"

Melissa had no intention of taking her place as Peter's mother, but she had made an enemy of her simply by dating the man who had broken her heart. Melissa cringed when she heard the hostile mes-sages that Shanna continued to leave for Dirk. Shanna was not happy that Melissa was in his life, and she made her feelings clear. Shanna was such a complete opposite of her that Melissa wondered how in the world Dirk had been attracted to them *both*. Melissa was a hard worker, but Shanna didn't have a job. Melissa was bubbly and optimistic, while Shanna always seemed angry. Even their hair-styles were about as different as they could be. Shanna's black hair was cropped short, while Melissa's long, straight hair was blond.

Shortly after she began seeing Dirk, Melissa was at his second-floor apartment one day while he was at work. "I was watching TV in the living room when I started to hear noises. It sounded like someone was banging on the wall outside of the apartment." At first, she was more curious than concerned. "I didn't think it had anything to do with me. I thought, 'Oh, someone's moving.'"

But it was not as if someone carrying furniture occasionally bumped against the outside wall. It was an intense racket, and it seemed deliberate. She got up and moved toward the door, hoping Dirk had remembered to lock it when he left. Suddenly she saw the doorknob wiggling and realized that someone was trying to open the door! "I was terrified!" But the door *was* locked, and whoever was outside gave up on trying to get in. Melissa crept to the door and peered out the peephole. "I saw items in the hallway, but I couldn't really make out what they were. I wasn't going out there to see! After a minute I heard the banging again."

Through the peephole, she saw Shanna come into view with an armload of stuff. "She just threw it all down and then left, banging away. Shanna knew my car, and I'm sure she saw that I was there. About two or three minutes later, she came back with more stuff! I didn't realize it at the time, but it was stuff that Dirk had left at her place. She was going crazy with it, throwing it against the door. It was like someone was literally banging down the door."

Trembling, Melissa wondered when it was going to stop. Shanna continued to make trip after trip. Nearly half an hour later, the noises ceased. Had she left, or was she waiting out there for Melissa to open the door? There was no use looking through the peephole because something was blocking her view. "I didn't know what she was capable of at this point. I felt she was so unstable, and I thought, *Who knows what she'll do?* I called my friend, Valerie Ness. I said, 'Valerie, I don't know what to do! I think Shanna is going crazy! She piled a bunch of stuff outside! I can't even see out into the hallway anymore!'"

Valerie arrived within minutes, but she didn't knock on the door. Instead she called out, sounding somewhat muffled. "Melissa, can you hear me?"

"Yes!" Melissa yelled, wondering why her friend sounded so far away.

"Shanna's not here!" Valerie shouted. "Go ahead and open the door!"

The door to the apartment opened inward, and when Melissa opened it, she was stunned to see that the doorway was completely blocked. "Shanna had piled everything in front of the door. It was weird things like barbells and dumbbells and mini cabinets and bookshelves. She pretty much built a fort! I wouldn't have been able to get out of the apartment without help!"

Valerie had to dismantle the wall of items stacked seven feet high. She moved it, piece by piece. Finally, the doorway was clear, and Melissa was free. "I called Dirk and left a message. I said, 'I don't know what you want me to do. Shanna left a lot of stuff in the middle of the hallway. I'm assuming it's yours.' He ended up leaving work early and came home."

Dirk glanced at the cluttered hallway. "Yup. This is the stuff I left over at her place." Melissa was clearly rattled, and while Dirk tried to be sympathetic, he couldn't understand why she was as upset as she was. He agreed it was rude of Shanna to return his things in such a reckless manner, but she hadn't done any real damage. But Melissa felt threatened on a visceral level. Shanna's dark energy was almost palpable, and the jilted woman wore it like a heavy coat. Melissa tried to avoid her, but that was not always possible. Whenever they crossed paths, she felt drained afterward.

The only person who understood was Valerie. While Dirk told Melissa she was overreacting, Valerie agreed she had good reason to be frightened. But Shanna had to remain in Melissa's life because she was Peter's mother, and *he* was Dirk's child. Melissa was growing increasingly attached to Dirk, so it looked like they were all in the mess together, one big unhappy family! Melissa hoped that Shanna would settle down, but her rage seemed to just keep building.

"Whenever Peter was with us, Shanna was always getting stranded somewhere. She would call Dirk and say that her car broke down, and she needed him to come get her. She would do anything she could to interrupt our relationship. Sometimes she had Peter with her when her car broke down, and Dirk did not like the idea of his child being stranded in the middle of nowhere, so he'd rush to help."

Melissa loved the fact that Dirk was such a devoted father, but she was bothered that Shanna used that to manipulate him. They had been together about two months, when they were jolted from a sound sleep at 2 A.M. "There was a big bang on the front door," Melissa recalls. "Dirk said 'Who was that?' and I said, 'Who do you *think* it was? It's Shanna! Go get the door!' But she wasn't at the door." Melissa glanced out the window and saw Shanna in the moonlight, running across the yard toward the parking lot. "She's there!" she cried. "She's running to her car!"

"Well, I guess she's gone," Dirk said, and they went back to bed.

The next morning Melissa went out to her car, a black Mitsubishi Eclipse. She took one look at it and gasped. "My car was keyed, and I mean, really, really keyed. The scratches went up and down and all around. I loved that car, so of course I was upset. It ended up being $3,700 worth of damage." But no one had actually *seen* Shanna vandalize the car. "My mom used to work at the police station, so I asked her if anything could be done. She said I could report it, but nothing would come of it, because no one had witnessed the vandalism. I felt like there was no point in reporting it." Melissa wanted Dirk to see the damage, but he was at work. She called to say she was on her way over.

"Shanna's here, too," he told her.

"Oh *great*!" Melissa snapped sarcastically. "That's just wonderful!" Sure enough, Shanna was there, in the parking lot with her toddler in her car with her. Melissa parked her Eclipse, and Shanna approached and said, "I want you to know I didn't do that to your car."

"I think you did, Shanna!" Melissa responded with a concerted effort to stay calm. "I think you lie a lot. I think you are a confused, troubled woman."

Soon another message was left on Dirk's answering machine. "Melissa," Dirk said. "I think you're going to want to listen to this." He pushed the button to replay the message, and Shanna's remorseful voice filled the room, her apology punctuated with sobs. "I just want to let everybody know that I'm sorry for how poorly I've been reacting. I just remember what it was like when we were a family, and how you played with the kids, and I just miss you!"

"She sounded sincere," Melissa recalls. "It was genuine. It made sense. The man you love had a family with you, and he doesn't want to be with you anymore, and it hurts. *I get it*." Was Shanna truly sorry? Melissa wondered if Dirk's ex was mentally ill. Maybe she had no control over her actions. She had compassion for her, but that didn't make her less afraid.

Shanna followed up on her apology with a special treat. Home-baked chocolate chip cookies, six in all. Four were in a container marked "Dirk and Peter," and two were in a container labeled "Melissa." All six cookies appeared identical, and a chill tiptoed down Melissa's back as she considered a possible reason why Shanna had segregated two for her. "Dirk!" Melissa cried. "She's trying to poison me!"

He laughed. "She's just trying to show her nice side."

"I don't think so," said Melissa. She threw her cookies in the trash. She has no idea if Dirk ate his cookies but doesn't remember anyone getting sick. Shanna's presence seemed constant. Sometimes she parked outside and sat in her car. Sometimes they glimpsed her driving by. Even when she wasn't keying Melissa's car, leaving antagonizing messages or presenting her with suspect cookies, the threat was always there. It was almost worse when things were quiet. What was she planning to do *next*? Melissa's normally calm demeanor was replaced by a chronic case of the jitters. "At the time I was a pharmacy tech. And all of a sudden, guess who's in the pharmacy tech program at Vatterott College?"

The college had recently established a new campus in Omaha, and Shanna Golyar enrolled there and began training to become a certified pharmacy technician. Of all the careers she could have pursued, why did she pick the exact one Melissa had chosen? Was it just a weird coincidence?

When Melissa looks back on her relationship with her stalker, she divides it in her mind into phases. "First it was the rage period," she explains, adding that the next phase was so peculiar she wasn't sure how to classify it. It began when Shanna decided to become a pharmacy tech. Melissa tried to shrug that off as a fluke, but then Dirk mentioned that Shanna had extensions put in her hair.

"What does it look like?" Melissa asked him.

"Well," Dirk said slowly, "now that I think about it, it kind of looks like *your* hair."

Melissa felt a prickle of dread. Surely *this* was not a coincidence! The same job and now the same hair? *What was Shanna up to?* "I never saw the extensions because they didn't last long. They fell out. Dirk said that they were put in by a friend of hers who was in cosmetology school. She was still learning, and it didn't turn out right."

The fact that Shanna's extensions had fallen out didn't give

Melissa pause, but the mention of a friend did. Somehow, she could not picture the hostile woman hanging out with a pal, sharing giggles and gossip. "She has a *friend*?" Melissa asked.

"Well, they're not really *friends*. Shanna doesn't really have friends," Dirk said, explaining that the budding cosmetologist was an acquaintance who lived in the same apartment complex.

"Don't you find it weird that she never has friends?" Melissa pressed.

He admitted that it struck him as little odd but that he hadn't given it much thought. He also felt that there was nothing alarming about the fact Shanna was shopping for a black Mitsubishi. Dirk was relieved to know his son would be riding in a more reliable car, and he agreed to cosign on it.

"But *I* have a black Mitsubishi!" cried Melissa. "Dirk, can't you see what's going on here? She's going to have the same car as I do, she tried to make her hair like mine, and she's going to college to be a pharmacy tech!"

"What's your problem?" Dirk countered. "She's trying to better herself!"

Melissa was frustrated that he couldn't see what was so obvious to her. She told him, "I don't have any problem with her wanting a better car. I don't have a problem with her wanting an education. I don't have a problem that she's trying to make herself feel better by looking nice. But it bothers me that she's doing all of these things to portray *me*! Dirk, there is something really, really wrong with her! This is so unhealthy. She needs help!"

"You're overreacting," said Dirk. "She's just jealous of you because you're with me, and she wants to be with me. That's all it is."

Except for their difference of opinion on Shanna, Melissa and Dirk got along great, and in the middle of the stalker drama, they married, and Melissa gave birth to a baby boy, Craig. Melissa was thrilled to be a mother, but now she had a biological link to her stalker. Their sons were brothers!

When they moved to a bigger apartment, Melissa had strict criteria. "Me being the nervous wreck that I was, I said 'Okay, I want an apartment that requires controlled access. I don't want it on the *first* floor. I want it on the *second* or *third* floor.' I wanted it higher up, so that she couldn't just get in through a window. She would need a ladder—if she were going to go to that length. After we moved to the new apartment, we got letters from her about how much better her life was now that she was no longer with Dirk."

It would have been nice to believe that Shanna was sincere, that she'd finally let go of her obsessions and was enjoying a fulfilling life. But it was obvious she was still focused on them when she sent a letter to Melissa at the drugstore where she worked. Prickling with apprehension, Melissa ripped open the envelope and read the enclosed note. She would have been devastated if she'd believed Shanna's lies. "I didn't believe a thing that came out of her mouth! Not one thing!" Melissa stresses. "She claimed that Dirk was cheating on me with her. And she sent pictures." Melissa scrutinized the blurry images, allegedly of Shanna and Dirk in bed together. "It looked like them, but for all I knew, those pictures were from the time they were together."

The envelopes of photos of "the affair" continued to arrive over the next week. Melissa trusted Dirk. She figured that Shanna was just trying to get between them again, though one of the photographs startled her. "It was a photo of Dirk without his shirt on, and it showed the *new* tattoos on his arm. He was in bed, but it wasn't our bed. Dirk was upset when I got all of those pictures. He went into a state of disbelief." Melissa assured him she didn't believe the lies. She assumed the photos were altered in Photoshop, with the new tattoo added. "'This is right up Shanna's alley,' I told him. 'Why are we so surprised? She has no boundaries. She has no limitations. She's always coming up with something.'"

The stalking rattled them both, though Melissa was far more bothered by it than her husband. The hostility, after all, was focused on *her*. Shanna had never keyed *his* car or trapped him in the apartment with a barricade of furniture. Dirk, however, did not like seeing his wife so troubled. He, too, wished Shanna would stay out of their lives, but the fact she was the mother of his son meant that he was forever connected to her. Despite the troubles with Shanna, Melissa and Dirk had some good years together. He was attentive and loving to both his sons, and she was impressed by what a wonderful father he was. She remembers how he patiently tolerated the kids' TV shows he found so annoying. "Peter loved Barney, the purple dinosaur. Dirk *hated* that dinosaur, but whenever Barney came on the television screen, Peter would get so happy, and jump up and down, waving his fists in the air with approval, that Dirk couldn't help but smile."

When he was a preschooler, Peter helped them ready the room for the new baby. Melissa agreed with her husband that it was important to make the child feel secure. They didn't want him to be jealous of the new baby, so they did what they could to make Peter feel included. Dirk held Peter up, and one by one, Melissa put the colorful Baby Toons decals in the little boy's hands. The youngster then "smacked the stickers to the wall to help decorate for his new baby brother."

Dirk would continue to be a devoted father, but there came a day when he was no longer devoted to Melissa. He asked for a divorce. They'd been together nearly four years, and she'd hoped their union would last a lifetime. "I didn't want my marriage to end. *He* did. I remember thinking, 'Well, at least Shanna will be gone.' That's what I *thought*." Melissa was wrong.

Dirk moved out and eventually became engaged again. If his new fiancée had problems with Shanna, Melissa never heard about it. While Dirk and Melissa shared custody of their son, it seemed *Melissa* had gotten *full* custody of their stalker! Shortly after the split, Melissa took her Eclipse for an oil change. "I think I'm already in your system," she told the shop's receptionist.

"Oh, here you are," said the receptionist, checking the records. "You were in here not too long ago."

"It's actually been quite a while," said Melissa.

"No, you were here recently. You brought in your 2001 Mitsubishi Gallant."

A Gallant? Her car was a Mitsubishi *Eclipse*, but Shanna drove a 2001 Gallant, a similar model to the Eclipse. "I'm sorry?" Melissa said, so stunned she wondered if she'd heard right. "*What* kind of car?"

Someone claiming to be Melissa had the Gallant serviced at the shop. It had to be Shanna—Shanna who'd copied her hairstyle, followed her into the pharmacy field, and purchased a car so similar to hers—was now using her *name*!

Possibly the most disturbing thing about the incident was the fact that it had occurred *after* Melissa's breakup from Dirk. Why would

Shanna continue with her strange stalking of Melissa? Shanna had initially picked on her because she was jealous of her relationship with Dirk. But Shanna was well aware of the divorce and knew Melissa was no longer an obstacle. Why was she continuing with her campaign to harass her? The one shimmering lining in the dark cloud of Melissa's divorce was her knowledge that she'd be free of the stalker who had kept her on edge for nearly half a decade. But Shanna was not yet done with her. "I always thought she was going to leave me alone after I was no longer with Dirk because I thought that was the reason for the stalking. But she kept at it. After I found out she had used my name, I was worried about identity theft, so I signed up for identity-theft protection."

The program Melissa chose made it easy for her to check her own credit history for discrepancies. "I recognized everything on the report, except for one thing. A year prior someone had opened an account for a five-hundred-dollar credit line. It was maxed out, and nothing was ever paid. Then the account was closed." It was a black mark on Melissa's otherwise perfect credit. "I looked up the company online and saw it sold cleaning supplies." For a fraction of an instant she wondered if Shanna was the thief but quickly dismissed the idea. "It could have been anybody. I couldn't think of any reason why Shanna would need five-hundred-dollars' worth of cleaning supplies."

Years later she learned Shanna had started a house-cleaning business, and only then would she realize her stalker had used her credit, but at the time she discovered the fraud she had no evidence of that. Melissa never saw a bill for the unpaid debt. "My guess is that she used my name, my information, but her address, so I was never aware I was being charged for those things."

Melissa moved in with her mom after her breakup with Dirk. One of the more peculiar things occurred about a year and a half after the divorce. Dirk was picking up their son when he mentioned, "Oh, Shanna said that she saw you at the grocery store, and she says, 'Congratulations.'"

Melissa regarded him quizzically. *"Excuse me?"*

"Shanna says you're pregnant."

"I can assure you, I'm *not* pregnant!"

"She just wanted me to tell you that."

"Okay!" said Melissa. "Whatever." She forgot about the odd exchange until three weeks later when a package arrived for her in her mother's mailbox. It was a sample from an infant formula company, and more samples began to arrive regularly. Puzzled, she phoned the company and asked why she was on their mailing list. She was told, "You signed up online for free monthly samples."

"I'm sorry for the misunderstanding," Melissa said. "But I didn't sign up to get samples. I don't have a baby and have no use for formula." The company representative thanked her for calling and said they'd remove her from the list. She tried to shrug it off as a mistake. "But about two months later, I started getting the samples again!" Could Shanna be behind it? She had, after all, made a point to ask Dirk to congratulate her on her nonexistent pregnancy just weeks before the first formula packet arrived.

Melissa didn't want to jump to paranoid conclusions. "I thought maybe it was a fluke." Still, she couldn't overcome the eerie sensation that someone was watching. If Shanna *was* behind the formula confusion that would mean she knew Melissa's parents' address. How would she know that Melissa was living with her mother, and how would she know the address? Could Shanna have *followed* her there? The idea heightened Melissa's anxiety. She couldn't drive to the grocery store without glancing in her rearview mirror to see if she was being followed. If a strange car turned when she did, her heart dropped a beat, and she held her breath until she could be certain Shanna was not behind the wheel of the vehicle on her tail.

It had been a long time since Melissa could relax without worrying someone was watching. Craving tranquility, she rented a cute studio apartment on the top floor of a high security building. She would continue to live with her mother on the days she had her son, but now she had a cozy nest she could escape to when Craig was with Dirk. She didn't tell Dirk about her getaway place for fear he'd inadvertently mention it to Shanna. She got no mail there, and all of her bills were still sent to her mom's home. "I felt safe there at first." Then a small package, addressed to her, arrived at the new apartment. The formula company had sent her another sample. Melissa felt queasy. She'd taken extreme measures to keep her address secret. Someone had gone to a lot of trouble to make sure she received that package. Her stalker was sending her a message, and that message was frighteningly clear: *I know where you are.*

It was the last "gift" from her stalker. Apparently, Shanna lost interest in her sometime after that, though it's hard to pinpoint when. It was many months before Melissa realized she no longer had to glance over her shoulder to see who might be watching.

While Melissa Strom and Amy Flora had never met, they had some things in common. Both were wonderful mothers. Both worked hard at their jobs. Both had had a healthy sense of fear when it came to Liz. And both had been chastised for that fear to the point where they were made to feel as if they were foolish and paranoid. The similarities did not end there, for each had a loyal friend with amazing wisdom.

Melissa had Valerie. Amy had Brandie.

The stalker targeted Brandie Bates with some odd messages from a Facebook page, identifying herself as Cari Farver. They weren't insults or threats, but requests. Could Brandie babysit for "Cari's" child?

How in the world did "Cari" know that Brandie babysat? She sometimes watched kids, including Dave and Amy's kids, but that was *not* public knowledge. She never posted about it on Facebook, and only a small circle of people was aware of it. Not only was it odd that "Cari" had known Brandie babysat, it didn't make sense that she'd contact her. Brandie had heard that the missing woman's son was a teenager, way too old for a sitter. She felt the hairs on the nape of her neck prickle to attention as she recalled Dave had once brought Liz along when he picked up his kids. Something clicked. In a solemn voice, she told Amy, "I don't think this is Cari messaging me. I think it's Liz. *Cari is not alive.*"

The friends pondered the possibility for a moment and then brushed it off. "We decided we'd watched too many *Lifetime* movies," says Amy. The Lifetime Network's slogan is "Lifetime— Television for Women," and the channel features dramatic films about women in jeopardy. The heroines often find themselves in harrowing and bizarre situations, and while many of the stories are based on real-life events, few viewers expect to find themselves in similar scenarios. Lifetime movies are popcorn-chomping escapes, and the danger vanishes the instant the TV is turned off. Even when the movies are touted as true stories, few believe that such things could happen to *them*. *Not to them*. *Not to anyone they know*. The ninety-minute dramas are carved from the tragedies of women living far, far away—women they have never met and never *will* meet. But for a sober moment, Amy and Brandie wondered. Could they be living in a world as scary as a made-for-TV-movie? *No!* The idea was ludicrous! They laughed, but their laughter was leaden, weighed down by an underlying dread.

CHAPTER FOURTEEN

GARRET SLOAN REMEMBERS the moment he first suspected his girl-friend was cheating on him. It was the Fourth of July 2012, and he'd taken her and her two kids to watch the fireworks at Lake Manawa State Park in Council Bluffs. The park was crowded with spectators. Some had brought lawn chairs, and many had spread out blankets to sit on. It had been hot that day, with the temperature peaking at a sweltering ninety-five degrees. The sun had long since dipped below the horizon, and it was cool enough now that people slipped into sweaters and jackets as they watched the spectacular show over the lake.

Most of the crowd had gathered by the water's edge to watch the dazzling lights exploding in the black velvet sky, but Liz suggested they sit on a grassy area, halfway between the lake and the car. They could still see the fireworks, had the space all to themselves and could get to the car quickly to avoid the traffic jam when the show was over.

Garret was accustomed to Liz's aversion to affection in public, especially around her kids, but that night she was more aloof than usual. "She was texting somebody all night. I could see it. She was trying to be sneaky about it. I asked her about it, and she said, 'Oh it's a guy I met, and he's helping me with my car.'" It was his first hint that David Kroupa had entered their lives, though Garret didn't yet know his name and was only beginning to suspect that his girlfriend had been unfaithful.

* * *

"I have never thought that someday my life may be written down on the pages of a book, and if I *did*, I can certainly tell you I never thought it would be in this capacity," Garret confides, adding that it's "not really the thing a person wants to think about in regards to the legacy they will leave and how their story will be told."

Garret had indeed found himself written into a real-life script that was more nightmare, heartache, and drama than he could have imagined. Decent folks don't expect to be swept up into the dark plots of dangerous people, and Garret is about as down-to-earth, honest, and kind as a human being can be. He'd lived three and a half decades of a relatively calm existence before Shanna Elizabeth Golyar stepped into his life and slowly attempted to dismantle it. Her mistake was confusing his kindness with weakness, maybe because kindness was something she did not understand. She had certainly been on the *receiving* end of kindness many times, but *being* kind was a foreign concept. It is only in retrospect that these observations can be made, for Garret would have to wander through a baffling maze of deceptions before he could comprehend the depth of her duplicity.

Garret Sloan's story began in Council Bluffs, where he was born in 1973 and has lived most of his life. The Sloans were the typical nuclear family, and Garret had a sister, four years older. His parents' marriage remained intact until long after he was grown. His father's second marriage would give Garret a beloved little sister, one who is young enough to be his daughter, but he "was the baby of the family" throughout the 1970s and 80s. The kids were smart, college bound from the beginning, his father made a good living, their house was comfortable, and the family went to the Lutheran Church every Sunday.

Garret achieved "decent grades" with minimal effort, and he spent his time after school hanging out with friends. "It was back in the day when you really didn't have to worry about kids being abducted," he notes, describing a quiet, suburban neighborhood where the ranch-style houses were built close together. "When your parents wanted you to come home, they wouldn't call you on a cell phone or text you. They would walk out onto the deck or the front porch and yell across the neighborhood for you."

The family loved dogs and usually shared their home with a four-legged, furry member. Garret fondly remembers two bulldogs, Ginger and Pebbles, and a Boston Terrier named Angel. Up until fifth grade, Garret was thin "as a stick. That's when the genetics kicked in." All the Sloan males had a tendency to gain weight in their teens, and he was no exception. He had more padding than he would have liked, but his bigger challenge was dealing with Perthes Disease, a rare childhood condition that affects the hip. "I had to wear braces that made me look and walk bow-legged." Complications included a slight discrepancy in leg length that resulted in an uneven gait, despite surgery in the ninth grade to slow the growth of the longer leg. That leg experienced another growth spurt after the operation, but he learned to compensate, and now no one notices the difference unless he points it out. It may have been that physical anomaly that sparked his interest in the workings of the body and inspired him to earn his Bachelor of Education in Exercise Science.

As Garret entered the workforce, computers were becoming ubiquitous, and career opportunities in electronics were abundant. Not only was he drawn to computers, he also had the ability to grasp the complexities of Information Technology (IT), and he soon found himself working in that field. Hired by Pottawattamie County in 2006, he has been employed by their IT department ever since.

For most of his life, Garret has been unattached, and that may have something to do with the fact his weight has yo-yoed over the years. During periods his weight peaked, he felt less comfortable meeting women. In September 2010, he had just dropped fifty pounds but was still a husky 250. He planned to lose more weight, but he was feeling fairly confident when he posted his profile on an online dating site. When it comes to Garret's most attractive physical qualities, women like the fact he is tall, has a strong chin and warm gray eyes. A nondenominational Christian who is true to his values, he hoped to meet a woman who shared his beliefs. It wasn't long before he met Liz via the dating site, and they made plans to get together.

On their first date, Garret and Liz watched a movie at his Omaha apartment. "We were intimate, but we didn't have sex," he remembers. Liz had made the first move, and after she went home, she texted him and implied he wasn't interested in her. It was his body language that had tipped her off, she told him. His body language spoke louder than words, and it had practically shouted that he did not find her appealing. He couldn't understand how she'd gotten that impression. He was actually very attracted to her, so he figured she must be insecure to need so much reassurance. "I had to convince her I liked her."

Maybe Liz felt rejected because she'd expected him to be more sexually aggressive, but he was looking for a relationship, not a one-night stand. It was their *first* date, and he wasn't the kind of guy to take advantage of a woman. Soon they were seeing each other regularly, and he was flattered that the slender, lovely lady wanted to be with him. He was thirty-seven, had not had many relationships, and it had been a couple of years since his last one had ended. Liz seemed to be into him, and he was pleased with "the attention she was giving me." Oddly, she pulled away from him in public, but he admits, "I was just enjoying any kind of affection, even if it seemed like it was being hidden."

Though they saw each other just a couple times most weeks, he knew he was on her mind, because she texted him so often. It made him smile to see her constant messages pop up in his phone, and unless he was working, he dropped whatever he was doing to answer her. After two years alone, it felt good to be the focus of an attractive woman's attention. They soon became sexually intimate, but Garret didn't find her to be particularly passionate, and, in fact, describes her as "a robotic" lover. Was she self-conscious because of her strict upbringing? Liz had described a stifling childhood, raised by adoptive parents who gave her no freedom. She told him that her family was extremely religious, but he wasn't clear on their beliefs. Had she been shamed for her sexuality? Maybe she would become less inhibited as time went on.

It seemed to Garret that Liz had had a very hard life. She confided that she was disillusioned by relationships because every man she'd ever been with had mistreated and used her. He vowed to be different. "I was determined to be the guy who didn't use her." After everything she'd been through, it was understandable she had some insecurities, and she definitely had her jealous moments. Once, early on in the relationship, Garret had been talking on the phone to his sister when Liz became suspicious. He quickly put her fears to rest. "That was my *sister*," he told her and assured her that he had no interest in pursuing other women.

He saw her jealousy as a sign she cared about him—cared so much that she was afraid of losing him. Was he going to cheat on her like the others had? He didn't want Liz to worry, and she calmed down as he reassured her. Garret was honest and loyal, not the type to stray. He believed in monogamy, and as he points out now, "I never gave Liz any reason to be jealous." He also believed that trust was important in a relationship and that it should go both ways.

Something unsettling occurred about two months after he met Liz, before they were officially exclusive. It was Garret's understanding that she was single and free to date, but he was in for a shock when he got a text from Allen Motts. "Allen contacted me through Yahoo Messenger. Somehow he had broken into her account and gotten my name."

According to Allen, Liz was *his* girlfriend. Not only that, they were living together. Stunned by the news, Garret confronted Liz, but he soon felt like the world's biggest shmuck. She vehemently denied she was still involved with Allen. How dare Garret accuse her of such a thing? Didn't he trust her? What was wrong with him, anyway? He had found himself apologizing for insulting her. "It was her typical fashion to put it back on me—to attack me, and somehow make it my fault. It was really weird. But somehow, she convinced me that he was her ex."

He tried not to think about the fact he'd never been to her place, never seen for himself that she lived alone with her children. "It was a long time before she invited me over." She had been so indignant at Garret's accusation, that he figured Allen had to be lying. Liz convinced him that Allen was nothing more than a jealous ex-boyfriend who was trying to make trouble. A few weeks after his email exchange with Allen, Liz sent Garret a text, announcing that she couldn't see him anymore because Allen was moving back in with her. While Garret was not exactly heartbroken, he was disappointed and admittedly a little sad when Liz dumped him. He was sorry to see her go, but he accepted that it was over.

"Just after New Year, I got a text from her, wanting to know if we could meet for lunch and talk." They met near Garret's apartment, at the Red Robin Restaurant. Liz told him she'd fought with Allen, kicked the guy out, and this time it was over for good. Garret was happy to hear she missed him and wanted to try again. At the time, he didn't question anything she told him. He wanted to trust her, and he didn't think he had jealous tendencies, but Liz implied that he could be quite irrational and paranoid. She never let him forget his accusations about Allen Motts. Garret was sorry he had been so quick to believe the guy when he'd claimed Liz was two-timing them. The last thing Garret wanted was to come off as an insecure jerk. But another questionable situation arose about nine months into their relationship in the early summer of 2011 when he was still living in his Omaha apartment.

Though he'd never met any of Liz's friends, she sometimes brought her sister, Marcy, along to swim in the pool. While her kids swam and splashed about in the water, Liz stretched out on a chaise lounge. She wore sunglasses to protect her eyes, but she let her skin bake until her tan turned brown. The bikini she wore testified to the fact she was in great shape. It was fun to have Liz and her kids there, and it never occurred to him that they came for the pool. Liz was his girlfriend, and she was there to visit *him*. Why shouldn't she enjoy the pool when she came to see him?

Then one afternoon he was alone when he decided to take a dip. He rounded the corner with his towel rolled up under his arm and stopped short. He had hoped there wouldn't be many people using the pool, and he certainly did not expect to see this one. It was Marcy, relaxing in the sun, drying off after a swim. She seemed surprised to see him and a little flustered as she explained that Liz had gone to pick up fast food at a nearby restaurant.

Garret was irritated when he realized that his girlfriend had come to use his pool but hadn't even bothered to say hello to him. "I was pissed while I was sitting there, waiting for her to get back." Liz soon returned, but she was not alone. Garret was shocked to see she had a guy with her. "At that point, I felt sick to my stomach." Liz didn't appear embarrassed that Garret had caught them. She didn't apologize or bother to introduce him to the man she'd invited to swim. She chatted and laughed with the guy, ignoring Garret. "She never paid any attention to me. It was like I was invisible."

Anyone observing the group would have assumed that Liz and Garret were strangers to each other. The interlopers proceeded to picnic by the pool as if they were in a public place. Liz didn't offer food to Garret. The scent of the greasy takeout fare mingled with the sharp odor of chlorine, and Garret no longer felt like swimming. He said he wasn't feeling well and excused himself, but they didn't seem to care. Liz barely glanced up as he got up to leave.

The next time he talked to Liz, he attempted to express his hurt feelings, but she suggested he had a problem. Why couldn't she talk to a guy without him getting jealous? The dude was a *friend,* and she never dreamed Garret would mind if she brought someone over to swim on a hot day. If she was going to cheat on him, why would she do it right under his nose? Garret ended up feeling guilty for jumping to conclusions. "She was very good at making you doubt what you'd seen." He didn't want to dwell on negativity and concluded it was a misunderstanding. He decided to put the incident behind him. He knew couples didn't always agree, and he made an effort to look at the world from her perspective. But sometimes she criticized him for things that made no sense. "She tried to make it seem like I had memory problems. If I ever forgot something, she'd say, 'Well, you do that *all* the time.'"

Garret knew that wasn't true. He prided himself on his excellent memory. Sure, he forgot something once in a while. Everyone did that. Why was Liz so set on convincing him that he was becoming feeble-minded? It wasn't worth worrying about, and he tossed it off as a personality quirk. No relationship was perfect, and he tried to look at the bright side.

In June 2012, Garret bought his first house. It had belonged to his grandmother, and when she moved into a nursing home, it was offered to him at slightly below market value. He liked the quiet neighborhood in Council Bluffs and was glad to live closer to both his family and work. The two-bedroom, one-bathroom home with a daylight basement had enough space for a roommate, so his long-time buddy, Gabe, moved in.

Garret and Liz were coming up on the two-year anniversary of the day they'd met, and overall, he thought things were pretty good between them. He didn't mind that she leaned on him, and he helped her out whenever he could, sometimes giving her money to pay her bills. It felt good to save the day—to be the guy who stepped up to pay the electric bill she'd been anguishing over.

Liz was petite, and when she looked up at him with her big brown eyes, she could appear so vulnerable, it brought out his protective instincts. His heart went out to the single mother who seemed to struggle so hard to get by. Garret didn't hesitate when she asked him to watch her kids when she had to work all night. They were good kids and easy to get along with. Trina was usually engrossed in a book, while Peter played video games. They stayed over at his place often. Liz hadn't told him any specifics about her cleaning business, but it couldn't have been easy on her to work all night. Not only that, it apparently was not lucrative.

Garret remembers that Liz had told him she had a lot on her plate. She had claimed that in addition to her housecleaning business, she was taking classes to become a dental hygienist and that she was also working as a nurse. He assumed it was true because he had seen her dressed for work in scrubs. He wasn't sure *where* she worked, but he does remember the macabre joke they shared about her odd mix of careers: As a nurse, she would know how to kill Garret, and she could get away with it because she could use her cleaning expertise to wash away evidence. It was a ridiculous idea, and they'd chuckled about it. He couldn't have imagined that he'd one day look back upon that "joke" with an icy shudder.

Despite the many hours she claimed she worked, Liz seemed constantly worried about money. His natural inclination was to offer help, though she usually made half-hearted attempts to protest. He didn't have to help, she told him. She didn't *want* him to pay her bills for her. She would just have to figure something out on her own. As she continued to mope and fret, he kept insisting until she accepted his help. She was his girlfriend, and he was glad to do what he could to make her life easier. It was gratifying to see her relieved smile when he made a problem disappear. Liz, of course, knew if she complained to Garret about her money woes, he'd want to help. She also knew that if she appeared upset enough, Garret would insist upon helping, even as she protested.

As time passed, she became no more comfortable showing him affection in public, but she showed him she cared behind closed doors. Overall, he felt they got along pretty well. But he sensed a shift in their relationship, beginning with that Fourth of July 2012, when she texted for hours "with her mechanic." Somehow, she was able to convince Garret that the texting during the fireworks was innocent. He had no proof to the contrary, so he shrugged it off, trying to ignore his stomach-churning doubts. "I wanted to believe it. But what mechanic has your personal phone number and talks to you at nine or ten o'clock at night?"

It was hard to fathom that Liz and her mechanic were texting about car repairs for hours at a time. Electronic messaging has become a modern-day mating ritual, and Garret and Liz had once indulged in marathon sessions. That was in the beginning, when their romance was new. "We texted constantly. Even late at night. It was nonstop."

Suddenly she was texting with someone as fervently as she'd once texted with Garret. She didn't tell him she'd met her so called mechanic on an online dating site, and that while he *did* fix cars for a living, the nature of her relationship with him was anything but business. She didn't tell him that the guy's name was Dave Kroupa and that they were dating, just as she didn't tell Dave about Garret. Dave would have been *relieved* to know she had another boyfriend, but she kept Garret a secret. Liz had a very specific image she wanted to paint for Dave, and that picture left no room for other men. She presented herself to Dave as his loyal girlfriend, patiently waiting for him to realize that she was the only woman he needed.

Meanwhile, if Garret ever voiced his suspicions about other men, Liz instantly flipped the conversation, so he ended up feeling like a jealous fool. By the time the autumn's cool breezes began to blow the dying leaves from the trees, Garret had all but forgotten his worries that Liz might be interested in another guy. She was, after all, still with him. Why would she stick around if she wanted to be with someone else?

Garret had been unable to keep off the weight he'd lost before he'd met Liz. He was gradually gaining more weight with each passing month, and though he did plan to go on another diet, he was procrastinating. With his degree in Exercise Science, he knew how to get in shape and was confident the pounds would fall off when he was ready to focus on his health. His girlfriend didn't seem to mind his expanding middle, and he figured that was a good sign their feelings for each other went beyond the superficial.

October 26, 2012, was a cold Friday in Council Bluffs, with temperatures falling below freezing. Garret doesn't remember what he was doing that night, but he was definitely not at the Freaker's Ball. Liz had *not* invited him to the big Halloween Bash at Harrah's Casino, and he was unaware she was there with another man. Most likely, Garret was watching one or both of her kids that night and was probably staring at the TV as his girlfriend of two years posed for a photo with David Kroupa. She didn't show Garret the photos of them, snuggled together in matching togas, and he had no idea that she'd been dating the freewheeling mechanic for months. He still believed that he and Liz were in an exclusive relationship.

Three days later, on October 29, Garret had no inkling that his girlfriend, who did *not* cook, had become hysterical over pots and pans left in Dave's cupboards, and that she had caused an embarrassing scene, interrupting Dave's date with Cari Farver. Garret, of course, didn't know Cari, and Liz had never mentioned her. As October turned to November, and the lives of Dave and Cari and Liz intersected in a horrific collision, Garret was oblivious. For him, it was just another November. The days were short and icy. He spent most of the daylight hours at work, and later he relaxed in the warmth of his home, curtains drawn against the long winter nights as he read, worked on his computer, or watched television.

He saw Liz regularly, often taking care of her kids when she said she had to work at night. There was nothing about Liz that indicated anything out of the ordinary was occurring that November 2012. Sometimes she appeared stressed, but that was often the case for the single mother who seemed to work so hard. He continued to help out as much as he could, giving her cash, paying some of her bills, and taking her to lunch.

He would one day look back on that November in astonishment, wondering what he'd been doing when Cari vanished and why he hadn't noticed that anything was wrong as Liz carried the burden of a secret so heavy it would have crushed a normal human being. She didn't tell Garret her secret and said nothing to him about vandalism in her garage, stolen checks, or the fact she'd reported to police that someone was threatening to kill her.

Though Garret saw no evidence that Liz was upset, he does re-member a peculiar incident that may or may not be significant to whatever was going on with his girlfriend. He can't be certain of the exact day, week, or month, and he can estimate only that it occurred in the fall or winter of 2012. He discovered it by accident, on one of his rare visits to Liz's home when he noticed a distinctive burning odor and commented on it. She quickly explained that she had had a get-together with a few friends, and some of them had lit cigarettes. They had put them out as soon as Liz asked them not to smoke in her house, but the smell still lingered.

His feelings weren't hurt that she'd had a party and not invited him, but two things struck him as strange. Liz didn't have friends as far as Garret knew. At least, he'd never met them, and she had not men-tioned them to him. There was her sister Marcy and the guy they'd brought to his pool, but other than that, he didn't think she had enough friends for a party. He couldn't figure out why she would lie about the source of the odor, but it didn't smell like cigarettes. Something had definitely burned, but it wasn't tobacco. There was no reason at the time for Garret to suspect something sinister had occurred. It didn't seem important, and he put it out of his mind.

The winter of 2012 swept upon Council Bluffs with frigid winds blowing as Garret and his family celebrated the holidays together. He often invited Liz to join them for Thanksgiving and Christmas, but she didn't seem interested in fraternizing with his relatives. Even so, Garret included Liz and her kids on his Christmas shopping list. Liz was easy to shop for because she was a gamer, so he usually got her video games for Christmas and her birthday. She rarely recipro-cated, though one year she gave him "a cheap ring," for Christmas, and he remembers that "she got me a card once for my birthday." Garret didn't expect Liz to give him gifts, and he wasn't offended when she didn't. He knew she had to shop for her kids, and he pre-ferred she spent her money on presents for them. For the most part, it seemed like an ordinary December, and before he knew it, the hol-idays were over, a new year had begun, and he had made a strange new friend.

CHAPTER FIFTEEN

ON NEW YEAR'S DAY, 2013, a text from an unfamiliar number popped up in Garret's phone. It was a friendly greeting, but he was confused. "Who is this?" he asked. The texter explained that she was a friend of Liz's, and that Liz had given her his number as a backup in case she needed to get a hold of her and couldn't reach her. He texted Liz. "Do you know a Cari? She just contacted me, looking for you. She said you gave her my number."

Liz replied, *All my friends have your number. If I'm not working or with them, then I'm with you.*

Okay. Well, she is looking for you I guess.

Okay, thanks! I will call her soon!

K, hon, Garret texted. *She asked me when we started dating. Hope it's okay. I told her we met a couple of years ago.*

LOL, Liz replied. *You don't have to tell me everything. I trust you.*

"Cari" began to text Garret regularly. Over two hundred texts were exchanged between them in the first nine days of January 2013. Often Liz and "Cari" would engage him in simultaneous texting marathons, and he'd jump from one conversation to the other as their messages popped up, intermixed.

It was mostly small talk, but "Cari" occasionally texted comments that seemed designed to provoke him. She wrote that Liz *barely ever mentions you. We didn't even know you two were still dating.*

Garret replied: *Hey, the good news is you knew at one time. LOL.*

I don't know what to say. Like I said, you would have to ask her about that.

In another text, "Cari," wrote, *Seems to me you like women who treat you badly.*

He asked, *Are you guys good friends?*

We used to hang out all the time, but not so much anymore. Why do you ask?

Because of your last text, he typed. Didn't this "Cari" realize that she was badmouthing his girlfriend? Why was Liz's friend trying to make trouble? Disturbed, Garret reported the comments to Liz, warning her that her good pal did not seem to have her best interests at heart. Apparently, Liz then confronted her friend, because "Cari" texted him an apology: *Sorry if I made you uncomfortable. Liz talked to me. You could have told me.*

Always the good sport, he replied, *Sorry too. You're right. I should have said something. Guess it kind of got to me—some of the things you were saying about Liz, and I don't know you very well yet.*

Sometimes "Cari" asked him for advice. *How do you get someone back you care about, even though they've started dating someone else?*

I don't know, he responded honestly. *If they have moved on, I guess I would ask if you were sure you would want them back.*

That's not helping. If Liz left, wouldn't you want her back?

Wary of getting into a personal conversation about his relationship, he changed the subject. The lovelorn texter continued to dwell on her broken heart, and in a later text, she told him that she and her ex and his new girlfriend all worked at West Corp together. *I don't want him with this girl,* she texted. *I wish I could meet a guy like you, sweet, handsome, smart, and we have a lot in common. Not trying to hit on you.*

I don't know about the handsome part. LOL. You've seen me?

Yes, Liz showed me a picture of you. You are very handsome. I would like your arms around me, just saying. I would be proud to have you as a guy I could show.

Garret was embarrassed. Liz's friend was obviously flirting with him, and that didn't seem right. Then again, maybe she was just being nice. He felt obligated to respond. *I appreciate the compliment.*

You're welcome, but I mean it.

The texting conversation with "Cari," was interrupted a moment later when a message from Liz popped up, and they discussed the Yorkie she had adopted. Garret had loaned her the $140 adoption fee, after she had promised to pay him back. She had borrowed a lot of money from him, and she had never once paid him back, but he had a soft spot for animals and loaned her the money because he figured she would give the little dog a good home. The pooch was adjusting, Liz assured him and ended with, *Painting my nails. Can't talk now.*

He went back to his text conversation with Liz's troubled friend. She mentioned her ex again, and Garret wrote, *You still care about your boyfriend and want him back?*

Guess so.

That gave him pause. Liz often gave the identical text response. *Guess so.* It was somewhat unusual, and he was compelled to point that out. *LOL. Sounds like Liz. She always says that.* It was easier to type a plain old "Yes," than to go to the trouble of tapping out "Guess so" with clumsy fingers on a cell phone's tiny keyboard. Why did both ladies make "Guess so" part of their standard texting lingo? He didn't have time to ponder it because he was too busy responding to the dozens of texts filling up his phone. His new phone pal was most curious about things that weren't her business. *How is your relationship?* she asked. *Is it what you want it to be?*

His response was evasive. *Are they ever?*

Yes, she answered.

Things aren't perfect, he admitted. *But we are working on them.*

Wow, you're as bad as her, but her words are, "It's fine, I'll live with it" LOL.

I figured you'd know everything because you guys talk, he wrote.

We do talk. She just seems quiet about you.

Why didn't Liz talk about him? And why was her friend so intent on communicating that fact to him? He didn't know what to make of it. The texts continued with so many popping up over the next week that Garret was often too busy to answer. "Cari" seemed bothered by this and in pouting mode suggested that he didn't want to "talk" with her. He told her that wasn't so and graciously explained he had to work and could not spend every minute of the day texting.

On January 9, 2013, Garret took Liz out to lunch, and the conversation took an interesting turn when she mentioned that someone had been harassing her. She had talked to a detective at the Sheriff's Office about it, and they were trying to help her. "They had downloaded her phone," he remembers. "So, she asked me casually what they could get from the phone—can they download everything from it, from the SD card if you had one in there."

Though Garret worked in the county's IT department, he was uncertain how much data a phone dump could acquire, and he told her so. After lunch, he was surprised to get a call from Deputy Randal Phyllips at the Sheriff's Office. Garret and the detective were acquainted, though they didn't know each other well. After five and a half years working for the county, "I had gotten to know a lot of people there, even at the Sheriff's Office."

When the deputy asked Garret to come in for an interview, he was puzzled and called Liz. "I contacted her because I had just talked to her about this, and I said, 'Why are they contacting me?' I didn't get to talk to her very long about it, and that's when I went in and found out about everything that was going on." Garret was escorted to a small room where he met with Deputy Phyllips and Lieutenant Dwayne Riche. He got the sense that something serious was happening, and it felt a little like being summoned to the principal's office. Garret had always been an honest guy who tried to do the right thing, and now he had an added incentive to cooperate. Pottawattamie County was his *employer,* and he would never do anything to jeopardize his career. It was an odd, almost surreal situation, as the detectives asked him personal questions. They asked about his relationship with Liz, and Garret explained that she was his girlfriend.

Remembering Liz's question, Garrett asked how much information a download could glean. They explained it depended on the type of download, but it was possible to absorb everything. In fact, they'd learned about his association with Liz when they recognized his photo among images on her phone. The detective handed Garrett a picture they'd printed of him with his family. He was shocked when they told him that Liz had labeled it "fat ass." The printed image had no label, and he wasn't sure if he believed the investigators but could think of no good reason for them to lie.

"Are you and Liz exclusive?" Phyllips asked.

Garret confirmed that they were. "That's when they started telling me about Cari, about this missing woman. They told me about what was going on with at least Liz, that she was allegedly getting threats."

Deputy Phyllips revealed that Cari appeared to be jealous of Liz because they were both dating Dave Kroupa. It was the first time Garret had heard the Kroupa name, and the first time he'd heard that his new texting pal was a stalker. He felt queasy. They were implying that his girlfriend was cheating on him! That was bad enough, but the punch they delivered next nearly knocked him out of his chair. "I was told that Liz and David devised this plan to give my information to Cari and hopefully 'sic' her on me, diverting her attention away from them to me." If the scheme unfolded as planned, Garret and "Cari" would fall for each other, and the crazy lady would no longer feel the need to terrorize Liz and Dave.

It was a lot to digest. Had Liz really been unfaithful to him? And did she think so poorly of him that she believed he could actually develop romantic feelings for a woman who, by all accounts, was stark, raving mad? Was he nothing more than "a fat ass" to the woman who swore up and down that he was her one and only? The idea that Liz was plotting against him with the guy she was cheating with was both insulting and hurtful.

The interview with the detectives lasted about an hour, and halfway through Garret got a text from "Cari." "If I remember right, it was something as simple as, 'Hi. How was your day?'" She also had a new phone number, and she texted that to him. He immediately relayed the information to the investigators. Whatever "Cari's" reasons for her bizarre behavior, she was a human being, and Garret felt, "She needed help—which is why I agreed to keep texting her and talking to her, to help the investigators try to find her, so that they could know it was actually her, and she was okay." He agreed immediately when the detectives asked to download his phone. It was new, with virtually no history. Most of his communication with "Cari" had been on his old phone, and he promised to bring it in the next day.

He left the interview in a fog. The scenario the investigators had painted was so different from the reality Garret knew. In this new twisted version of his world, Liz's good pal, "Cari," was threatening to kill her, both women were sleeping with some guy named Dave

Kroupa, and his own girlfriend was involved in a devious plot to set him up with the nut who'd been terrorizing her. Liz was indignant when Garret confronted her. The cops had it wrong. Dave was a guy she'd dated years ago. Sure, they were friends. They saw each other when their kids played together. How dare Garret suggest she was cheating? It wasn't *her* fault that Cari had flipped out. *Of course,* she knew Cari was gaga over Dave. But there was *nothing* romantic between Liz and Dave. If Garret believed that, he was as delusional as "Crazy Cari!"

"Essentially, Liz said she was kind of caught up in the deal, just because she was friends with Dave, and Cari was someone he'd dated. They broke up, and Cari wasn't happy about it." As for labeling his photo "fat ass," Liz was insulted that he would accuse her of such a thing. And the idea that she was trying to dump her stalker on him was ludicrous. Hadn't she just got done telling him at lunch that there was a problem with someone bothering her? It was *Cari.* She sounded surprised that he hadn't realized that, when she thought she'd made that fact perfectly clear. Garret really needed to listen better.

As Liz spun her words around him, he felt almost foolish for doubting her. He told himself he'd overreacted. None of it was Liz's fault. If anything, she was more distressed than he was by the whole mess. If she hadn't been, she wouldn't have gone to the police. This Cari person was obviously a basket case if she was freaked out because Liz had dated Dave a lifetime ago. If Garret allowed himself to be jealous of their bygone relationship, then he was just as unreasonable as the nut who was causing all the trouble.

It crossed his mind that the cops could have deliberately misled him about the situation to throw him off balance. Maybe they thought he was hiding something and wanted to rattle him. It was kind of a low blow to falsely claim his girlfriend was cheating on him and that she'd captioned his photo "fat ass." But Liz sounded genuinely offended by those accusations. Garret wasn't sure what to think about the baffling situation.

He was just beginning to see tiny, blurred fragments of a tragic mystery that he now played a part in. He did his best to make sense of it, but he knew only what police and Liz had told him. The detectives knew a lot more than Garret did, and Liz knew more than all of them put together, though she had managed to make everyone believe she was as mystified as they were.

If Garret had seen the email Liz had received six days earlier, he would have been even more bewildered:

Hey, Cari and I would like Dave and you to come out to dinner Friday night. It's on me. I would like to meet him. Plus, it will be a good chance for me to sort out if they have feelings for each other. Cari says she doesn't have feelings for him, but that he still has feelings for her. So, I would like to see for myself if she is telling the truth. So, if it's no inconvenience, do you think the two of you could come to dinner Friday? Let me know as soon as possible. And thank you, Liz.

Sincerely,
Garret

The email address contained Garret Sloan's name and was registered with Yahoo. It was *not* Garret's email address, but it certainly looked like it could have been. Garret didn't write the email and was not aware of its existence. It had, in fact, been written for Dave Kroupa's benefit. Liz showed Dave the email she claimed Garret had sent her, along with her brusque reply to him: *One, Friday is Dave's date night—or alone night without me. Second, I really don't want to double date with you and Cari. You two haven't even met yet.*

In the bizarre, alternate universe where Garret's cyber-double was developing a romantic interest in "Cari," the two apparently met two days later, after Liz had coolly pointed out to "Garret" that he and "Cari" had yet to meet. If the email sent to David on January 5 was any indication, the set up between the digital versions of Garret and Cari was working beautifully: *So, Cari is here and said I had to email you. So, me and Liz talked a while ago about you, and what she was looking for. So, I just want to say she deserves someone good. She has been hurt so much the last 10 years from abusive to verbal-abusive relationships. I know it's not my place to say shit, plus Liz isn't talking to me, and this will piss her off more. Well, Cari won't let it go, and you know how it is when a beautiful woman asks you to do something. All I ask is that you don't hurt her, and if you*

don't want her, to let her go. I am not going to tell you to leave her
or anything. So, what is going on with you and my girl?
   Garret

   Garret was unaware emails were being sent in his name, and Dave
gave them little thought. Dave was a drowning man, swept away in a
deluge of words, a tsunami of bizarre emails and text messages that
washed over him in an inexplicable, never-ending wave of hate. He
could make no sense of "Cari's" motives, and the weird emails from
"Garret" had all the impact of a drop of rain on a sinking swimmer.

   It didn't dawn on Dave that *Liz* had written the emails from Garret, just as he didn't guess that she was behind the thousands of
threats. In reality, Liz was having a grand time dreaming up nightmares for the men in her life. Dave was no more plotting to sic the
stalker on Garret than Garret was sending Dave emails because "you
know how it is when a beautiful woman asks you to do something."

   When we scrutinize Liz's concoctions with the wisdom of an out-
sider's retrospect, they quickly disintegrate as fakes, particularly in
the case of the Garret letters. What man proposes setting up a double
date so that he can see if his new love interest still has feelings for
another? It's the kind of scheme a pair of giggling preteen girls
might come up with, not a forty-year-old man. And why would a casual male friend of Liz's write to Dave, begging him to treat her
right? For someone so good at manipulating males, Liz had some
curious gaps in her understanding of them. What was Liz trying to
accomplish with the Garret letters? While it's possible she had a
complex plan that went beyond the obvious, a reasonable guess at
her motive suggests two goals. One, she hoped Dave would take to
heart "Garret's" plea for him to treat her better. Maybe it would be
just the nudge needed to inspire him to embrace his true, deep feelings and finally commit to her.

   Also, Liz hoped that the letters from Garret would confirm for
Dave that Cari was alive. If he believed Cari was hanging out with
Garret, then he'd have no reason to suspect she had died. While
Dave showed no sign that he doubted the stalker's identity, Liz
needed to make sure that he would never question that. So far, Dave had
told the police exactly what Liz had wanted him to. He had unwittingly
served as her alibi. He was so sure Cari was terrorizing him, that he
spoke of it as fact, with all the certainty of an eyewitness.

While the phony emails that Liz had written in Garret's name showed an embarrassing lack of understanding of male behavior, they didn't exactly radiate insight into female behavior either. The second fake Garret letter claimed that Cari was pestering him to ask Dave to treat Liz better. Why would the so-called stalker, so wildly jealous of Liz, suddenly become her advocate and implore upon Garret to convince Dave to embrace Liz? Dave didn't question the discrepancy. The world had stopped making sense to him six weeks earlier on November 13, 2012, when the wonderful woman he'd clicked with had seemed to morph into a vicious enemy. Dave was already so overwhelmed that he didn't stop to ponder the lunacy of the Garret letters. Liz was confident that she had Dave and Garret fooled so thoroughly that their heads would never stop spinning.

While she continued to control Dave by making him feel guilty, she was unaware that her grip on Garret had somewhat loosened. He admits he was still unsure. He would waiver over the next months. "But the seed of doubt had been planted," he confides. The meeting with the detectives made a lasting impact, and he could not completely dismiss the things they'd told him.

Garret still had a helluva ride ahead of him. It would not be fun, but he would do it again if he had to, for he believes God placed him in the middle of the horrific situation for a reason. He had a noble role that he would not recognize until much, much later. He would never ask for fame, fortune, or even for thanks for the part he played. Though he won't step forward to make the claim, it would certainly be within his rights to do so. Few people can say, "I helped stop a killer."

CHAPTER SIXTEEN

SHANNA ELIZABETH GOLYAR'S HANDS were stained with blood—figuratively speaking. No one would glance at her soft little hands and see anything amiss. They appeared just like every other thirty-eight-year-old woman's hands, though her fingers were quicker than most as they danced over her cellphone's tiny keyboard because they had had so much practice.

When Shanna's dainty hands were not engaged with a cellphone, they did all of the things that most hands do. Delivered food to her mouth. Gripped a steering wheel. Curled around a doorknob. Waved hello and good-bye. Caressed her lovers. Brushed a strand of hair from her child's eyes.

Yes, Shanna's hands did normal, everyday things, but they had also done something shockingly *abnormal*. They had killed a human being. While only metaphorically stained in blood today, there *was* a day when they were likely covered in actual blood. Tuesday morning, November 13, 2012, to be precise. Probably before 11 A.M. detectives would one day pinpoint that morning as the dark window of time when she brutally took the life of an innocent person.

Perhaps more frightening than the realization that Shanna's soft hands committed murder, is the idea that her heart felt no sorrow over what her hands had done. She went on with her life as if nothing at all had happened. No one could have looked into her eyes and guessed the truth. Because she fooled so many people, she probably believed she was brilliant. She had, after all, gotten away with *murder*. But the reality is, she wasn't brilliant. She wasn't even smart.

Some areas of her intellect were sadly lacking. Liz was no genius. But she did have two things going for her that helped her conceal her evil deeds. First, she could count on our ignorance. We don't expect females to be dangerous. This writer includes herself among the ignorant masses, because even though I went to many trials with my true-crime-author mother, and had a front-row seat as deadly women took the stand, I *still* can't grasp the fact that women can and *do* kill.

Certainly, I can understand on an intellectual level that females can be just as dangerous as males, but if a murderous woman with a smiling face walked up to me on the street tomorrow and said hello, I would not shrink away. My natural inclination would be to trust her. I'd likely feel a warning on a gut level, because most of us do when confronted with evil. But we almost always ignore it, because we allow our eyes, and what we perceive to be our common sense, to override our intuition. If we see a dangerous but feminine, smiling creature with soft, little hands, most of us dismiss the cold, prickle of warning that shivers down our necks. Female sociopaths *know* this. They have spent their entire existence incognito as gentle beings, and they know how they are perceived. Many heartless sociopaths are mothers, and that intensifies the illusion of softness. Shanna Golyar was well aware of the fact that no one would expect her to be dangerous.

She also had a big bag of tricks—or *rather*, a big bag of electronic applications—to aid her in the concealment of her malicious charade. She favored an app called Letter-Me-Later that does exactly what the name implies. It allows a message to be written in advance and sent at a chosen time. Often when she was hanging out with Dave and nowhere near her phone, he or she, or both, received threats from the stalker. Dave had no idea that Liz was sending herself threats.

Even as we embark upon the third decade of the twenty-first century, we are still as naïve about the many ways that electronics can be used to deceive us as we are about the deadly females who walk among us. Liz was two steps ahead of most of us. She educated herself about the myriad cyber applications designed for deception. In January 2013, she still had many more months of freedom ahead of her, many more months to play vicious games and harm innocent souls. No one looked at her and saw a killer. Not the detectives. Not David Kroupa. And not Garret Sloan.

While Garret suspected that his girlfriend wasn't always truthful, he wasn't aware of the depth of her treachery. He was hesitant to flush the relationship down the toilet over things he couldn't prove. He *wanted* to believe in her. And that's why he agreed to help her out again about three weeks after his disturbing meetings with the detectives. Liz told him she had to work all night. It was Wednesday, January 30, 2013. Peter was with his father, but Liz had no one to watch Trina. As usual, Garret allowed her to stay at his place. He didn't mind. She was a nice girl and spent most of her time reading. He was blissfully unaware of the significance of Wednesday.

Liz had insisted that Dave was nothing more than a friend, and while Garret was not entirely confident that that was true, it was more comfortable to believe her than to doubt her. He had no idea that his girlfriend was David Kroupa's Wednesday Girl. Trina spent the night while Liz "worked" on Wednesday night. When Garret left his house early Thursday morning, Trina was waiting for her mother to pick her up and take her to school. They expected Liz to arrive any minute.

Garret arrived home that night to an unpleasant surprise. "When I got off work, I came home, and the first thing I noticed when I walked into the living room was the TV was missing." After looking around and noting more missing things, he called the police and then his roommate. The missing items included the TV, a PlayStation, a computer monitor, a laptop, and, oddly, some of Gabe's clothing—a pair of jeans and his favorite Notre Dame sweatshirt he'd had for years.

There were no broken windows, no sign of forced entry. Had Trina forgotten to lock the door when she left? If so, then why was the door locked when Garret got home? *Someone* had locked that door, and it seemed unlikely that a stranger would burglarize his home only to conscientiously lock up when they were done. He was also puzzled by what he discovered in his garage. "I noticed this big black thing behind a piece of wood, so I pulled it out and, lo and behold, it was the television. Apparently, when it was being taken out of the house, it was dropped and the screen was broken. They had attempted to hide it behind a piece of wood." Garret had kept meticulous records of his valuables and gave police the serial numbers for the stolen electronic equipment. The numbers were added to the lists circulated to local pawn shops.

Other than the burglary of his home, nothing much about the first months of 2013 stood out, though Garret was on the list of people contacted on April 17 by someone claiming to be Cari. It was the same Siena/Francis House hoax that the others had been drawn into. Garret had passed the information along to police, and it was the last time "Cari" contacted him. He was unaware that Dave Kroupa and Liz continued to report cyberstalking and vandalism in the following months. Though he'd hoped to help detectives locate the missing woman, he wasn't privy to any part of their investigation and wasn't told about Phyllips's search of Cari's Macedonia home, the suspicious activity on her fake Facebook page or the vicious threats against Dave's new friend, Jessica McCarthy.

As the summer of 2013 approached, Liz complained to Garret that she was unable to pay her bills and might become homeless. She received a deep discount on the rent from the Omaha Housing Authority's Section 8 program, and as part of the agreement, it was her responsibility to pay the utilities. Garret had already picked up so much of Liz's slack that this time he didn't offer to help. She fell so far behind on the electric bill that the power was turned off. She managed to have it turned back on by using an alias, but the company caught on and shut off the power for good. She knew that once the landlords caught on that she'd breached the contract by failing to pay utility bills, they could evict her, but they were required to give her a 30-day written notice. She expected to be kicked out but knew she had weeks to find a new place to live.

Though Garret wouldn't realize it for some time to come, Liz was still seeing Dave, and she was always warmer to Garret during the times Dave pulled away from her. Dave was doing his darndest to break free from her. Suddenly, Liz was smiling more at Garret, listening more intently to him and was much more affectionate than she'd been in a long time. To Garret, it seemed like their relationship was improving, and he began to feel closer to her. When he saw how hard she was struggling to make ends meet, he not only worried about her, he was concerned for the kids. "I knew they needed a place to stay." His roommate had recently moved out, and Garret had lots of space. When he asked Liz to move in with him, he saw it as a commitment "to take the relationship to the next level." Around the end of June 2013, Liz and her kids moved in. She took her time moving her things out of the old place, well aware that the eviction process could take weeks. As it turned out, the eviction notice was not sent until July 30, so she had until August 30 to collect the rest of her possessions.

While Garret had expected his girlfriend to stay in his room, she immediately laid claim to the basement, and he got the sense he didn't want him to invade her space. The warmth Liz had radiated in the previous days was replaced by cool indifference. It became painfully obvious that she saw the new situation as a roommate arrangement—one where she didn't have to pay rent.

He was dismayed to discover that she didn't clean up after herself. Soon her space downstairs was buried beneath heaps of dirty clothes and trash. Crumpled up fast food bags, with the leftovers rotting inside, became a permanent part of the décor. "There was crap everywhere. You couldn't see the floor. It was a complete mess. For somebody in the cleaning business, she was not a clean person. When she moved in, I immediately regretted it. I was thinking, 'Okay, how do I get her out?'"

But Liz couldn't afford to live on her own. Garret figured if he helped her out for a while that she could save enough money to move out. With that in mind, he didn't ask her to chip in for utilities. It was another generous move that he hoped would help her build her savings faster so that he could get her out of his house. But no matter how much he helped, Liz always claimed to be broke.

One of the kids stayed in a room on the main floor, and the other slept in a downstairs room "that was not intended to be a bedroom. It was essentially a storage room, so it wasn't very big." They switched around from time to time, and though they shared some of their mother's sloppy habits, the children were never the problem. Liz spent most of her time downstairs. "She usually confined herself to the basement, or more specifically, to her room in the basement. She was down there roughly eighty to ninety percent of the time she was home."

As time went on, Garret realized that he and Liz had few shared interests. One thing they definitely did *not* have in common was their taste in movies. "Liz loved horror movies." He recalls how she gravitated toward gory films. In the past, he'd had no aversion to horror films, "but I hated what they had become—which is a gore fest!" The realistic special effects and the emphasis on killing didn't appeal to him. He preferred Hitchcockian suspense that focused on psychological tension. But Liz relished violent scenes. "Everyone else would be bothered by the blood and guts, but it never affected her at all." He found himself cringing as they watched one of the ultra-violent *Purge* flicks that Liz had chosen for the night's entertainment. He didn't want to see people hurt even if it wasn't real. He glanced at his girlfriend during a particularly gruesome scene and was startled to see her staring blankly at the TV without a flicker of reaction. He soon realized that was her standard response to violent scenes. "She was emotionless," so unaffected that she sometimes fell asleep in the middle of a shocking movie. "She was almost proud of the fact that horror movies didn't affect her," he remembers, adding that she claimed she found them funny in the same way that most people would be amused by a comedy.

Liz also enjoyed crime programs and once posted on a social media site that *Criminal Minds* was a favorite show. She was also a big fan of *Dexter* and watched the show regularly with her kids. The TV series features a most unusual character who both solves murders and *commits* them. A vigilante killer, Dexter chooses victims he feels deserve death. "*Bones* was another one she liked." The popular drama centers around a forensic anthropologist who studies victims' bones for clues about their lives and deaths. As for books, Liz liked true crime, but Garrett can recall the subject of only one book he noticed on her nightstand. It was the story of the Craigslist Killer. Philip Markoff, a clean-cut Boston medical student, had a dangerous side few were aware of. He met his victims via online ads for massages on Craigslist. His arrest in 2009 opened the public's eyes to the hazards of meeting strangers on the Internet.

When Garret and Liz were first dating, he wasn't disturbed by her fascination with murder. Millions of people, after all, are drawn to movies and books with dark subjects. If they weren't, producers wouldn't make violent films and publishers wouldn't print crime books. But most people also have *other* topics that intrigue them. It's only in retrospect that Garret wonders why Liz didn't occasionally choose a comedy over a horror film or a coming-of-age novel over a murder story. Why was she interested *only* in horrific things? He acknowledges that he wasn't with her every minute and that it's possible that Liz *did* sometimes choose lighter fare. He isn't the only one, however, to say that Liz favored the most gruesome of horror flicks available.

After Liz moved in, Garret noticed that she didn't like to cook and rarely made dinner. When she *did* cook, it was just for her and the kids. He hadn't expected her to make his meals or clean his house. She was his girlfriend, not his servant. He wished, though, that she would pick up after herself and the kids.

She loved fast food, and when she was hungry, she often texted him from the basement, dropping hints until he got the message. "A lot of times I got suckered into driving to McDonald's." Liz expected him to pick up the tab, and while fast food should have been easier on his wallet, the cost tripled because the children needed to eat, too. He always bought enough for everyone. At least Liz purchased her own groceries, so Garret didn't have that expense.

Even though they were under the same roof, most of their communication was through text. "When she texted me, our conversations were typically very pleasant." Face to face, she was usually cold and distant. The friendly person texting him was "almost never the same person when she was physically around me."

The house had just one bathroom, and Liz went out of her way to dodge him when she came up to use it. "If I was in the living room, she would go through the kitchen and dining room to the bathroom. If I was in the kitchen, she would go the opposite way, through the living room to the bathroom. Either way, it was to avoid me. She would be short with me or barely even look at, talk to, or notice me, unless she wanted something, and then the sweetness really came out."

The situation was confusing because she claimed she wasn't seeing anyone else. And while Liz and Garret did not *sleep* together— not literally—they continued with their sexual relationship, though it was somewhat infrequent and still not particularly passionate. With kids around, not many opportunities for intimacy presented themselves. It was clear that Liz's kids weren't aware that Garret was her boyfriend. He'd learned not to show affection when they were watching because she'd instantly tense, pull away and glare at him.

He never considered marriage because she'd said from the start she wasn't interested. But she pouted when Gabe got engaged, and she was angry that Garret hadn't proposed to her. She pointed out to him that they'd been together longer than Gabe and his fiancée. "She was upset by this, and I literally laughed," says Garret. The fact that Garret's friend had fallen in love shouldn't have been an issue for Liz. Yet, it seemed to draw her attention to the fact Garret had failed to make the ultimate commitment to her. Garret remembers thinking, "Was she serious? Why would I get engaged to someone who had made it clear she had no intentions of getting married anytime soon?"

Garret didn't want to marry Liz. He cared about her, but he wasn't in love with her, and he didn't completely trust her. But it would have been nice if his girlfriend wasn't so uptight about showing him affection.

When Liz and Garret were alone in the house, and she was in the mood for sex, she would let him know in an unusual way. She wore a revealing outfit, such as a skimpy nightgown, and joined him as he watched TV in the living room. "She'd pretend to fall asleep," Garret recalls. As she played possum, she would twist around until her clothing became "accidentally" rearranged to strategically reveal parts of her body. It was an obvious invitation, but for a reason Garret could not quite fathom, she didn't want it to appear she was making the overture.

While he sometimes made the move that he knew she was waiting for, and they would end up tangled together in intimacy, other times he ignored her and went to bed by himself, leaving Liz feigning sleep with her private parts exposed.

CHAPTER SEVENTEEN

DAVID KROUPA. GARRET SLOAN. NANCY RANEY.

Though their lives were irrevocably connected by a web of seemingly tenuous strands, none of them realized how tightly they were bound in the same intricate trap. They were vaguely aware of the others' existence but still so unfamiliar that if they had passed on the street, it would be as strangers.

The predator sat smug, smack in the middle of the web that only she could see. She amused herself, spinning lies, entangling her victims as she fed on their confusion and distress. She was so like a spider with her invisible snare, but for the fact a spider's intention is not cruelty. A spider is driven by instinct to survive.

Shanna Elizabeth Golyar was deliberately cruel.

In the thick of the summer of 2013, she plotted new ways to deceive, to harm, and destroy. Her victims were numerous, but in this evil spate of deceptions, she favored David, Garret, and Nancy. Three innocent people, their destinies intertwined, endeavored to struggle free of the trap without realizing exactly what it was that held them. Sometimes one of her victims wiggled free, and she had to work extra hard to trap them again. Dave seemed to be slipping away from her that summer. He'd once again become fed up with her jealous nagging and dumped her. While no one can guess exactly what was going on inside Liz's head, the plan she concocted and was about to implement indicates her desperation was immense.

She would do anything to get Dave back. *Anything*. She would *kill* for him. That is not just idle talk but the raw and hateful truth.

She had killed for Dave before, and her plan had worked out exactly as she'd hoped—*for a while*. But every time she almost had the guy where she wanted him, a fat-assed whore would waddle in and ruin everything. She warned them again and again, but they never learned.

Yes, she had killed for Dave once and was about to kill again. No one is sure exactly when Liz crept into the dark house and set the fatal fires, but it was probably very late at night on Friday, August 16, 2013, or very early the next morning. Omaha Fire Department's Station 61 was alerted at 8:14 A.M. that Saturday to a possible house fire, two miles south of their facility. The crew rushed to their big ladder rig, donned safety gear, climbed aboard, buckled their seatbelts, and radioed dispatch that they were en route to the fire. It was 8:15 when they pulled out of the station—well within their one-minute turnout time goal.

Truck Captain Mark Sidener, with the Omaha Fire Department since 1998, worked twenty-four-hour stints, along with the rest of the crew. They started each shift at 7 A.M. and finished the next day at the same time and were only an hour and a quarter into their day when the alarm sounded. "On a possible house fire, we have a standard protocol for how many rigs we send to a fire call," he explains. "Three pumps, a truck company, two battalion chiefs and a med unit."

The Station 61 crew arrived at the scene in five minutes and six seconds—twenty-one seconds after first responders from Station 60. Slightly closer to the emergency destination, Station 60 had had a head start. In the firefighter's world, speed, of course, is crucial. A few seconds can make the difference between life and death. Neither team had wasted a moment, but this morning, it made no difference. The fire was already out, the victims long dead.

When Sidener's rig pulled up to the house just south of Omaha's West Center Road, "I hopped out of the truck with my firefighters. There was a female standing in the front yard area, and I made contact with her and asked if anybody was still in the house." Shanna Golyar told Sidener that while no humans were inside, four pets were in the home—two dogs, a cat, and a snake. When firefighters entered the house, it was no longer burning. The atmosphere was hazy with smoke, and much of the interior was charred and blackened with soot. They searched the building from top to bottom for

Cari Farver was a loving daughter, a devoted mother, and a loyal friend.
Her future was bright until she crossed paths with evil.
Photo by Stefan Stroebel.

Cari was a tomboy who c[...]
keep up with her big brot[...]
Adam (*right*), in [...]
rough-and-tumble gar[...]
Photo by Barbara Bisbee Peder[...]

In nursery school Cari could already read and would later be the star pupil of her kindergarten class, where she often read to the other children.

Cari at about age five with her cat named Kitty. She loved both people and animals. *Photo by Barbara Bisbee Pedersen.*

Cari, age nine, with her mother and stepfather, Nancy and Mark Raney, in 1983. Cari was thrilled with her dolls—including the popular Cabbage Patch Doll that nearly every girl in America asked for that Christmas.
Photo by Nancy Raney.

Cari at age three with her brother, Adam, five.
Photo by Dennis Farver.

Cari and Maxwell through the years.
Mother and son were always close.
Photos (clockwise from left)
by LuAnn Smith, Nancy Raney, Cynthia R. Weisz.

As an adult, athletic Cari could still look the part of tomboy, but she could also appear glamorous for a night out on the town. *Photos by Nancy Raney.*

Amber Jones (*left*) was Cari's best friend. The two were so close they often read each other's thoughts. *Photo by August Siefken.*

Cari Farver loved the little Iowa to
of Macedonia and never imagin
that evil would stalk her he
Photo by Leslie Ru

Amy Flora, a dedicated mother
and hard worker, was shocked to find
herself the target of a violent stalker.
Selfie by Amy Flora.

Dave Kroupa was an easygoing mechanic and
father of two. His life was turned upside down
when he realized someone with evil intentions
was watching, waiting, and planning to kill.
Photo by Leslie Rule.

anna Elizabeth Golyar told acquaintances that she feared for her safety
d was angry at police for doing little to protect her from a vicious stalker.
hoto by Tayandy Braver.

Cherokee Montoya, Shanna's loyal friend,
took this picture. She trusted Shanna
to care for both her children and pets.

Shanna Golyar flashed a dazzling grin
as her pal snapped this shot.
Photos by Cherokee Montoya.

Cherokee (*right*) shot this selfie as she and Shanna prepared to go out on Halloween night.

Cherokee (*left*) and Shanna turned heads when they hit the bars together. *Photos by Cherokee Montoya.*

When Shanna received threatening texts, Dave was overwhelmed with guilt
for inviting a cyberstalker into their lives. But Dave and Shanna had fun this night,
engaging in flirtatious play at a restaurant.
Photos by Cherokee Montoya.

Dave and Shanna at the
2012 Freaker's Ball,
a big Halloween bash held
at a Council Bluffs casino.

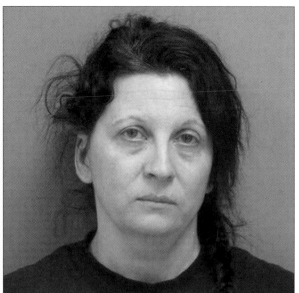

Shanna Golyar was yanked from
a sound sleep on a December
morning in 2016. She was not
expecting to have her photo taken
and had no time to brush her hair.

Shanna Golyar in the hospital
after she was shot. She said she
recognized her attacker's voice
and couldn't understand why police
were slow to make an arrest.

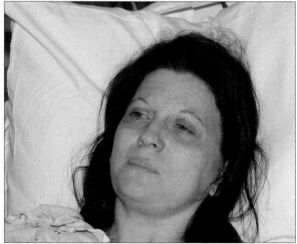

Big Lake Park, in Council Bluffs, Iowa, is beautiful in the daytime but creepy after dark. Authorities rushed to the site on December nights in 1975 and 2015—first when a UFO reportedly crashed here, and later when a call to 911 reported a violent act.

Murky waters at Big Lake Park may hide debris from a UFO crash and, detectives suspect, a gun stolen from David Kroupa. *Photos by Leslie Rule.*

The Pottawattamie County Sheriff's Office overlooks the south side of sprawling Big Lake Park.

Shanna Golyar ventured into Big Lake Park on a cold black night. She later told police she recognized the voice of her attacker. *Photos by Leslie Rule.*

Pottawattamie County Special Investigator Anthony Kava worked thousands of hours to track a sadistic killer.

Omaha, Nebraska, Detective Dave Schneider joined forces with Iowa detectives to crack a case that had stumped many before them.

Detectives Ryan Avis (left) and Jim Doty set a clever trap to outsmart their suspect and saw the fruits of their labor realized here, at Omaha's Douglas County Courthouse.
Photos by Leslie Rule.

Douglas County prosecutors Brenda Beadle (*left*) and Jim Masteller had a scant four months to prepare for one of the most challenging cases of their careers, but they were determined to get justice for Cari Farver.
Brenda Beadle photo by Alison Clark; Jim Masteller photo by Ann C. Miller.

naha's award-winning defense attorney nes Martin Davis represented the killer Cari Farver, with his efficient assistant, eyann Parr, by his side. As usual, vis gave his client the best defense ssible, but he never received his fee. oto by Leslie Rule.

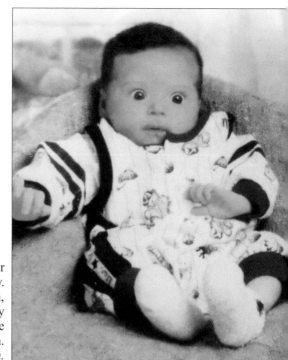

Cody Nathaniel Golyar
was a colicky baby.
Cody's father, Raymond Strahan,
pictured here with infant Cody
in the winter of 1998, was the
only one able to soothe him.
Photo below by Shawn Flanigan.

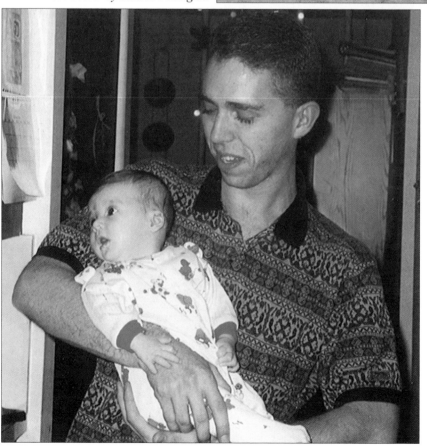

possible victims. The only victims they found were the poor pets, discovered in the rooms where Liz had said they would be. All had perished from smoke inhalation.

Garret Sloan would not learn of the deaths of the animals until years after the fire, and when he did, he was heartsick and angry. "I helped her get the dogs," he remembers bitterly, explaining that he had "loaned" her the adoption fee. He had met the dogs just once, a pair of small breed canines. According to Garret, the snake had belonged to Peter's father, Dirk. Garret didn't know the pets' names or anything else about them. As an animal lover, it was painful enough to learn of their deaths, and he preferred to not know the details.

Whatever heat the fire had generated had dissipated by the time firefighters arrived. Sidener verified that fact with his thermal imaging camera, a device that reads the temperatures of materials, and the rescuers determined that nothing was burning. They measured the temperature of the walls, too, to be sure nothing continued to smolder within them. Readings showed that all surfaces had cooled. No flames, no burning embers remained.

"After we did the primary search of the residence, we went downstairs and checked that too and found nothing down there. And we came back upstairs and started opening windows to assist with ventilation to remove some of the smoke out of the building." Positive pressure fans were placed in the exterior doorways to push fresh air into the house, forcing the smoky air out the open windows.

If a fire is deemed suspicious, investigators are called upon to determine the cause. Two fishy things had immediately jumped out at the first responders—a gas can on the floor of the living room, and evidence that the fire had originated in multiple spots. Sidener noted two couches with fire damage in the basement. Clothing and other material, now somewhat charred, had been piled in front of the furniture. The couches were not close together, and it was obvious that the fire had not spread from one to the other. The area surrounding the sofas was untouched. Sidener points out, "A fire doesn't start in different areas unless it's *made* to start in different areas. It starts in one spot and travels across material."

Even a perfunctory assessment of the damage screamed arson. The suspicions were relayed to dispatch, and Battalion Chief Michael Shane McClanahan was sent to investigate. By the summer of 2013, he'd been with the Omaha Fire Department for seventeen years, and had spent the last four assigned to the Fire Investigation Unit. McClanahan's extensive education includes a degree in fire science, intense studies with the National Fire Academy, and multiple courses related to the forensics of fire.

McClanahan must determine the source of each fire he investigates, assigning a cause from one of four classifications—incendiary (intentional), accidental, undetermined, and natural. An accidental cause could be an electrical malfunction, while a natural cause might be a lightning strike. Incendiary fires are deliberately set, and when an investigator cannot identify a fire as accidental, natural, or incendiary, it is classified as undetermined.

Chief McClanahan arrived on the scene at 8:37 that Saturday morning. After he was briefed by the commander on duty, he "did a quick walk-through of the structure to familiarize myself with the layout and what was inside." Most of the smoke had cleared, and the structure had cooled, so no protective gear was necessary on this day. With a notebook and pen in hand, he made notes on everything that stood out, paying particular attention to burn patterns.

The Chief noted that heavy soot covered everything on the main level of the house but that he saw no signs of thermal damage—damage resulting from intense heat—on that floor. "As I moved to the basement of the structure, the smoke damage became heavier, and I found multiple points of origin," he recalls. The basement also showed signs of thermal damage. An aquarium, holding the deceased snake, sat on a desk, and the structural framing of the container had "been degraded and warped due to the heat damage, and the glass of the aquarium was actually cracked and broken."

Liz still waited, and she soon joined the Chief in his vehicle for an interview.

She sat beside him and shared her tragic story. She explained that she was in the process of moving to a friend's house in Council Bluffs, but she failed to mention the fact she'd been evicted. She said that she'd stopped by the house the day before, sometime between 1 and 3 P.M., to collect some things for herself and the kids. She confirmed that the big garage door had been unlocked at that time, but that she was certain she had locked the door that led to the house, as well as all the other exterior doors.

After arriving that morning between 7:30 and 8:00, "She stated that she went to the front door, unlocked it, opened the door and encountered a large volume of smoke, immediately shut the door and called 911."

Liz told the frightening tale of the woman so insanely jealous that she'd stop at nothing to destroy her and win the love of David Kroupa. She handed McClanahan a business card for Detective Prencer, explaining that the OPD had been working with her to catch "Cari."

McClanahan asked Liz standard questions and took careful notes. How many sets of house keys did she have? "She stated two, one that she possessed and one that her daughter possessed. She then told me there were originally three sets of keys to the house. The locks had been changed by the owner of the house, the Omaha Housing Authority, sometime near the end of 2012 or the beginning of 2013, when she had reported the stalking incidents. They changed the locks for her, and she was given three sets of keys at that time. Shortly after receiving the three sets, she stated, one of those sets came up missing."

Did any of the residents smoke? Had anyone lit candles or incense? She confirmed that while her boyfriend, Dave, did smoke, it was always outside because she didn't allow smoking in the house. No one had recently lit candles or incense.

The investigator asked about recent utility work or remodeling that might have been done in the home. Liz told him that other than some plumbing repairs ordered by the home's owners, there had been no recent work on the house.

When McClanahan inquired about the home's utilities, "She stated that she had the power turned off on Wednesday," August 14, but that the gas and water were still on. Liz didn't mention that the electric company had turned off the power because she'd failed to pay the bill.

She also answered questions about the gasoline container on the living room floor and a bottle of charcoal lighter fluid found on the kitchen counter. Both items were out of place, she insisted. A gas can was kept on the back porch for the lawn mower, and the bottle of lighter fluid was normally kept next to the grill on the back patio.

According to Liz, "Cari" had set the fire, intending to murder her and her children. She had proof, a threatening email that she now pulled up on her phone and showed to the Chief. It had been sent at 12:56 A.M., about six hours before Liz opened the front door to find her home thick with smoke.

Nasty whore, Dave doesn't want you talking to him anymore. He wants to be with me. We are trying a new relationship. We have had sex recently. He loves me and always will. He doesn't want you back, you nasty, fat, whore, Liz. Hope you and your kids burn to death.

The last line of the email was "a red flag," as far as the investigator was concerned. He took a photo of the email and began his comprehensive evaluation of the scene. The rules of fire investigation are orderly and strictly followed. To avoid cross-contamination, all equipment is thoroughly cleaned after each incident, and disposable items are not reused. A fresh pair of gloves is donned before each piece of new evidence is examined. Everything is photographically documented. Rooms are shot from various angles, and each step of the evidence-collecting process is recorded as proof that protocol was followed. Even the discarded gloves are photographed to show that the investigator did indeed wear new gloves before handling evidence.

Investigators measure depth of char and examine fire patterns to identify areas of origin. One indicator is known as a flash point. "We use that to describe an area where potential accelerant may have been, and it flashed, burning off the gas from the accelerant, but did not burn long enough for the surrounding combustible materials to start consuming themselves and continuing combustion."

McClanahan explains that when it comes to examining a burned structure, he first looks at the areas where there is the least amount of damage, and ends by scrutinizing those with the most damage. With Liz's house, "We started with the exterior of the structure where there was virtually no damage and moved to the interior towards the basement."

Absorbable gauze is used to extract liquids from vessels holding possible accelerants. McClanahan took samples from the gas container on the living room floor and also from the bottle of charcoal lighter fluid, leaving the containers themselves behind. Each piece of gauze is first removed from an individual sterilized package before it's dipped into the vessel holding the questionable liquid. After it soaks up some of the liquid, the gauze is placed in a sealed metal container, labeled, and later sent to the lab for testing.

McClanahan identified six separate areas where fire originated in Liz's house. All were in the vicinity of the basement. One was on the staircase leading to the basement—the third step from the bottom. Another was on the threshold of the door leading to the garage. Two piles of clothing in the laundry room were also determined to be places where fires originated. In addition, McClanahan found that the two couches, noted earlier by Sidener, were also areas of origin.

There was no question that this was an intentionally set fire, but the arsonist was obviously an amateur. Because all of the windows in the house had been shut, the fire was starved for oxygen and quickly squelched.

Dave was at work at Hyatt Tire when he answered Liz's frantic phone call. "She was distressed, upset, telling me her house is on fire, and there are fire trucks there. I was at work, and it was very, very busy. She asked me to come over." He was hesitant to leave work when it was so busy but felt guilty when Liz told him "Cari" had set the fire. When things slowed down a little, he left for a while to check on Liz. Three or four firetrucks were parked on the street, and he saw "fire hoses all over the place" as firefighters entered and exited the house. "Liz was standing in the middle of the road, crying." She was a forlorn figure, all alone, staring at her house as tears streamed down her cheeks. Dave put his arm around her and tried to comfort her.

It's all gone, she told him, hopelessly. She had lost *everything*.

"Do you have renter's insurance?" he asked.

"No." Liz's lower lip trembled as she swiped at her tears with the back of her hand. Dave stood by awkwardly. He wanted to be supportive but was unsure of what to say. "It's hard to be comforting in that situation, so you try to just be there."

It was obvious she needed him. Though they'd broken up, he couldn't abandon her in the middle of this latest trauma and did what he could to help over the next days. While some of her possessions were charred, others were salvageable. The couches were destroyed, but some pieces of furniture just needed a little cleaning. Dave helped her drag them out onto the lawn to hose down. Liz made it clear she blamed him. "Your stalker did this to me," she reminded him more than once. As usual, he felt guilty, and they began to spend time together, sliding back into their usual pattern. Dave's Wednesday Girl was back.

He didn't know Liz had moved in with Garret weeks before, and she'd left nothing she treasured behind. Nothing destroyed in the fire, including her pets, mattered much to her. In her mind, all of it was replaceable.

Two days after the fire, on Monday, August 19, Detective Paul Prencer was in his Omaha office on Harney Street, when Liz asked to speak with him. "She said she had found some sort of cleaning fluid or a bottle on a table in her house that may have been used in the arson." She showed the detective a photograph she'd taken of the bottle in question. She told him that she was familiar with the brand of cleaning fluid, and the color was wrong, as if someone had replaced the original solution with another liquid.

"She said it didn't quite match what it was supposed to look like, and she thought it might have been used to start the fire," Prencer remembers. He wasn't involved in the arson investigation "and was very hesitant to pursue that too much. I wanted to contact the arson investigator." He called Captain McClanahan, and the two of them went to the burned house. Liz met them there, and inside pointed at the kitchen table. It was blackened with soot, but there was a round, clean spot, in the place where the suspect bottle had been. Photos taken earlier clearly showed a bottle sitting in that spot.

"That bottle was now missing," remembers McClanahan.

Liz denied removing the bottle, and she expressed concern about the situation. Someone had come in and taken the bottle containing the very liquid she suspected had been used to start the fire. She seemed to be suggesting that the arsonist had returned to the scene to get rid of incriminating evidence. The timing was odd. No sooner had Liz discovered the suspicious liquid, photographed it, and rushed to report her findings to Detective Prencer, than the damned thing disappeared. It was almost as if the arsonist had been *watching* Liz and had seen her discover the evidence. In the time it took her to go see Prencer and for him to alert McClanahan and meet her at the house, the stalker had slipped in and snatched the one thing Liz hoped could convict the maniac.

Chief McClanahan was no slouch. He had thoroughly investigated the scene, gathered the appropriate evidence, and sent every
potential accelerant to the lab for testing. Gasoline was the obvious
choice, and he had discovered traces of it when examining the fires'
points of origin. Careful lab work would soon confirm the presence
of gasoline in suspect areas. The seasoned investigator certainly did
not need Liz's help.

In the days following the fire, Dave did his best to comfort Liz.
She told him she was frightened. What would the maniac do next?
When Liz refused to give Dave her new address, he couldn't really
blame her. "I don't want your stalker to know where I am!" she exclaimed. Dave wasn't all that interested, anyway. He was just making polite conversation when he asked her where she was going. He
thought she was smart to not tell him, because his tormentor seemed
to have the ability to peer over his shoulder and see everything he
was doing. If he jotted Liz's new address on a slip of paper, somehow the stalker would find it.

Dave couldn't guess Liz's real reason for being secretive about
her new place. She was living with her boyfriend—the boyfriend
Dave didn't know she had. He had heard her mention Garret's name,
and they had the long-standing joke about setting "Cari" up with the
unsuspecting guy. It was actually Liz's joke, and Dave laughed
along with her to be a good sport, but it wasn't all that funny. He
didn't know much about Garret. He was just some guy Liz knew,
and Dave wouldn't wish his stalker problems on his worst enemy,
let alone an innocent bystander.

If Dave had known Liz had another boyfriend, he would have
been elated. He was very tired of feeling responsible for her and
longed for the day he could be free of his obligation to try to fix all
of the problems his mistake had caused her. Liz never missed an opportunity to remind him that if he hadn't been as horny as a tomcat
on the prowl, her life wouldn't be in shambles.

CHAPTER EIGHTEEN

BY LATE AUGUST 2013, Liz seemed to have sprouted permanent roots in Garret's basement, and she was not budging. She was very comfortable, and her focus was on producing hundreds of emails and texts each week, most designed to taunt Dave. The more off-balance he became, the easier he was to control, and Liz was constantly scheming to come up with new ways to keep him off-kilter. She had accomplished quite a bit that month, and capturing his attention was at the top of her list.

When she had summoned fire to solve her problems, most likely it was not with the sole purpose of winning back her lover. She was so far behind on her bills that she was being evicted, and the fire might have been an act of spite. *If I can't live in this house, no one can!* Whether it was her intention or not, when she freed herself from the burden of the house, she had gotten revenge on the "jerks" who'd evicted her. It would not be cheap for the Omaha Housing Authority to pay for the repairs necessary to make the home suitable for the next renter.

It's also possible that the house held secrets—ghastly, unthinkable secrets that, if discovered, could threaten Liz's very existence. As long as she had stayed at that house, she could monitor who came and went. She had invited police in when she reported the vandalism, allegedly caused by her stalker, but it had been on her terms. The cops hadn't been nosing around, searching for evidence of murder. They had come in to take Liz's reports, and she had always directed the conversations. In her mind, the police had been as easy to fool as Garret and Dave.

If the house contained evidence that she feared she could not scrub away, she would have been reluctant to give up her control over the environment. As Liz surely must have learned from the many crime shows she watched, blood can seep into cracks in a floor, splatter across a ceiling, or drip down a wall, carrying with it DNA that can settle into crevices, waiting to be discovered weeks, months, or even years after a murder. If her victim had died in the house, Liz might have feared what future residents could uncover. If the house *had* held evidence of a homicide, Liz had quite possibly incinerated some of those clues right into the belly of oblivion.

Liz could also congratulate herself for finding a place to live rent free with a built-in-babysitter. She no longer had to worry about paying bills. Garret would take care of everything! Not only that, she had what she believed was an excellent excuse for her unemployment. Her business had been destroyed in the fire. She claimed she had to give up cleaning because all of her supplies had been destroyed. Considering that housework relies mostly on elbow grease and that the cost of a broom, a mop, and a can of scouring powder is not prohibitive, some wondered what prevented her from working. Others wondered exactly *when* it was that she had last worked—if she had ever worked at all. Many times, when she had told Garret she had to clean houses all night, she had really been on an overnight date with Dave.

Dave! Liz had guilted him right back into her arms when she complained to him that *his* stalker had burned her out of her home. She reminded him more than once, "Your stalker could have killed me and my kids!" Each time she had taken drastic measures to turn Dave's attention to her, it had worked exactly as she had hoped. It was almost *too* easy for her to manipulate him.

The fire also bolstered Liz's victim image, and many felt sorry for the single mother who had lost so much. In reality, she'd removed everything she wanted from that house before lighting the first match, and she'd acquired a few more items of value *because* of the fire. Every expensive thing Garret had loaned her was "lost in the fire," including an iPod Touch.

With nothing to distract her, Liz had countless hours to cyberstalk Dave, and the sheer volume of texts and emails she sent him suggests that she probably didn't sleep much. But she did not forget about Nancy. She also took the time to jab at her.

On August 28, 2013, Nancy received the following text: *I'm in Omaha. I'm not hurt, Mom. I miss everyone too. I just had a breakdown, and I think I'm getting over it. I should have come to my senses sooner and realized the guy wasn't worth it.*

Nancy stared at the message. As usual, it was filled with grammar errors, and she doubted that Cari was the one texting her. Despite her reservations, she felt a rush of excitement. Her heart pounding, Nancy texted back, "Is this really you? I need to hear your voice! I'm not going to answer texts."

The texter agreed to talk to her, typing, "Let me pull over."

Nancy could not stop her hopes from soaring. Maybe this *was* Cari! Maybe her daughter was about to call her! She waited, and as the minutes passed, she knew it was once again someone playing a sick game.

Nancy, of course, had never heard of Liz and didn't know she was the one impersonating Cari. Liz wanted Nancy to believe that Cari was driving along the highway and texting at the same time, an awkward and dangerous habit. It's possible that Liz *was* driving when she decided to taunt Nancy. She seemed to enjoy causing pain. She had no qualms about her slow torture of a grieving mother and wasn't worried that her reckless behavior might cause an accident that could harm or kill someone. Or perhaps Liz was not driving at all, but lounging in her messy basement quarters, compulsively texting away as Garret made another McDonald's run to fetch her the greasy meal she craved.

In addition to giving Liz a place to live, he'd been helping her out with her transportation for quite some time. Her credit was bad, and early on in their relationship Garret had cosigned on a loan for a Jeep Liberty and had also put her on his insurance. Liz had ended up totaling the Liberty when she crashed it. Garret is unsure how the car was wrecked, but she claimed that the accident had happened while she was on her way to a cleaning job. She said she had clients who wanted her to clean their place in Utah, so she had followed them there on a long drive, and very early in the morning she had fallen asleep at the wheel.

She next purchased a brand new 2012 Honda Civic, partially paying for it with the insurance payout for the wrecked Liberty. Garret cosigned on that loan, too, and he continued to carry her on his insurance. "Liz loved that Civic!" he remembers. She was driving it when a red-light camera captured her ignoring a traffic light. A ticket was automatically issued to Garret because the car was in his name. The ticket arrived via mail, and he got online and followed the instructions to view the video of the Civic as it zipped through the red light. It was clearly Liz's vehicle, though the driver wasn't visible because the view was from the rear.

She was the only one who drove the car, and he knew for a fact she had been in the area on the day the camera caught her. When Garret told her about it, she shook her head. She would *never* run a red light, she insisted.

"But you did. There's a video of you!"

"I didn't do it!" Liz swore that it could not possibly be her, and she refused to look at the online images that proved her guilt. It was not the first time she'd failed to take responsibility for a mistake despite irrefutable photographic evidence. A few years earlier, a boyfriend who had dumped her discovered that shortly after their breakup, someone had used his debit card to take cash from his account. The bank had images of every withdrawal, and sure enough, their camera had snapped a picture of Liz taking the cash.

The guy confronted her, but even when faced with photographic evidence of her theft, she would not acknowledge that she had stolen the money. "It wasn't me," she said as she looked him straight in the eye. It was a blatant lie, and the evidence would have stood up in a court of law, but he didn't want the hassle of getting authorities involved. Garret, too, opted not to fight Liz. He paid her traffic fine and let it go. Not long after that, Liz wrecked the Civic, and the insurance company notified Garret that they would no longer cover her on his policy.

Liz used the last insurance payout to fix the car. Concerned about the liability of having his name connected to a car she was driving, Garret paid off the loan and gifted the Civic to her. "I told her to get her own insurance and title. That's when I washed my hands of ever helping her get another vehicle."

Dave Kroupa's days always started early at Hyatt Tire. One morning in the middle of October 2013, he was there, as usual, long before the sun was up. As he pulled up to the shop, he was stunned to see a message, spray-painted in fluorescent orange across the big front windows. He realized this was not a random act of vandalism. *He* was the target. He felt sick as he read the words, "Dave beats women." The accusation wasn't true, but that didn't matter. The store's owner was not the easiest person to get along with, and Dave knew that the guy would blame him. "Luckily the paint was really fresh. One of my oil change guys, a friend of mine, had gotten there early, too. We were able to wipe it off, but I would have been out of a job if it hadn't come off. The owner would have canned me on the spot if I hadn't been able to clean it off."

Whenever his stalker vandalized property, she sent a gleeful text or email, claiming credit for her destruction. Today was no exception. It was maddening! He felt threatened no matter which way he turned. Whether he was at work or play, he couldn't relax. He couldn't predict what the stalker would do next. He could be sure of only one thing. It would *not* be good.

It was around this time a year earlier when the lady with the sparkling eyes had come into the shop. He remembered how his heart had quickened as they stood in the parking lot, smiling at each other. Now, as the sun came up, he stood in that same spot, scrutinizing the windows as daylight hit the glass. He had to be sure he'd wiped away every last trace of the tell-tale paint.

He reported the vandalism, and Omaha Detective Paul Prencer responded. He was as baffled as Dave. How had the stalker managed to strike again without being seen? The men contemplated the odd situation. The culprit had to be watching, because she seemed to know Dave's every move. Where was her hiding place? "I surveyed the area to try to ascertain if there was someplace where someone could have been living that had a view of his place of employment," Prencer recalls. Dave's residence was to the east of the shop, and there were also apartments to the west. Detective Prencer went to there to talk to the manager. "I showed a picture of Ms. Farver, and they said she didn't live there, they didn't recognize her. Nobody by that name lived there. They didn't know who she was." The stalker was as elusive as a ghost in the autumn mist.

The close call had nearly cost Dave his job, and he was upset. At least he had Liz to talk to. The attacks brought them closer together. "That's what kept bringing us back together so to speak, because I broke it off numerous times. And then something would happen. A window would get broken, there'd be fresh threats, or there'd be a house burned down."

He felt obligated to Liz because, "Of course, I'm the bad guy who brought this crazy lady into our life, and it's my fault." Liz never let him forget that. She asked why he couldn't have been satisfied with *her*? Didn't he realize how good he'd had it? Why did he have to go out and hook up with a nut? Dave felt defeated. He hardly recognized his own reflection. He'd gained forty pounds, and dark circles had formed beneath his eyes. In the past, he'd been a casual, social drinker. "I had one drink that lasted me four hours." Months of vandalism and nonstop threats had made him jittery and depressed, and now he drank to numb his anxiety. "There was a bar between the shop and my apartment, and I got to the point where I knew all of the regulars, and I knew the owner real well. I knew what day of the week it was by who was coming through the door! I spent too much time there. Too much time and too much money."

As the one-year anniversary of his first date with Cari approached, Dave remembered how thrilled he'd been to meet such a lovely and brilliant woman. Now, he could hardly believe it was the same person sending him twisted messages.

On November 1, 2013, an email arrived at 7:54 P.M., sent from leakroupa@gmail. Lea was Cari's middle name, and he assumed she'd combined that with his last name to make it appear she was his wife. The email began, "To my husband, David Kroupa." She claimed she'd purchased a knife and had been creeping around "in your building." The attached photo showed a large knife, Cari Farver's driver's license, and an envelope for a bill with her name on it. Was she attempting to prove it was really her tormenting him? He'd never doubted the identity of his stalker and didn't question it now.

Was the photo of the knife supposed to be a threat? Once again, he escaped to the familiar bar and grill and drank more than he knew he should.

It was hard for Cari's family and friends to accept that a year had passed since she'd disappeared. The holidays were upon them again, and they went through the motions, but none of them felt much joy. It was a difficult time for Cari's friend Amber. After months of disturbing texts from someone claiming to be Cari, Amber could take it no longer. It had become clear that whoever was texting her was definitely *not* Cari. "My *main* problem with it all, was she never once mentioned my child. She was so, so, *so* excited about my pregnancy," she explains, adding that her friend couldn't wait to "be Auntie Cari." Amber changed her phone number.

Cari's birthday came and went, uncelebrated on November 30. If still alive, she was now thirty-nine. December 10, was Maxwell's sixteenth birthday, another huge milestone that he knew his mother would not have missed if it were within her power to be there. The little house Cari loved had sat vacant for too long. Her family packed up her possessions and moved them to a storage unit. Nancy didn't like driving past the house. It appeared cold and dark and so obviously empty that it gave her a lonely feeling in the pit of her stomach. They rented it out to a nice young woman, Marina Estes, and she moved in that December. She would take care of the place, and it was somehow comforting to see the windows lit at night. The family had little hope that Cari would ever return, but if she did, her home would be in good shape.

December 12, 2013, was the one-year anniversary of Denny Farver's funeral. It was also the day that Police Officer Tim Huffman was dispatched to Dave's apartment at 1:10 P.M. Huffman had been with Omaha Police Department's Uniform Patrol Bureau since July 2000. He handled crimes reported via 911 calls and had started his shift that morning at 6:00. The dispatcher advised him that a break-in had occurred in the first-floor unit of a large apartment complex. Officer Huffman went to the scene where he was greeted by Dave and Liz.

Liz told him she'd left earlier that day and returned to a shocking mess. "She said she was at the apartment until approximately 10 A.M."

Huffman recollects. Liz said she'd returned "sometime around one o'clock in the afternoon. She found a screen to a bedroom window on the floor and then some items that were destroyed and writing on the wall."

It appeared an intruder had crawled through the window, tracking in the leaves that littered the dresser top. Liz pointed to a pile of clothing, slashed with a sharp instrument and dumped in a heap on the floor. An angry message, clearly aimed at Liz, was scrawled on the wall in red crayon: "Go away whore." Liz's destroyed garments included two shirts and a pair of sweatpants, but Dave's clothing had not been touched. This latest vandalism would eat up many hours of Omaha law enforcement's time. Detective Prencer soon became involved, and investigators processed the scene. Officers canvassed the area but couldn't find a single person who'd noticed anything suspicious on December 12. Not only were there no witnesses, the intruder had left no fingerprints. The police didn't guess that *Liz* had staged the scene, that she'd cut her own clothing, removed the screen from the window, and written the message on the wall. She had everyone fooled and told her dark secrets to no one.

Most of the people in Liz's life were aware she had problems but had little understanding of how deeply those troubles ran. They didn't really know who she was, and as of this writing, neither does *she*. Liz is unaware that the middle name she has embraced as her own for most of her life is not the one her mother gave her. She was not born Shanna Elizabeth. She was Shanna *Kay*. Her mother called her that, all in one breath. Never just Shanna, but always Shanna Kay.

Liz was very young when she was separated from her biological family. She knows of her mother's fate, but not her mother's birth name. She is unaware of her father's identity and might be surprised to realize he was alive until 2007, residing in Kalamazoo, Michigan, in the same apartment he'd moved into with her mother three decades earlier.

Liz is still unaware her aunts have been searching for her since the state of Michigan cut their ties with her in 1978, days before her third birthday. After long hours of research, I found one of those aunts. I wrote to her, hoping my letter wouldn't come as a shock. I wasn't sure if I had the right family, but if I did, I figured they surely must be aware of Shanna's conviction. Even so, I chose my words cautiously. I mentioned prison but not murder. I gave the aunt my phone number, and sent the note off to the ten different email addresses I had found online, hoping that one of them was correct.

Fifteen minutes later, my phone rang. Shanna Kay's Aunt Camila had no idea what had become of her, and it was up to me to tell her. She knew that Shanna was in prison but was aware of that fact only because she'd just learned it from my email. I stalled, reluctant to speak words I knew would hurt her. "It's pretty bad," I warned. "A tragedy."

"My whole life's been a tragedy," Camila replied with a sigh. "I can take it."

"Shanna was convicted of murder," I said.

Camila gasped, and I was relieved when she didn't ask for details. She was remembering the sweet little girl she'd spent decades searching for. How could I tell her that that child had grown up to be a monster? Over the next days, we spent hours on the phone. Little by little, Camila began to ask questions, and I gave her the answers as gently as I could, never volunteering details she had not asked for. I knew she needed to digest the information slowly, but it didn't take long for Camila and her sisters to find the episodes about the murder produced by NBC's *Dateline* and the Oxygen Channel's *Snapped*.

In my long conversations with Shanna's aunts, we talked about what causes an innocent child to grow up to be a killer. Is it nurture or nature? They, too, hope to find answers and opened their hearts to share some very personal and painful things. While I knew they'd be shocked by the things I had to tell them, I wasn't expecting to be shocked by the things they had to tell me.

CHAPTER NINETEEN

MOST OF WHAT I'VE LEARNED about Shanna's roots came from her birth family. While they did their best to recall the past, their memories of long-ago events sometimes differed from each other's. Scandalous accusations were made against relatives, both living and dead. Pseudonyms are used for most of Liz's birth relatives, and some horrendous details about things impossible to prove have been omitted. The dead can't stand up and defend themselves, and it would be unfair to repeat some of the worst and possibly untrue things told to me.

By exploring Shanna's past, I hoped to find events that might explain why she had traveled such a stormy and treacherous trail. Was violence in her genes, or was she warped by early trauma? I found ample evidence of both.

Despite their sometimes contradictory viewpoints, Shanna's relatives agreed on one thing: Her mother was kind and gentle. It was in the spring of 1978, a lovely afternoon in Kalamazoo, Michigan, when Delores "Dee" exited the laundromat. She carried a big basket of laundry, still warm from the dryer. She didn't have a car, but it was only four blocks to her apartment. Many people were out and about that Monday, enjoying the sunshine as temperatures climbed into the seventies. It's not known what Dee was thinking, but it's unlikely she was concerned for her safety. She was in the middle of the sidewalk in broad daylight, doing the most ordinary of tasks. No one expects a trip to the laundromat to be hazardous. But for Dee, on that tragic day, it was.

Troy Samuels knew he wasn't supposed to be driving. The eighteen-year-old was epileptic and couldn't predict when a seizure would overtake him. He had no warning on that ghastly afternoon, and probably no memory of what occurred. His car left the road, veered onto the sidewalk, and plowed straight into Dee.

She was twelve days away from her twenty-ninth birthday, but her young life ended on that sidewalk, with the freshly laundered linens scattered around her. Because of Troy's bad decision, many lives were altered. His selfishness caused a chain-reaction of dark events with consequences that reached into the next century.

Dee's sisters remember that she was happy on the day she died. She was about to be reunited with her two youngest children, Shanna Kay, almost three, and fifteen-month-old George. Employees of the state of Michigan had removed the toddlers from her home two months earlier because of her abusive boyfriend, Alva "Al" Jenkins. Al was also Shanna Kay's father, and while Dee's sisters insist that he never physically harmed the children, they recall that he beat Dee daily. She was caught up in the classic cycle of the battered woman, trying and failing repeatedly to break free from her abuser. But this time, she had somehow mustered the strength to convince Al to move out. Social workers had approved the return of the toddlers, and Dee was elated to learn they'd be coming home soon. She wanted the place to be perfect for their return and had walked to the laundromat to wash the children's bedding.

How did Dee become involved with a violent man? It probably seemed normal to her, her sisters suggest. Abuse was a family pattern, and Dee witnessed her father's cruelty to her mother. Fabian Zaragozate was born in Puerto Rico in 1917, the twenty-third child of Adela Zaragozate. His siblings had all arrived via multiple births, twins and triplets. Adela's first singular birth should have been easier, but there were complications, and she did not survive. Fabian was raised by his older sister, Francis, an allegedly abusive woman who took her anger out on him with harsh punishments. They moved to Michigan, where Fabian met Ruthie Anne Maples at a Kalamazoo bowling alley where they both worked. "My mother was a pin setter," Camila explains. It was her job to set the pins upright after each game.

Fabian was a musical genius, and according to family lore, he could play any instrument without training and quickly mastered the horn, piano, and guitar.

He was a dozen years older than eighteen-year-old Ruthie Anne, and her parents didn't approve of him because of his dark skin. But she rebelled and married him in the summer of 1948. They had seven children in quick succession. "We were stairstep kids," Camila notes. "Some of us weren't even a year apart. Before I was born, my father ran the dump here in town, and our family lived next to it. My mother told my father that it wasn't healthy for kids to be playing around all that garbage, so they moved to a house on twenty acres on the outskirts of town."

Camila's earliest memory was captured on film—seven beautiful children, posing in front of the Christmas tree. Three brothers and four sisters, most of them grinning for the camera, appear excited about the holiday. "It was Christmas Eve," she remembers. "Our mother let us each choose one present to open that night." The two oldest sisters, Dee and Isabella, picked the biggest gifts with their names on them. The boxes contained matching dolls with tight, blond curls and blinking, blue eyes. The girls are proudly holding their new dolls in the old black-and-white photograph. The children's father was absent that night, but he returned on Christmas morning.

"I remember it because of all the blood flying around," says Camila. "My father broke my mother's nose." Fabian hit his wife because he was enraged that she had given the dolls to the girls without him there. "He left us that day. I heard he already had a new girlfriend, and he had kids with her, too. Sometimes he came around to see my brothers, but he told them he didn't want to see us girls."

Ruthie Anne was not even thirty, and she was all alone with her brood of seven with no one to support them. "We were her slaves," Camila recalls bitterly, alleging that not only did her mother force the kids at a young age to cook all the meals and clean the house, she also beat them. At least one of her children "hated her," though one daughter seemed to have a good relationship with her. The other siblings claim that that daughter was their mother's favorite and not treated as badly as they were.

Camila was humiliated when she was a young teen and had a friend over for a visit. "We were laughing about something, and I said, 'That's funnier than sin.' My mother started hitting me, screaming, 'You think sin is funny? Sin isn't funny!'" Ruthie Anne was a strict Mormon and took sin and hell very seriously. Camila remembers that they had a record album with a song that mentioned hell. "My mother inked out the word 'hell' on the album cover, and when the song played, she pushed the record player's needle down to scratch the record wherever the singer said 'hell.'" As a result, the record forever after skipped over that part of the song, and Ruthie Anne's ears were spared the sound of the offensive word.

Camila confides that her mother whipped her most often with an old electrical cord with copper woven into the cloth coating. "When I was in labor with my first child, they told me to lie on my back, but I couldn't do it. It hurt too much." The nurses were shocked to find that Camila's back was imbedded with little bits of copper, pieces that had broken off during the many whippings with the old cord. "They picked the copper out of my skin while I was in labor."

While some of her offspring describe Ruthie Anne as sadistic, at least one of her kids is less critical and "marvels at her strength in raising seven children on her own." While many today view corporal punishment as abusive, when a 1954 Gallup Poll asked Americans about the most effective punishment of their youth, *forty percent* answered "whippings," a category that included everything from spankings to beatings with a stick. The fact that corporal punishment of children was common doesn't mean it was *not* abusive, but it *does* mean that some of the abuse discovered in Liz Golyar's biological family was not so unusual that it could be convincing evidence of a genetic predisposition toward violence.

Horror stories about the Zaragozate family include accusations of incest, rape, and murder. All of Camila's brothers have rap sheets, and some of their offenses are violent. These are Shanna's uncles, men she's never met, and one has been described as an evil genius. He escaped from prison *twice*, once eluding authorities for five years before he was recaptured when an acquaintance snitched. "His

IQ is just two points below Einstein's" says Camila. "He could have used his brains to accomplish something positive. But he went down a different path."

Their sister, Dee, however, was a joyful soul. Though her given name was Delores, when she was little, everyone called her Dee Dee. As she matured, she thought it sounded babyish, so the nickname was shortened to Dee. She loved to laugh, remember her sisters. "And she was a fixer. If someone had a problem, she wanted to fix it." When a pregnant dog in the neighborhood was killed by a vicious dog, a veterinarian delivered the puppies in an emergency cesarean section. "Dee got one of the puppies, and it was so tiny. I remember she stole my doll's bottle, so she could feed him!" Dee named the puppy Duke, and with her nurturing, he grew to be a big brown dog, resembling a chocolate lab.

Dee also loved horses, and when she was a teenager, she often skipped school to ride Patches, the family's black-and-white horse. "Dee didn't like school," Camila recalls. "She didn't do the work, so she flunked a grade and ended up in the same class as one of our sisters who was almost a year younger. She wasn't dumb, but she had trouble in school. She was restless, and it was hard for her to focus."

Dee fell in love with Greg Carowe, who was a couple of years ahead of her in school. They married when she was eighteen and soon had two sons. Dee was excited when they bought a cozy house with a yard for the boys to play in. The new home was in Comstock, Michigan, on Azuba Avenue, a quiet street, shaded by trees. Greg worked as a cook at a psychiatric institution, while Dee cared for their sons. One night, Greg failed to come home, and Dee was frantic with worry. "She tried to find him and called his relatives," remembers Camila. "They told her he was okay but wouldn't tell her where he was. She never saw him again."

Greg abruptly stopped supporting his family and filed for divorce. He moved to Florida and married a woman Camila suspects he'd been carrying on with while married to Dee. History was repeating itself. Dee's husband had left her and the children, just as her father had abandoned his family. Not only was Dee emotionally shattered, she was all alone with two small boys and no way to support them. She lost the house, applied for welfare and moved to an apartment.

When Dee met Alva Jenkins, six years older than she was, he might have told her he was one of ten kids, but he probably did not mention that he was an ex-con. A few years earlier, in November 1967, he'd been convicted of taking indecent liberties with a child and had spent nearly three years behind bars. The age of Alva's victim is unknown. Perhaps he'd molested a small child, or maybe he'd been intimate with a teen just weeks shy of the legal age of consent. These are two entirely different 'types of scenarios, and without more specific information, Al's trustworthiness in interacting with children is difficult to gauge. But that wasn't the only issue. He was a violent alcoholic. That alone was a good enough reason for Dee to avoid him. If she recognized that Al had problems, she might have believed she could help him. She was, after all, "The fixer." While he appeared sweet in the beginning, she soon realized he had a temper and no qualms about hitting women. Dee came to fear Al, but it seemed safer to stay with him than to test the limits of his rage by attempting to flee.

"They didn't have shelters for battered women back then," Camila stresses. When authorities became aware of Al's abusive presence in Dee's home, they took her sons away. Greg's new wife didn't want the boys, so they were placed in foster care. Dee was devastated. She wanted her sons back and tried to break up with Al. It was a difficult situation. She had lost her welfare benefits when the kids were taken, and Al was supporting her with his job at a foundry. Dee couldn't go home because her mother was furious at her for "living in sin" with Al.

Sometimes Dee got her hopes up when Al promised to change. He would quit drinking. He would never hit her again. Together they would fix everything and bring her boys home. But he always broke his promises, and she blamed herself for making him mad. "It's my fault," she told one of her sisters. "Everything that's happened is my fault." As much as she wanted her sons with her, she may have felt they were better off in foster care.

Dee's situation became more complicated when she got pregnant again. "But Dee was excited when Shanna Kay was born," says Camila. "She was so happy to have a daughter." The birth of his daughter brought out a tender side of Al. He adored Shanna Kay and was gentle with her. The little girl was still in diapers when Dee got pregnant with George. Camila insists Al was good to the children, but he was cruel to Dee. The smallest thing sent him into a rage.

Dee often asked her sisters to come get the kids so that they could play with their cousins. Camila believes she did this to prevent her toddlers from witnessing Al's drunken rampages. But the children *did* witness violence. Even if they were in another room when he attacked their mother, the little ones heard Al's shouting and Dee's shrieks when he hit her. Once, when Camila and her husband, Gary, were picking up Shanna Kay and George, Dee handed Camila a change of clothing for the kids. Al barked, "I don't want them wearing those old clothes!"

"They're going to be playing outside," Dee explained. "I don't want them to get their nice clothes dirty."

"He hit Dee hard in the face," Camila remembers. "I started crying, but she told me, 'Don't worry. I'll be okay.' My husband told Al that if he ever hit Dee again that he'd beat him up." Al backed down when Gary challenged him. But Gary couldn't always be there to protect his sister-in-law, and Al didn't change his ways. Sometimes Dee feared Al, sometimes she pitied him, and too often, she blamed herself for making him angry.

One of the most traumatic moments of Camila's life was identifying her sister after the accident. She recognized her only by her hair style and was still reeling from the shock when her family gathered at the hospital. The ambulance had brought Dee there, even though she hadn't survived. "My little nieces wanted to know where Dee was," remembers Camila. "I tried to comfort them and said, 'Dee passed away. She's in Heaven now.'"

"Don't lie to them!" Ruthie Anne snarled. "She is in *Hell!*"

Camila stared at her mother. How could she say such a horrible thing about her own daughter? Why couldn't she forgive her, even in death? Did she really believe that kind hearted Dee was in a place so horrible that their mother had had to scratch the word for it off the record album cover?

Camila was overwhelmed with grief over the loss of her sister, and it hurt even more when the facts came to light. She alleges that her sister's tragic death was not covered in the news and that Troy Samuels faced no criminal charges because his family was influential in the Kalamazoo community. "The Samuels were from Illinois.

Troy was not allowed to drive there because of his seizures. They moved to Michigan so that he could get a driver's license, and he lied on the application about his medical condition."

Dee's family sued the negligent driver. "My mother asked for $50,000, and the settlement was to go to Dee's children. But Troy's attorney stood up in court and said my sister wasn't worth anything." Camila was standing near the attorney, and when she heard him make his callous statement, she was so infuriated, "I smacked him in the face."

Troy's insurance company settled for $20,000, but it's unknown if the money was set aside for Dee's kids. Grandma Ruthie Anne and two of Dee's sisters wanted to adopt the kids, but the social workers refused to allow any of them to see the children again. Dee's sisters claim that Troy Samuels continued to drive and worked delivering beverages for his parents' business. Dee's sister, Victoria, ran into him once at the grocery store when he was making a delivery via his van. "He was so shocked to see me, he dropped the case of drinks he was carrying." Dee's family is understandably bitter about her fate, but no documentation has been found to prove or disprove their allegations.

Victoria was the last to glimpse Shanna Kay and George. Weeks after Dee's death, Victoria was at a Kalamazoo bowling alley when she heard the sweet peal of children's voices, calling "Aunt Victoria!" She turned to see Shanna Kay and George, running toward her, their faces lit with joy. The children threw their arms around her knees, but an angry woman was right behind them and roughly grabbed the kids by their arms, "yanking them away." She spoke harshly to Victoria, "You stay away from them!"

Victoria stood frozen, dumbfounded, as her niece and nephew were dragged away. The children were sobbing and must have been so confused. Their entire family had vanished from their lives, and they had been so excited to see their aunt. Victoria assumed that the hostile woman was the children's new foster mom, but there hadn't been time to ask questions. Victoria never saw the kids again.

If Alva Jenkins tried to get custody of the motherless children, Camila and Victoria never heard about it. Despite his alcoholic stupor, he surely must have been aware that his prior conviction and history of violence would preclude him from gaining custody. While online records of his address history are unclear, Camila insists that Al stayed in the apartment he had once shared with Dee—that for nearly three decades he mourned the woman he'd mistreated, eventually "drinking himself to death," as the walls closed in around him. Whenever Camila ran into Al around town, he was always drunk and mistook her for her dead sister. Overcome by emotion at the sight of Camila, Al cried out, "Dee! Dee! I miss you, Dee!" It was a pitiful display and made Camila extremely uncomfortable.

If the man carried a crushing guilt, it was well deserved. Dee had lost all four of her children because of his abuse, and probably would not have been on the sidewalk at that deadly moment if not for that. Dee had, after all, gone to the laundromat as part of her preparation for the children's return.

But when it comes to fate, so many things must occur to achieve a particular outcome, and the smallest event can change everything. If Dee had dallied at the laundromat another moment, she would likely be alive today. Nothing can change the past, though Shanna Kay's aunts wish that they had the power to alter it. They were surprised to learn that their niece eventually ended up with the Parsnoll family in Battle Creek, Michigan. Not only did they know of the Parsnolls, Victoria had been to their home on more than one occasion, and had met foster parents, Jack and Nannette Parsnoll, but it had never occurred to her to look for Shanna there.

Before Shanna landed at the Parsnolls' home, she first spent time with at least one other foster family, and many years later, she would claim she suffered abuse in at least one of the homes she'd been placed in. If indeed she had been abused, it probably did *not* occur at the Parsnolls' home. Victoria knows for a fact that Shanna didn't live with the Parsnolls until at least a year after Dee's death, because in a strange coincidence, Victoria's own two daughters were placed with the Parsnolls before Shanna Kay was sent to live there. Victoria realized only recently that the niece she'd spent so many years searching for had lived for most of her childhood with people Victoria had met.

Shanna Kay's aunts claim that a male social worker, who was later accused of abusing children, had unfairly picked on their family, removing some of their kids because of urine stains on mattresses and other so-called offenses they consider minor. Victoria's two daughters, Christie and Gillian, were sent to the Parsnolls' home, and Victoria was allowed to visit them there. "I can't say the Parsnolls abused us," says Christie, who was not yet school age when she spent months living there. "But they were kind of unusual." She recollects that her little sister was forced to stand in the corner, facing the wall because she refused to eat the split pea soup they had served for dinner, and was later sent to bed hungry. Christie also recalls that Patsy Parsnoll, Nannette and Jack's biological daughter, picked on Gillian. Whenever Patsy pinched Gillian or pulled her hair, Christie rushed to protect her little sister and retaliated by doing the same to Patsy. But Christie usually got caught and ended up getting punished.

The most upsetting thing to occur in the foster home nearly cost Gillian her life, though Nannette Parsnoll claims she doesn't remember the incident. An older foster child, Shelly, a girl of about nine or ten, allegedly tried to drown Gillian in the bathtub. According to Victoria, Nannette Parsnoll walked in and discovered Shelly, holding the little girl's head under the water. "Gillian had turned blue," Camila remembers. "She went to the hospital by ambulance."

When Victoria learned her daughter had nearly died, she raised a ruckus, and says the disturbed girl was removed from the Parsnolls' home. Prior to the near drowning, the Parsnolls were apparently unaware that Shelly was dangerous, and Victoria doesn't blame them for what occurred, but she was very glad to regain custody of her children. Shanna Kay's aunts insist their children were safer with them than in any foster home, and they believe that Shanna Kay would have been far better off with family than with strangers.

But Shanna's aunts concede there may be a genetic component to their family's violence, for she is not their first relative to be incarcerated for brutal crimes. While several male relatives have violent histories, it is interesting to note that Shanna has a first cousin, a few years younger than she, who is currently serving time for a vicious attack. Henrietta was arrested in Michigan in 2016, a few months before Shanna. At one time a beautiful woman, fresh faced with even features and long, dark hair, a series of mugshots show a quick progression of aging, probably a result of hard living. In the summer of 2016, Henrietta attacked her boyfriend, Bob, with a board, splitting his head open and breaking his ribs.

"He pulled a knife on her first, and they were drunk," Henrietta's mother, Jean, explains. "Bob didn't want to press charges, but it wasn't up to him." Henrietta was given a maximum sentence of ten years. Bob has forgiven her, and he is patiently waiting for her release. He is about thirty years older than Henrietta, but only five feet tall, and at 5'8", Henny not only towers over him, she outweighs him by seventy pounds. "I don't know what happened to her," Jean says sadly. "She used to be normal. She was in the Peace Corps."

While Jean recalls that her daughter was once a gentle soul, another relative remembers that this was not the first time she reacted violently, and they claim that when she was a young girl, Henrietta once hit another child with a shovel.

While Shanna's biological family seems to have more than their share of dysfunction, there are a number of relatives who were very good people, including Camila's only daughter, Sherry, and granddaughter, Arianna. Camila lost both in separate accidents, just one month apart in 2014.

Arianna would *literally* give someone the shirt off her back. The teen was waiting for the school bus one icy morning when she noticed a girl, shivering, without a coat. Arianna peeled off her sweatshirt and gave it to her. When Arianna was only twelve, she heard about a campaign to encourage people to become organ donors. She immediately wanted to sign up, and she took it upon herself to get the paperwork and fill it out. At her young age, parental consent was required, so after her mother signed, Arianna mailed the form.

When Arianna lost her life at age fifteen in the car accident, several people's lives were saved because she was an organ donor. Camila is rightfully proud of her granddaughter. She taught good values to her kids and granddaughter, and she believes that if she had been allowed to raise Shanna, things might have turned out differently. If indeed Shanna's problems are a result of both nurture and nature, it's possible that the right nurturing could have made a difference. Would Shanna have lived a more gentle existence if her Aunt Camila had raised her? No one will ever know.

CHAPTER TWENTY

WHEN THE WIND IS RIGHT, Battle Creek, Michigan, residents can step outside and inhale the sweet scent of toasting cornflakes. The brothers Kellogg invented the cereal by accident in a Battle Creek sanitarium in 1894 while trying to create healthy meals for patients. Will left some boiled wheat out too long, and when it got stale, he and brother John tried to turn it into dough but ended up with flakes. They toasted it, the patients loved it, and breakfast of the future was born.

Also known as Cereal City, Battle Creek is still the headquarters for Kellogg's, the breakfast giant currently employing over 35,000 worldwide. Over the years, thousands of locals have toiled in the Battle Creek plant, including Shanna's foster father, Jack Parsnoll. He and Nannette raised a houseful of kids, most foster or adopted, and Shanna would one day complain she felt stifled by her foster mother's religious views. It couldn't have been too uncomfortable, however, because Shanna continued to depend on the family into adulthood, even living with them for a while after Kellogg's transferred Jack to Omaha in the mid-1990s.

The Parsnoll family had suffered losses over the years, and Nannette credits her faith for giving her the strength to get through it. She was a teen in 1975 when she lost her older sister in a snowmobile accident, and the family was rocked again when Shanna's foster grandmother, Elsie Parsnoll, was murdered at age forty-six in January 1981. Elsie's ex-boyfriend, Drake Leeds, was ten years her junior, and in what sounds very much like stalker behavior, followed her into a Battle Creek lounge, pulled out a gun, and shot her in the side. Elsie was rushed to the hospital but died during surgery. Leeds pled guilty to second-degree murder and was sentenced to ten to fifteen years in prison. Shanna was five when her foster-grand-mother died, too young to fully understand the tragedy.

When Shanna was barely twenty, she married Arthur Drune, and the couple lived for a while in Delton, Michigan. She was divorced by the time she was twenty-two, but didn't bother to mention her past to Raymond Strahan when they began dating. Raymond had always trusted the opinions of both his mother and his stepmother. They were smart women, and he knew they had his best interest at heart. He appreciated their advice—until the day he introduced them to his new girlfriend. Neither of them liked her.

It was the spring of 1997, Raymond was twenty-two and infatuated with the dark-haired lady, so petite he says "she weighed ninety pounds, soaking wet." He thought the elder ladies were wrong about Shanna, and he was offended. Shanna, too, was insulted when he relayed their comments to her, something he now realizes was not his smartest move. "At the time I was naïve," he recalls. Shanna was mad when she learned his family didn't like her, and her interactions with them grew more tense.

Ray couldn't understand why his moms didn't like Shanna and hoped they'd change their minds when they got to know her. He and Shanna had met at the plastic factory where they both worked in Battle Creek, Michigan. She ran the press, and he was attracted to her from the moment she first smiled at him. He'd just moved from Tennessee, where it seemed that all of the women he'd met were gold diggers, not interested in a guy without a lot of money. After being on his own for a couple of years, Raymond was flattered by Shanna's flirting.

But he soon realized his new girlfriend had problems. "She was a cutter, but I think she did it for the attention." Her wrists were often covered with razor scratches, but he never saw signs she'd done serious damage.

Shanna was unreasonably jealous of female coworkers. Once, after Ray had an innocent conversation with a woman at work, Shanna snapped, "What did that bitch want?" He realized his mothers had been right, but he'd become too attached to Shanna to walk away. The fact she was living with him at his dad's house made it even harder to break up. They bickered frequently, but when they were getting along, they liked to go to the movies or to their favorite restaurant—Battle Creek's Big Boy Fast Food. One afternoon, in early 1998, they were eating at Big Boy, when Shanna smirked triumphantly and announced, "I'm late."

It was a shock, but Raymond was determined to take care of her and his baby. "Let's wait for the right moment to tell my parents," he urged. She nodded but blurted out the news the minute she found herself alone with his stepmother. Ray was annoyed but tried to overlook Shanna's quirks. The baby was due in August, and he focused on getting things ready. He bought a trailer, so they could have their very own place to raise their family. It wasn't exactly a mansion, but it was clean and cozy and located in a trailer park with friendly neighbors. He expected Shanna to be pleased, but she had other ideas. She was eight months pregnant when she suddenly moved into twenty-one-year-old Neil Munson's house.

"He's just a roommate!" Shanna insisted. Raymond wanted to believe her, but Neil glared at him when he visited. Shanna told Raymond not to worry about it and invited him to spend the night. Neil rushed outside and got into his car, loudly revving the motor outside their bedroom window. Neil was behaving like a jealous boyfriend, but Shanna insisted there was nothing romantic between them, and she had no idea why he was acting so strangely.

Instead of settling into nesting mode, as most pregnant women do, Shanna was restless, flitting about from place to place and man to man. Sometimes she stayed with Ray, sometimes with Neil, and sometimes at a women's shelter. Raymond couldn't help but wonder if the baby was really his. But when Cody Nathaniel Golyar entered the world on August 25, 1998, Ray realized the six-pound infant looked exactly like his own baby photos. This was his son, and he loved him instantly. But it soon became clear that Neil was Shanna's boyfriend. The betrayal stung, but Ray wanted to be in his son's life. Things were so strained between Shanna and Ray that he saw Cody only a few times over the next months. "He was a colicky baby," Ray remembers, "But I was able to soothe him."

Raymond and Neil had something in common. Both had mothers who'd taken an instant dislike to Shanna. "I got a bad vibe from her," remembers Gloria Munson, adding that she could see Shanna was manipulating her son. "He's slow. He believes what people tell him. He was always kind of naïve. If he thinks that you know what you're talking about, you could tell him the sky is really fluorescent purple, and he'd believe it."

Gloria and her husband, Stan, owned an old house they rented to Neil and his brother, Larry. When Gloria discovered Shanna had moved in, she asked her to pay rent. But Shanna was always broke, despite the fact she'd gotten a job at the convenience store where Neil worked. She barely contributed to the household but lived with Neil, off and on, after Cody was born. Neil had his own baby, Gavin, a few months older than Cody, and he helped Shanna take care of her newborn. The oldest of Gloria's six kids, Neil had helped care for his younger siblings from the time he was school-age and had also helped with the many foster children the Munsons raised. Neil and his ex, Rachel, shared custody of baby Gavin, but Neil wanted full custody. Rachel had almost agreed to it, until she saw something that alarmed her. "Rachel called me," Gloria recalls, "and she was upset because Shanna was swaddling Gavin, and he was seven months old—much too old for that." It was as if the baby were wearing a little straitjacket, his arms bound to his sides, unable to move. "Shanna didn't want the kids moving. She didn't want the kids to do *anything!*"

When Gloria confronted Neil about Gavin's swaddling, he explained, "Shanna says it's the best thing for him." Gloria put her foot down. She would not allow her grandson to be subjected to any more of Shanna's peculiar mothering and told Neil "Rachel is going to keep your son until we know what's going on."

Gloria has powerful maternal instincts, and in addition to her biological and foster kids, she adopted a special-needs child. A hands-on grandma, she helped Neil care for both Gavin and Cody. She worried about Cody, who seemed to be a very unhappy baby. Shanna said he was just colicky, but he should have grown out of that by the time he was three or four months old. Cody cried incessantly—until January 29, 1999. Neil and his mother went grocery shopping at about 9:15 that morning, taking Cody along while Shanna worked. Gloria was struck by how unusually quiet the infant was.

Later, back at Neil's place, they set Cody down on the rug and played baby games with him. He was oddly subdued but didn't look ill. Cody hadn't cried the entire time Gloria was with him that day, and she still hadn't heard a peep out of him when she left after noon. When she returned around 5 P.M., she stepped straight into a nightmare. Neil was dozing in a chair, and when she checked on Cody, she realized he wasn't breathing. She shouted at Neil to call 911. As Gloria performed infant CPR, she could hear Neil on the phone. "I remember him trying to give his address, and he couldn't do it totally," she says adding that her son seemed confused by whatever the dispatcher was asking. Stan arrived and took over the CPR while Gloria grabbed the phone and gave directions to the emergency operator. Police beat the ambulance to the scene and took Cody to the hospital in their squad car.

Gloria was worried sick about Cody and asked Neil if anything unusual had happened. He said Shanna had called him at work the night before and cried, "I dropped the baby! Get home!" But Cody had seemed okay when Neil got home. He was definitely *not* okay when officers rushed him to the Battle Creek Health System Emergency Room. The baby had no heartbeat. Doctors administered two courses of resuscitative drugs to restart his heart, but he couldn't breathe on his own, and his pupils were fixed and dilated. He was intubated and transferred to Bronson Methodist Hospital. Dr. Robert Page pronounced Cody Golyar dead at 12:40 A.M., January 30, 1999. The cause of death was "shaken baby syndrome (SBS)."

Neil was devastated. The infant had gotten sick on his watch, and the young man suffered both guilt and grief. At 5 A.M., cops put an exhausted Neil in the back of their squad car and grilled him. Neil acknowledged that he often playfully tossed Cody into the air to make him giggle. The police taped the conversation but admitted later that they didn't start recording until they'd prompted Neil to incriminate himself.

Neil was trying to be helpful. The mentally challenged man was sleep deprived, probably in shock, and had a tendency to get confused, especially in stressful situations. This was the second time in twelve hours he'd been questioned, and he'd already stated there was nothing unusual about his play with Cody that day. But they kept repeating questions and didn't seem pleased with his answers.

Neil eventually told them what they wanted to hear. He finally said he'd shaken the baby. Shaken him once. But Cody's death was not caused by a gentle jiggle or bouncing on a knee. Did Neil understand what they meant by shaking? Probably not. Dr. Page testified that Cody's injuries were the result of *twenty seconds or more of vigorous shaking*. Apparently, the officer didn't understand SBS either because he fixated on the tossing game—a potentially dangerous activity but *not* the cause of Cody's death. Officer Stone testified, "Mr. Munson told me that he often would play with the baby by tossing the baby in the air and catching the baby. He described it as setting the baby on a knee and kind of tossing him up in the air and catching him. He advised me this is how he often played with the baby. I asked him if anything out of the normal happened this day, if he had played with the baby any differently, and he said basically no . . ." Unsatisfied with Neil's response, Officer Stone pressured him. "When I asked him if he could've thrown the baby higher or whatever, he said, yeah, he could have. I tried to get—I asked him distance-wise and if it could have been a foot. He said, yeah, maybe it was—it was even a little over that. I asked him how many times he had thrown the baby in the air and caught him, and he said he would estimate five."

Neil had affectionately played the game with Cody to get him to smile, and while the National Center on Shaken Baby Syndrome (NCSBS) warns that activities such as tossing a baby in the air and bouncing a baby on the knee, "can be dangerous and are not recommended, they will likely *not* cause SBS injuries."

Someone had shaken Cody violently, but there was no proof Neil had done it. And no one could prove *when* Cody was shaken. SBS "symptoms can start quickly, especially in a badly injured child. Other times, it may take a few days for swelling to cause symptoms," reports Cigna, a global health service company.

Several people had interacted with Cody in the days leading up to his death. Cody's own mother had claimed she'd dropped him. Had she done *more* than that? Was Shanna fed up after five months of Cody's nonstop wailing? Had she shaken him and then concocted the dropping story to make possible injuries appear accidental?

No one knows the answer to that, but observers noticed that Shanna didn't behave like a typical grieving mother. Within a day or so of Cody's death, Gloria ran into her at Walmart and was shocked by her cheerful mood. Shanna was with an older couple, and the woman smiled at Gloria and said, "We're treating Shanna to a new wardrobe today!"

Gloria was taken aback when she saw how excited Shanna was about the shopping spree. "Shanna looked so happy, she didn't act like a mother who'd just lost her baby."

Raymond, too, was baffled by Shanna's behavior. Numb with grief, he was more confused than ever as she bounced between him and Neil. But Neil was soon out of the picture. Police decided Neil had hurt Cody, and they arrested him. After he went to jail, Shanna slept with Raymond. It was the night before the funeral. One of Raymond's darkest moments came as he watched Shanna by Cody's tiny coffin, with a small group gathered around her. She whipped out photos of Neil's baby. "They were passing the photos around," remembers Ray. It hurt him to see Shanna, smiling proudly at the photos of this other baby, when her own infant lay motionless, within her reach, but already forgotten. "It was so inappropriate," he remembers. "That was not the place to be doing that."

Today, Ray is a happily married father and an Army Sergeant First Class, and he regularly trains new recruits. In a poignant moment in 2018, as he checked his clipboard and glanced at the birthdate of a young man standing before him, he felt a lump rise in his throat. *August 25, 1998.* Cody's birthday! Ray realized if his son had lived, he'd be the age of this man, twenty and healthy with a long life ahead of him. Once again, he was rocked by the loss of all that could have been.

He's always suspected Shanna was involved in his child's death, and remembers that police, too, suspected her at one time. She may have been a suspect, but Neil took the fall. When he was arrested and charged with second-degree murder, the Munsons hired defense attorney Morris Astene. But the best attorney in the world can't help a client who isn't upfront with them. Neil was clearly under the spell of Shanna Golyar and trusted her word above all others—trusted it more than the advice of the attorney his parents had paid to save him.

As the December 1999 trial got underway at the Calhoun County District Courthouse, *The Battle Creek Enquirer* quoted Astene's opening statement: "Neil Munson didn't do it. The mother did. The night before, she called and said, 'I dropped Cody. Get home.' My client is covering for a dysfunctional, abusive mother." In a photo with the article, a bespectacled, baby-faced Neil appears dazed by the courtroom commotion.

He was as easy for Shanna to manipulate as a handful of Play-Doh. Today, a long list of intelligent and embarrassed men have been forced to step forward and publicly admit she duped them. If Shanna could trick experienced detectives and men with genius IQs, how could an intellectually challenged twenty-two-year-old who thought he was in love understand her games? Gloria Munson's first impression of Shanna had been spot-on. She'd sensed Neil's girlfriend's sneaky influence would hurt him, and she was right.

On the second day of Neil's trial, Gloria waited in the hall outside the courtroom, anxious to take the stand and share what she knew. But she never got the chance. That opportunity was snatched away by a questionable witness who brought the trial to an abrupt end and sealed Neil's fate. Gloria didn't recognize that witness when she first appeared. "If she hadn't turned and looked at me, I wouldn't have known it was Shanna."

Shanna was in *disguise!* She wore a wig, a dingy shade of dishwater blond that flowed past her shoulders, and a skirt with a hem that brushed the floor as she sailed passed. As it so happened, the grieving mother was a fugitive from justice! She would later insist that the felony warrant was nothing more than a misunderstanding. She hadn't *really* meant to steal a car. Even so, if the wrong person at the courthouse recognized her, she could go to jail. She was the state of Michigan's star witness in a murder trial, and she arrived incognito to avoid arrest in the other matter.

Shanna took the stand in her strange getup, and would spend the next seventy minutes destroying the young man who believed that she loved him. Assistant prosecutor Karen Ounst knew she had to air Shanna's dirty laundry before her opponent got a chance to. Morris Astene would surely use Shanna's crimes to discredit her, so Ounst diffused the impact by bringing them up first. With Ounst's prompting, Shanna acknowledged two standing felony warrants for "Unlawful use of my roommate's car" and "Driving while my license is suspended." She also admitted she'd been arrested for shoplifting in 1996.

The prosecutor next wanted to establish that Cody was healthy the morning Shanna left him with Neil—something Gloria was prepared to refute. Shanna testified, "He was fine, normal. Laughing. And I just got him out of bed to get him dressed, so I could go to work."

Ounst asked about the call to Neil on the night before Cody was stricken. This was the infamous "I dropped the baby" call, and records from the phone company could confirm a call was made at about half past eight, but only Shanna and Neil knew what was said. Ounst asked, "Why did you place a call to Neil Munson?"

"Just to see when he was getting out of work, and if he was going to need a ride home or what." Shanna next testified that Neil was careless, and it was up to her to pick up the knives and bullet casings he left lying around within the infants' reach.

Gloria, still waiting in the hall, would have been horrified to hear Ounst's next line of questioning. Apparently, sometime before her testimony, Shanna had reported that *Gloria* had confessed to shaking Cody. Gloria, who had raised a number of children and never had an issue, was now being accused of the worst thing imaginable by the odd little woman in the wig. Shanna claimed Gloria had phoned her the day after Cody's death with a startling admission. "I was just called and told that she could have shaken Cody."

"Okay. And when you called the police, why did you do that?"

"To inform them."

"Okay. Now, was that the first time Gloria Munson told you that she may have shaken the child?"

"Yes."

"All right. Did she indicate under what circumstances she may have shook the child?"

"No."

"What was your reaction when she told you that?"

"I was just upset and confused."

The first time Gloria learned of the accusation was in March 2019 when I read her parts of the trial transcripts over the phone. She wasn't really surprised to hear Shanna had plotted against her, but was floored by something else I revealed. For the first time, Gloria learned why she didn't get a chance to testify and why Neil's trial had come to a screeching halt. Shanna sat on that stand in her bizarre outfit and read

seven letters she claimed Neil had written to her from jail. Those letters convinced the jury that Neil was responsible for Cody's death and
allowed Shanna to dance out of that courtroom and flee the state of
Michigan. She hurried back to Omaha, far away from the felony
warrants and people who whispered that *she* had shaken her child.

There was just one little problem. It's unlikely Neil authored the
letters that sent him to prison. When I read them to Gloria, she
laughed out loud. "Neil would not have been able to articulate so
well," Gloria told me. "He has a learning disability."

While we *now* know that Shanna is a pathological liar, and that
forging confessions to frame others for her crimes is her M.O., no
one at that 1999 trial had the ability to peer into the future and know
that she would one day impersonate innocent people in over 20,000
emails. Certainly, Karen Ounst believed Shanna was truthful when
she questioned her about Neil's handwriting. "Did you recognize his
handwriting in every one of the letters?" she asked.

"Yes," Shanna testified. The writing on the envelopes bore information indicating they were mailed from the jail, but that, too, could
have been forged. The one-time suspect in Cody's death was permit-
ted to identify Neil's handwriting, and no one challenged her. Not
even Neil. As his client sat silently beside him, Morris Astene had
no reason to suspect the letters were fakes. They were supposedly
written in May 1999 and contained dramatic passages such as "I
wish I could have you in my loving arms one more time. Please understand I've lost something very special to me. I've lost a son that I
loved very much. Also, I lost his mother as well."

The flowery, romantic wording was as foreign to Neil as the complex sentence structure, Gloria insists. "Neil" wrote that he missed
Shanna's "beautiful face" and that he wished he could "hug and kiss
your beautiful body from head to toe and make sweet love to you all
over again." He proposed marriage, and even signed one of the letters, "Love your husband, Neil John Munson."

The fourth letter, dated May 10, 1999, contained the first damag-
ing passage:

> . . . *As my wife to be, I need you to come back up here and
> tell my attorney that on Thursday, the 29th of February the
> reason you called me from work at eight-thirty p.m. was*

*because you had dropped Cody from about four feet, which
then caused Cody to stop breathing. So then, you shook
Cody, not to do any harm, but to get him to start breathing
again. Please Shanna, this is what will set me free because
they are trying to pin it on me. Please, I love you with all
my heart and soul . . .*

Cody had actually died on *January* 29th, but the letter writer had
forgotten that. The fifth letter, dated May 11, made things worse:

*. . . Hi honey. Hey, what I said in the letter to you on May
10th, about what to say that you dropped Cody, forget
about it. That is wrong of me to ask you to say something
that you didn't do like that. I'm just scared, but I went to
court and it went well . . .*

The Battle Creek Enquirer reported that Morris Astene realized
that the letters destroyed the defense theory and quoted him. "You
could tell by the look on the jurors' faces. You could tell it was all
over." Astene spoke to his client during the next break, and together
they decided it was time to surrender. The young man pled guilty, and
the trial was over. If indeed he did *not* write those letters, he didn't
speak up for one of three reasons. One, he put Shanna's needs before
his own. Two, he didn't understand the significance of the letters. Or
three, he didn't think anyone would believe him.

Neil's apology with his guilty plea echoed the statements the cops
had coaxed from him during the ambush interrogation in the back of
the police car. He had learned then what he was expected to say. He
was probably greatly relieved the trial was over but didn't fully
comprehend what the future held.

The record of Shanna's testimony, including her reading of the incriminating letters that put Neil behind bars, was confined to a video-
tape that had slowly begun to disintegrate with the beginning of the
new millennium. When I ordered the transcripts of Shanna's testimony, I was told that no typed version of the trial transcripts had ever
existed. The transcriptionist would have to watch the old video and
type a transcript from that, but the tape was so fragile they could

make no guarantees. There was a chance the tape could turn to dust as the reels began to churn, and Shanna's lies would be swept into a dustpan with the fragmented pieces of a drama long past.

But as it turned out, the transcriptionist was very careful, and "babied the tape along." She recorded Shanna's every word, and presented me with seventy perfectly typed pages. I've tried to get copies of the actual letters, so the handwriting can be studied to determine if they're forgeries. As of this writing, the letters have not materialized and may have been destroyed when old files were cleared. The only solid evidence to show Neil Munson did *not* write the letters comes from comparisons of linguistic styles. But if anyone had been paying close attention, they would have noticed another odd thing. "Neil" had written in one letter that Raymond was wondering where Shanna had gone, implying that he and Raymond had had a discussion about her whereabouts. Not only were the two men *not* friends, Neil was in jail. Raymond is adamant that he never had that conversation with Neil.

While he served his time and was paroled years ago, if Neil *is* innocent, it's terribly unfair that he should carry the stigma of someone else's evil deed. It's possible Neil was manipulated into *believing* the death was his fault. The cops' obsession with his "tossing game" might have convinced him he had caused the injuries.

Neil spent eight and a half years in prison. His parents and siblings stood by him and never believed for a moment he could harm a child. A father of two now, his care of his children has always been above reproach. And yet, the *other* suspect in the baby's death was eventually proven to be a sadistic killer. All of this makes me question if justice was served in Cody's death.

According to Gloria, there was another important witness expected to testify, and she never got a chance to take the stand. The would-be witness was an acquaintance of Shanna's and allegedly claimed that Shanna had told her she'd had *another* child who had died of SBS, and this was relayed long *before* Cody was stricken. If Shanna really did tell that story, was it fact or fiction? Either way it's suspicious.

Shanna seldom returned to Michigan. She feared arrest and avoided the state. Ray remembers brief visits when she showed up incognito. She owned two wigs, one blond and one brunette, and when she ventured into The Great Lakes State, she did so as stealthily as a secret agent. The felony warrant for the car theft still stands. Authorities knew she'd moved to Omaha and could have extradited her, but the cost was prohibitive. She was a known fugitive from justice but didn't make it onto any "most wanted lists." No one realized she was dangerous.

CHAPTER TWENTY-ONE

DAVE KROUPA HAD A CLOSE CIRCLE of pals in Sioux Falls, friends he'd known since high school, and they'd kept in touch over the years. Some of the guys in the group dated some of the girls, but others were platonic friends. Tayandy Braver was a platonic friend, but her best friend, Heather, describes herself as Dave's "friend with benefits," though romance between them occurred only when they were both single. They cared about each other, but their relationship had never been serious. It was simply a fun, comfortable friendship with a strong physical attraction.

In January 2014, they were both single. Heather had recently broken up with her boyfriend, so Dave invited her to visit. She made the three-hour drive from Sioux Falls to Omaha and remembers that "It was the coldest day of the year." Shortly after she arrived, one of Dave's male friends stopped by. "We had a few beers with him," Heather remembers. The guy soon left, and she noticed Dave's cellphone was blowing up with texts and calls. "What's going on?"

Dave sighed. "This girl, Cari, won't leave me alone. She keeps stalking me. The cops haven't been able to do anything about it."

It was upsetting news! She wished he'd warned her. Dave tried to reassure her, and they moved into the bedroom but were interrupted by a rattling noise. "It sounded like someone was trying to open the patio door." Heather shudders at the memory. Dave told her not to worry. The stalker's shenanigans were commonplace. It might have been normal for *him*, but she was scared. She screamed as glass shattered. They found a brick on the bathroom floor, amidst shards of glass, as the icy winter air poured through the broken window.

Dave was surprised by how frightened Heather was, and she couldn't understand why he was so calm. "Call the police," she cried, but he balked. There was no point, he told her. The stalker was long gone by now. But Heather was adamant, so he made the call. The police showed up to take the report, but just as Dave had predicted, there was nothing they could do. The only sign of the stalker was a jumble of footprints in the snow, some outside the bathroom window, and others outside the patio door. Dave told Heather more of the story, explaining that "Cari" was also stalking Liz, one of his girlfriends. He added that he and Liz had an open relationship, but he kept Wednesdays reserved for her.

The whole scenario struck Heather as fishy, and she ventured, "Maybe Wednesday Girl threw the brick." It made no sense that this Cari would not want to see him face to face. If she was so in love with him, why hadn't he seen her in over a year? Dave knew it was a whacky situation, but it had been going on for so long he'd stopped trying to make sense of it. He shrugged off Heather's suggestion that Liz was the real culprit. He and Liz had been together many times when she'd received threatening texts, and he'd seen with his own eyes how frightened she was. He was worried about Liz now because it was unusual for the stalker to break a window when he was home. Why had she suddenly changed her pattern? The nut must be extra riled up. "We need to check on Liz to make sure she's okay," he said. They went by Liz's place, but there were no cars in the driveway and no tracks in the snow. No one had been there for hours. Heather found that suspicious, but Dave wasn't interested in her theories.

Heather was annoyed, frightened, and miserable. It was so cold with the broken window that it was impossible to sleep. She grew more irritated when she spent the next day alone in the freezing apartment when Dave went to work. She would have been even more frightened had she known Cari had disappeared from that very apartment. Heather felt the same visceral terror Melissa Strom had experienced a decade earlier when Liz trapped her in her boyfriend's apartment. Both Heather and Melissa had been dismissed by men who suggested they were overreacting. Both women survived because they trusted their own instincts. Heather cut her visit short, and she and Dave parted on a sour note. He knew she was shaken but didn't realize how angry she was at him for not warning her. He'd grown so used to the constant harassment that it was no longer a big deal to him. While they remained in touch, their friendship cooled, and their rendezvous during Omaha's coldest days of 2014 was to be their last romantic encounter.

A few months later, Dave invited Liz along to keep him company when he drove to Sioux Falls to see family and friends. It was a casual visit, he remembers, stressing that it was *not* a special trip to introduce his girlfriend to his parents. He still had no desire for a commitment. After Heather's unfortunate visit, some of his friends snidely referred to Liz as "Dave's Wednesday Girl," though most weeks she managed to see him on additional days not allotted to her.

Dave and Liz stopped by Tayandy's house. They'd first met as children, when Tay was best friends with Dave's older cousin. One day, when the girls were playing together, they were asked to sit on the porch and keep an eye on Dave. "Dave was in diapers," Tay remembers. She would know him forever, and they would grow up to be good friends, but her first impression of him was forever tattooed upon her memory banks. He was an adorable tyke with sunrays highlighting the ginger tones of his hair as he toddled around the yard. She would always think of him as a little brother.

Tay warmly welcomed Dave and Liz and would have been surprised to realize that Liz was jealous of her. An attractive blonde, Tay is a mother of two and has been married to her husband, David, since 1998. The walls of her home are adorned with photos of her kids and pets, and it should have been obvious to anyone visiting that her life was grounded in her family. After a pleasant visit, Tay walked them to the door and casually mentioned to Liz that she should come back sometime. It wasn't an actual invitation, just something polite that hostesses say without expecting to be taken seriously. Tay would come to regret her good manners.

Not long after the visit, Tay received an email from Dave, and when she opened the attachment, she was shocked to find herself watching a sex video starring Dave and a dark-haired woman whose face was not visible. Annoyed, Tay called Dave and demanded, "Why did you send me that?"

"I don't know what you're talking about," he replied.

She sent the video back to him, and he recognized the images. He was aware that Liz had used her phone to record a few seconds of intimacy between them, but he wasn't thrilled to learn that the X-rated flick was being sent to his friends. He figured that the stalker had hacked into Liz's phone and accessed the naughty movie. A few weeks later, Tay was looking forward to relaxing at home with her husband in the upcoming weekend when she got an unexpected call from Liz, who asked, "What are you doing this weekend?"

"Not much," Tay answered honestly. "Just hanging out here." Before Tay realized what was happening, her polite "invitation" from weeks earlier had come back to haunt her. Liz had taken the invitation literally and announced she wanted to visit for the entire weekend. Though disappointed that her plans were ruined, Tay always put other people's feelings first. She told Liz she was welcome to come, explaining now, "I didn't want to be rude."

Liz soon arrived with her packed bags but seemed surprised to find a house full of people. "I think she thought I was going to be alone here, because my husband often works away from home overnight. Also, she didn't realize that my father-in-law had moved in with us. I went around and introduced Liz to everyone, and she did not seem at all impressed. She asked, 'So, where are we going to go spend girl time?' I said, 'Here!' I had no intentions of going anywhere else. Where did she think we should go? To a bar? I'm not a big drinker, and I didn't want to go to a bar."

"Girl time" would just have to take place at Tay's kitchen table. Tay poured coffee as Liz launched into a monologue about "Crazy Cari."

"She said she was frustrated because Dave wouldn't do anything to stop Cari from stalking them, and she had to get out of town for a while because the whole thing was stressing her out." She told Tay, "The Omaha cops are stupid" because they couldn't catch the stalker. As Liz griped, Tay tried to sympathize but grew weary when it turned into an exhausting monologue. Tay was relieved when Heather dropped in.

"Heather, this is Dave's girlfriend, Liz," said Tay.

"Heather?" Liz's eyes narrowed. "Oh, you're the one who came

to see Dave. He should have brought you to my place when Crazy Cari threw the brick through the window."

"I don't even know you," Heather said coldly. "Why would I stay at your house?"

Flustered by Heather's attitude, Tay shot her best friend a warning glance. Why was Heather being so rude to poor Liz? But Heather ignored Tay, instead locking eyes with Liz, who asked her, "What were you doing at Dave's?"

"You know," Heather said slowly. "Dave and I have been friends with benefits for decades. I will always be here. I was here before you, and I will be here after you. You're just the Wednesday Girl." Then Heather walked out, leaving a fuming Liz glaring after her. It had been a tense exchange, but at least it got Liz's mind off of Cari. Now Liz wanted to talk about Heather, and she asked Tay how often Heather and Dave had sex. "I don't know," Tay told her. "I don't keep track of it."

Then Liz wanted to know if *Tay* had ever had sex with Dave. Tay laughed and said, "Kroupa is like a little brother to me!" She told Liz about meeting him for the first time when he was a toddler in diapers, but Liz was skeptical. "She didn't believe me, and she asked me over and over again if I'd ever slept with Kroupa. I kept telling her that we were just friends."

Liz said she was aware that Dave had been intimate with several other women in the group. If Dave had slept with those women, why hadn't he slept with Tay?

"We're not attracted to each other," Tay said patiently. "And I'm *married!*"

"Why aren't you attracted to him?" Liz prodded. "What's wrong with him?"

"There's nothing wrong with Kroupa, but he's like a little *brother* to me! And I don't think it's a good idea to sleep with your brother!"

Liz asked her to explain again about how she and Dave had met, so Tay repeated the story. "Seriously," Tay told Liz. "Kroupa is just a *friend!*"

"If he's just a friend, then why do you have a pet name for him?"

"A pet name? What do you mean?"

"You call him Kroupa."

"I call him Kroupa because I've got so many friends named Dave. Even my *husband's* name is Dave." Tay tried to explain that Kroupa was not a term of endearment, but a way to distinguish him from multiple Daves and reduce confusion.

"Why do you text him so often?" Liz asked.

Tay told her that she regularly texted a number of her friends, just to say hi or ask how they were doing. After a while, Liz switched gears and suggested they visit Dave's parents, who lived a few blocks from the Braver home. Tay phoned Dave's mom and asked if they could come. Patricia "Trish" Kroupa was surprised by the call. She didn't know either Tay or Liz well, but she graciously invited them over. Tay remembers that they sat down at the Kroupa kitchen table, drinking coffee, as Liz began to gripe about the stalker situation. Tom and Trish appeared worried as Liz told them that "Crazy Cari" was very dangerous.

The Kroupas were aware of the stalking and had been concerned enough that Tom had recently given Dave a gun for protection, but Tay recalls that Liz went on and on about it until she had the couple worked up into a panic. "Tom finally said that maybe Dave should have more guns, and Liz got excited and said, 'Yes, we need more guns!'"

Trish Kroupa recalls that the most peculiar part of the visit was when Liz started to obsess over Dave's child-support payments. Liz felt that Dave was handing over way too much of his hard-earned cash to "greedy" Amy and suggested that Trish speak to her son about it. Maybe with input from his mother, he would finally realize that Amy was taking advantage of him.

Trish was astonished by her gall but kept her voice level as she responded, "Dave is a grown man. He can make his own decisions." Trish had two other encounters with Liz that left her shaking her head. Once, Dave had gone to his parents' home to see his cousin, Trish (named after her aunt), who was visiting from out of town. They hadn't seen each other in a long time, and everyone was laughing and reminiscing when Dave got a call from Liz. Though they could hear only Dave's side of the conversation, it was apparent to everyone listening that Liz wanted to join him, but he very clearly told her not to come. They were shocked when Liz showed up a few hours later. She claimed she had been nearby, attending a meeting, and, since she was already in the neighborhood, had decided to drop in. Dave's mother remembers that her niece took her aside and with a worried look exclaimed, "There's something really wrong with her!"

On another occasion, Tom and Trish went to Omaha to take Dave and their grandchildren to a steakhouse for Calista's birthday. Though not invited, Liz showed up, ordered an expensive meal and expected Dave's parents to pay for it. They were taken aback by her rudeness but quietly paid the bill.

It was a pattern with Liz. She usually expected someone else to pick up the tab, and she rarely said thank you, as Tay learned during that impromptu visit. After they left the Kroupa house, Liz suggested they go out to dinner. Tay and her husband decided to take her to one of their favorite places, a nearby Chinese restaurant. No sooner had they ordered when Liz got up and left the table. The food came, but she didn't return. "David and I were sitting there, wondering what we were supposed to do. Do we start eating or wait for her? I said, 'Well, maybe I better go check on her.'"

She found Liz in the ladies' room, cellphone pressed to her ear, in a heated exchange with Dave Kroupa. Tay could hear his angry voice coming through the phone. "Kroupa's screaming, and she's screaming! I'm like, 'I don't even know what the hell's going on here,' and everybody was so mad!" Tay gathered that Dave was upset at Liz for infiltrating his gang of pals and stirring up trouble with Heather. When he hung up on Liz, Tay said, "Let's go, Liz. You can't sit in the bathroom all night!"

Seething, Liz followed her back to the table for a tense meal. "The conversation was weird," Tay recalls, describing lengthy, awkward silences with sudden outbursts from Liz. She had insisted they go to dinner but showed no interest in the food. When the Bravers paid the bill, she didn't offer to chip in or leave the tip. She also failed to say thank you, irritating Tay. "I'm pretty big on manners, and she didn't possess too many of those."

As infuriating as the dinner was, it was what happened later that Tay would never forget. The Braver family had a full house and were short on beds. Dave and Tay Braver normally slept together in their basement bedroom, but he'd been working graveyard shifts and wasn't tired when the ladies were ready to turn in. As he played games on his computer in a partially sectioned off corner of the basement, Tay invited Liz to share her queen-sized bed. They slid between the sheets, talked for a while, and then Tay drifted off to sleep. "At one point, I rolled over, and she was looking at me."

Liz appeared to be in a daze as she stared, unblinking. Tay felt sure it was her intense gaze that had woken her. "It was like she was boring holes through the back of my head." Tay felt a chill and asked, "Hey, everything okay?"

The light from Dave Braver's computer cast an eerie glow on Liz's face, and Tay was startled by her oddly blank expression. Suddenly, Liz blinked a couple of times, seeming to "snap out of it" and replied, "Yeah, I'm just having a hard time sleeping."

It wasn't quite 5 A.M., and Tay had barely slept three hours, but she got up with Liz. "We ended up coming upstairs and sat on the couch talking." When Liz announced she wanted to go home, Tay didn't argue and was relieved to see her walk out the front door. Liz was an odd duck and very rude, but she didn't seem dangerous. *Not then.* Today, Tay looks back on the visit with a shudder, certain that Liz had a dark plan for her. "She expected I'd be there alone, but thank God my husband was there."

It was not the last Tay heard from her. Liz called and texted Tay constantly, mostly to complain about "Crazy Cari" and the fact Dave was refusing to commit, even though, as Liz claimed, "I'm the best girlfriend in the world!" Tay also found herself a target of the stalker's rage, and was receiving fifty to a hundred emails and texts daily, all allegedly from Cari. The "Cari" texts spewed hatred and accused Tay of being one of "Dave's whores."

Liz repeatedly invited Tay to come stay with her in Council Bluffs, sometimes suggesting that Tay's teenage daughter come, too. "I think if I'd gone down there by myself that she would have tried to rub me out. Honest to God, there is not a *thing* anybody could say to me that would change my mind, but I think that if I had taken my daughter there, she would have killed her, too." But that was a revelation still years away in 2014, and while she found Liz to be extremely irritating, she had no fear of her. In fact, she was angry at *Heather* for being rude to Liz.

From the moment Liz had entered their lives, relationships had been strained all the way around. Heather was frustrated with both

Dave Kroupa and Tay for failing to see what was so obvious to her. They pooh-poohed her warnings that Liz was dangerous. No one bought Heather's theory that Liz had murdered Cari and was pretending to be her.

Though Liz bombarded Tay with texts, she got annoyed when Tay texted Dave—particularly on Wednesdays. "Wednesday Girl became Every-day-girl for a while," Tay wryly notes. Often, when Tay texted Dave a quick hello, she would immediately get a text from Liz with a pointed message: "I'm having alone time with Dave." That was Tay's cue to back off. Dave reported back to Tay that one of her "hellos" had prompted Liz to pick a fight with him. Tay remembers, "Nobody knew when it was safe to call. We ended up calling him at work because that was safer."

CHAPTER TWENTY-TWO

LIZ NEVER GAVE UP trying to get closer to Dave, and he continued to meet women. Connie was one of the ladies he met online, and though they hadn't talked on the phone, they texted quite a bit, and he was eager to meet her in person. She described herself as a slender blonde and said she liked to have fun. They arranged to meet in a restaurant in Omaha, and he showed up a 7 P.M., but there was no sign of his date. He waited and waited, but Connie didn't show up. Finally, he texted to ask if she'd be there soon. She replied, *Ha! Ha! Got you!*

The lady he'd been texting with wasn't Connie after all. *There was no Connie!* His stalker had created a fake identity to cat-phish him. He changed his number. He was more careful after that, and screened the ladies through multiple online chats before trusting them with his phone number. The next time he made a date with a stranger, they had a more extensive online friendship before he shared his information. He was looking forward to meeting Rita, and they set up a date at a coffeeshop, but she stood him up. He texted her and received a prompt reply: *Fuck you!* His stalker had gotten him *again!* Dave was cat-phished no less than six times, despite all his precautions. It was a frustrating waste of time.

Where did Liz get the energy to play her nonstop games? That's almost as baffling as her unbelievable cruelty. She played another mean trick on Cari's family in March 2014. It was Saint Patrick's Day, hours before sunup, when Deputy Karl Rhyster was dispatched to the former home of Cari Farver in Macedonia, Iowa.

Sixteen months had passed since Cari left the home she shared with Max, but it was the only address dispatchers could find for her after they were alerted to a possible suicide threat, posted by "Cari" on the social networking site, MeetMe.

Deputy Rhyster recalls, "There was a vehicle in the driveway, so I contacted dispatch with the plate number, and they advised me that it was registered to a Marina Estes." The Raneys' tenant was jolted awake by a rap on her door. It was barely 5 A.M., too early for someone to drop by for anything other than an emergency. Marina was startled to see a uniformed officer on her stoop. She opened the door, shivering as the cold, early morning air rushed in.

"I recognized her as a person I know," says Rhyster. "And I advised her of why I was there and talked to her about the incident."

Marina shook her head. She knew the Raneys' daughter was missing, and she hadn't seen her. Rhyster apologized for waking her and headed to his next destination, a four-minute drive away. He roused the Raneys and informed them of the suicide threat. Nancy and Mark verified that their daughter was still missing. The news both bewildered and shocked them. Did this mean Cari was still alive? If so, was she really threatening suicide? Had rescuers been sent to the wrong address as Cari lay dying? Or was this a cruel prank?

It had been thirteen months to the *day* since the Siena House hoax. The stalker often picked on Cari's family on holidays, and was at it again on Sunday, May 11, Mother's Day—another hard day for Nancy. She grieved for Cari *every* day, but this holiday rubbed salt in the wound. It was difficult for Maxwell to face this day without his mother, and difficult for Nancy to face it without her daughter. Watching her grandson suffer made the day all the harder for Nancy. The Mother's Day greeting came via text from an unfamiliar number:

Happy Mother [sic] *Day, Mom.*

Maxwell, too, got a message. Though both he and Nancy were wary because of the many letdowns, it was particularly hurtful to receive a phony message on what should have been a day of celebration.

"How is Max?" the texter asked Nancy.

"Call me, and I'll gladly tell you about him," she replied. "This is not talking. I need to hear your voice." As usual, no call came.

* * *

Spring of 2014 was eventful for some of the people in Liz's life. In April, Garret suffered chest pains late one night. He called his mother, who rushed over to take him to the hospital. He was hospitalized for several days for the "cardiac event," while doctors ran tests. When Liz didn't visit, it angered his friends and family. She *had* asked if he wanted her to come, and he'd replied it was up to her. He wasn't surprised when she didn't show up. If she possessed a nurturing side, he had never seen it.

Liz had zero empathy for living creatures, human or animal. Animal lovers will be relieved to read that the next trio of pets she adopted were brought to Garret's home, and as of this writing, they are alive and well, and he's vowed to always take care of them. Freedom, a German Shepherd mix, is black with a fluff of white on his chest and loves to ride in Garret's truck. When Liz had lived at his place, he'd had to remind her to feed her pets, clean the cat box, and take the dogs outside. He'd noticed that most of the time she seemed annoyed by the animals and coldly shooed them away when they approached her.

She could not be counted on to take care of the animals *or* him if he ever got sick, but luckily, Garret was healthy. The chest pains had apparently been caused by a flu virus he'd been fighting. The health scare was the wake-up call he needed. Determined to get in shape, he began exercising and making healthier diet choices. He soon began to lose weight.

On May 1, Amy gave birth to a beautiful baby boy, Mason. Though Amy's relationship with Mason's father would not last, she was thrilled to welcome her son. Calista and Trey, too, were excited about having a little brother.

In the autumn of 2014, Liz went to work at a distribution warehouse in Omaha. It's been said that she had no female friends, but that's not entirely true. Liz made a friend at her new job. Cherokee Montoya, a statuesque woman with high cheekbones and long, black hair, liked her immediately. No one knows why Liz switched between names, but she introduced herself as Shanna. To Cherokee, Shanna appeared to be a dedicated mom, working hard to make ends meet. Cherokee could relate to that, for she, too, had once been a struggling mom on her own. Widowed in her early twenties, she had been through some hard times. She was no longer single, thanks to a sneaky but loving scheme concocted by her younger sister, Celeste.

Worried her sister was lonely, Celeste had posted Cherokee's profile on an online dating site. "She would ask me questions," Cherokee remembers, "And I'd be like, 'What's this for?' and she'd be like, 'Just answer it.' So, I'd give her all my answers, and she'd just type them in.'" Celeste had found Tim Verbeek and noted how much he had in common with Cherokee. Both were attractive single parents in their mid-twenties.

Posing as Cherokee, Celeste messaged Tim, and he responded. "I went on to the dating site as a joke," he admits, explaining that one of his female friends, Marta, had ended up on the site after *her* family, too, had secretly posted her profile. After Marta discovered what they'd done, she'd decided to give online dating a chance. But she was encountering "pervy" guys and asked Tim to help her screen them. He signed up so that he could view the profiles of Marta's potential dates, but he wasn't expecting to meet anyone himself and reveals, "I'm not even sure if my profile was a hundred percent accurate."

Women immediately began to message him, but they weren't his type. They were elderly, "pervy," or lived in other countries. "The first lady that messaged me was seventy or eighty years old and from Spain." When Tim saw Cherokee's profile, he thought, "Oh, a normal person!"

In the beginning, Celeste posed as her sister but finally admitted to Cherokee what she had done. Tim seemed like a nice guy, so Cherokee took over. After six weeks of texting, they went on a date. It was the spring of 2011, and just like in the romantic comedy, *Yours, Mine and Ours*, they fell in love, got married, combined their brood and had another baby together. With Cherokee's five, and Tim's six, they are now the proud parents of a dozen!

While Cherokee insists that she'd never cheat on her husband, she is openly bisexual and admits that she and Shanna were very attracted to each other. Tim is not threatened by this. "We would tease each other," he chimes in. "She'd be like, 'I'm stealing your wife,' and I'd say, 'No, you're not! We're going to have to fight over this one.'"

One year, "She was my Valentine's date," Cherokee recalls. "She took me out to dinner at the Village Inn on Dodge Street, close to

downtown." While Shanna told her that she, too, had had relationships with females, that news comes as a surprise to others who
know Shanna well. Possibly, she was mirroring Cherokee's behavior to win her trust—a common ploy of manipulators. Not only do
they pretend to share the values of their targets, they sometimes mirror their body language, sitting or standing in the same position to
create a subconscious alliance.

Cherokee describes Shanna as an excellent housekeeper, so organized it was almost compulsive. She apparently didn't see Shanna's
filthy basement quarters. Garret kept the upstairs neat, and of course,
supported Shanna and her kids. Cherokee is sincere as she explains,
"Shanna was always looking to take care of the kids, always wanting
to have enough money, so the kids got everything they wanted. At
the same time, she was paying all of the bills. Working multiple
jobs. Trying to keep up with everything." But that was not *Shanna's*
life. That was *Cherokee's* life. *Cherokee* was the selfless, hardworking mother who kept a tidy house and was sexually attracted to
women.

The persona Shanna had created for her new friend's benefit was
nothing more than a reflection. But Cherokee didn't realize that, and
she was glad to have a new buddy who seemed to share her viewpoints. As far as Cherokee knew, Garret was a platonic roommate,
and Shanna's heart thudded only for David Kroupa. Shanna chat-
tered about him constantly and complained about his "cheating."
Remembering her friend's intense jealousy, Cherokee says, "I figured some girls are more jealous than others, just like some guys are
more jealous." When Shanna confessed she'd been going by Dave's
apartment to see if he had other women there, Cherokee advised her,
"Give up on him if you've had enough. It's not going to change."
She remembers how Shanna sometimes worked herself into a tizzy.
"I'm not good enough for Dave!" Shanna would sob, tears wiggling
down her face. "Nobody loves me! Nobody stays with me!"

Cherokee's voice rings with sympathy as she attempts to explain
her friend's distress. "She just wanted that one person to be with her
and stay with her."

When Shanna came up with a plan to make Dave commit, Cherokee was skeptical. Shanna thought that if Dave could just sow his
wild oats, he could get it out of his system once and for all. What if

they had a threesome? Would Cherokee join them in bed? Shanna was so excited about the idea that Cherokee pretended to go along with it. "I never would have done it without my husband's permission," she emphasizes, glancing at Tim who has been listening intently.

When asked if he would have granted that permission, the answer is a resounding, "No!" He didn't mind the jokes about Shanna stealing his wife, he didn't mind their cozy Valentine's dinner, and he didn't mind the kisses on the cheeks. But that was as far as it could go. Cherokee insists that she was only humoring her friend. The idea of the threesome had gotten Shanna's mind off her heartbreak, but Cherokee doubted Shanna would go through with it. She was too possessive to sit calmly by as Dave had sex with another woman.

But Shanna *did* broach the topic with Dave. He was mildly interested. "I've never had a threesome," he admits, adding it is *not* on his "bucket list." The idea didn't disgust him, but he was wary of his jealous girlfriend's plan. "I told her I'd have to meet Cherokee first."

Liz arranged a double date, and they met in a restaurant. While neither Dave nor Cherokee expected anything would come of Liz's kinky proposal, Tim was completely oblivious. He had no idea that anyone was contemplating a threesome and wasn't told the purpose of the get-together. He didn't have a particularly good time at that dinner and found he had little in common with Dave. He, too, had heard Shanna vent about how badly the guy treated her, and he felt kind of sorry for her as he watched them together. "He didn't pay any attention to her. I don't think he was emotionally there. He was like, 'Whatever.' It was like he'd rather be somewhere else. I don't think he was emotionally invested in Shanna."

Cherokee openly admits she's had threesomes in the past and can testify to the fact that Shanna's proposal was completely out of the norm. Shanna had planned to direct Dave's *every* move, throughout the entire sex act. He would not be allowed to kiss, caress or touch Cherokee anywhere until Shanna granted permission. "I didn't think Dave would go for that." In the end, Shanna fibbed to both Dave and Cherokee, telling each of them that the other had backed out. Neither had believed it was ever going to happen, and they were relieved that the topic could finally be dropped. Dave had been a little surprised to discover that Liz was very angry after the dinner. She was absolutely indignant when she told him, "Cherokee was se-cretly taking photos of you at the table!"

The photos snapped on Cherokee's phone appear to be candid shots and show both Liz and Dave, clowning around together. Maybe Dave didn't notice she was taking pictures, but he wouldn't have objected. Liz carried on about it as if it were an unthinkable vi-olation of his privacy. She couldn't have been more offended if Cherokee had sneaked into the men's room and photographed Dave at the urinal.

He soon began to receive messages, allegedly from Cherokee, suggesting that they rendezvous *without* Shanna. He sensed a trap and declined. He would one day learn that Liz had forged those notes. Cherokee had no idea that her trusted friend was impersonat-ing her. It was another weird game, a baffling, pointless game that only Liz understood.

She had a strange way of viewing the world and seemed intent upon stirring up trouble. Liz was threatened by the fact that Dave and Amy were still part of each other's lives. When the parents vowed to make their relationship as harmonious as possible, they had also agreed to share holidays with the kids. Calista and Trey wanted to celebrate Christmas with *both* their parents. "We always planned on spending Christmas together with the kids," says Amy. "And we'd always done it at my house." So far, the arrangement had worked out beautifully.

In December 2014 Mason was almost eight months old. His very first Christmas was coming up, and he was excited. While he couldn't really understand what the holiday was, he was mesmerized by the lit trees with the shiny, red baubles and caught up in the excitement of his older siblings. When Dave shopped for Calista and Trey, he made sure to get gifts for Mason, too. The presents were wrapped and heaped beneath the tree, and Dave was looking forward to watching the kids open them. The affection was mutual between Dave and Mason. When Mason learned to talk, he called his siblings' father, "My Dave." The little boy was a charmer, and Dave was fond of him.

"We'd always had Christmas at my house," Amy explains. "But that year Dave wanted to do it at his place. The little guy and I went over there, and the kids were waiting for us. We were all having a good time, the kids were opening presents and Mason was checking out everybody's stuff. And then Liz came walking in the door."

Her visit was unannounced, and she hadn't bothered to knock. Like Dr. Seuss's Grinch who stole Christmas, Liz seemed determined to destroy the holiday. Amy cringed as Liz stomped in. "You could just *feel* the negativity as soon as she got there. She took Dave into the dining room, and I could hear that she was angry that I was there." Dave spoke in a subdued tone, trying to keep the argument quiet. Liz sounded mad, her voice rising as she spoke Amy's name.

"It was very uncomfortable," Amy recalls. "I don't like confrontation, and it was *Christmas*!" Amy scooped up a protesting Mason. "I told the kids I'd see them when he brought them home later, and I left." They were disappointed to see their mom leave, but Amy knew if she stayed that Liz's tantrums would ruin what was left of the day. Though Liz had never heard of her Grandfather Fabian or his tirades, she continued his tradition of ruining Christmas for children. Just as Fabian had broken his wife's nose in a tantrum over dolls more than half a century earlier, Liz, too, was behaving badly, though no blood was spilled on that day.

CHAPTER TWENTY-THREE

AFTER OVER TWO YEARS of harassment from the stalker, Dave moved across the river to a place he hoped his tormentor wouldn't find him. On February 1, 2015, he settled into his new apartment in Downtown Council Bluffs, near historic Bayliss Park. He lived closer to his kids now, too, and looked forward to seeing them more often. Dave's stalker, of course, knew exactly where to find him, because *he* had given her his address. Dave was not stupid. And neither were the many other people Liz had fooled. Many, *many* intelligent people—mostly males—had been tricked by Liz. Some were professionals who dealt with criminals on a daily basis, but Liz managed to thoroughly manipulate them, too.

How is it possible that Liz got away with murder for so long? Some people who've read the news stories are bewildered by that, assuming that her crime was so obvious that *they* could have solved it, even if they've had no training in law enforcement. The truth is that the Golyar case is one of the most complex and confusing crimes to ever challenge detectives. It might have gone unsolved if not for those who spent months painstakingly untangling the killer's snarled web. They sorted out the facts and presented them in an exquisitely linear fashion that made sense out of nonsense. This was done first by the investigators who captured her, then by the prosecutors who convicted her, and finally by the media who parroted the professionals who worked so hard to get justice.

By the time the case was served up in a neat package for public consumption, the facts were so well organized that it appears far simpler than it actually was. Online chatter unfairly criticized the first round of investigators for being fooled by a killer. But those investigators reacted as probably 99 percent of their peers would have if confronted with the same crazy illusion, and they shouldn't be faulted for that. They didn't solve the case, but they *did* collect and preserve valuable evidence. This initial group of investigators did exactly what was expected of them. The second wave of investigators, however, did *more* than what was expected—much, much more! And it is *this* group that should be singled out as extraordinary.

In order to get justice for Cari Farver, they worked *thousands* of hours without pay, sacrificed important relationships and even risked their health. While several brilliant people worked endless hours to nab the killer, this complex endeavor called for so much more than brains and hard work. The case could not have been solved without vision, creativity, and *heart*. It took vision to see the truth that so many others had missed, creativity to devise traps to trip up the predator, and heart to feed the passion required to see a difficult case through till the end.

Detective Jim Doty always knew he wanted to work in a helping field. The Council Bluffs native graduated from York College with a Bachelor's in Psychology and was employed as a counselor in a group home for troubled children when he heard Pottawattamie County Sheriff's Office was hiring. He applied on a lark and wasn't expecting a written test. Applicants were presented with various scenarios that could arise on patrol and asked how they'd respond. He must have done well, because he was invited in for an interview. Two months later, "They called and said, 'We've got one spot, and we want to give it to you.'"

He hesitated. "I don't really know what you guys do," he admitted and asked if he could shadow a deputy before accepting the position. But they needed someone immediately, so he had to pass. He later signed up to go on a ride-along with a patrol deputy and realized "I could still help people like I wanted to as a mental health counselor, but I didn't have the monotony of doing the same thing every day." A few months later, in August 2007, another position opened up, and he went to work as a deputy.

Ryan Avis also went into law enforcement because he wanted to help, though his path was more treacherous than Doty's. Avis's parents struggled with drug addiction and ran with a dangerous crowd. "I had a really rough childhood. I saw a lot of things that most people don't see in their whole life before the age of ten. I never had good encounters with police when I was a kid because they would arrest my parents, and I went to that place where he worked," he says, nodding toward Doty. "That group home—that's where I would go for a night or two because I had no one to care for me."

The police he encountered as a boy were cold and indifferent. "I grew up with disdain toward police. They'd never helped me out." Born in Houston, Texas, Avis moved to Iowa with his family when he was four. Soon after, his parents divorced, his father overcame his heroin addiction and got custody of Ryan and his sister. The fact he survived "is proof enough of a higher power," says Avis. He lived in Treynor, Iowa, throughout most of his childhood. Morningside College in Sioux City offered him a scholarship when he was recruited to play football. Later, he went to Western, working to pay for school.

He was employed as a guard at the Pott County Jail for about a year and a half and went to work as a road patrol deputy in March 2008. He joined the Investigation Unit in May 2014 and was promoted to corporal in the spring of 2015, around the time Randal Phyllips was promoted to sergeant. Detectives Avis and Doty had heard "water-cooler talk" about the Farver case. They were intrigued by the peculiar mystery, and they asked to have the case reassigned to them. Sergeant Phyllips gladly handed over his case file.

When they teamed up to investigate the disappearance of Cari Farver, Doty and Avis devised a unique strategy to avoid tunnel vision. They approached the case from opposite angles. Avis worked it as if Cari were alive. Doty worked it as if she were dead. "We started from scratch," notes Avis. But they found nothing to suggest Cari was alive. She'd dropped out of the lives of her dying father, her teenage son, and everyone else who loved her. No one had seen or talked to her for two-and-a-half years. She had abandoned her house, her car, and all of her possessions. She had not withdrawn money from her bank or used her credit or debit cards. It appeared they were investigating a homicide.

If Cari was deceased, then who was sending messages in her name? Only the killer would have a motive to make it appear Cari was alive, but it was an unusual scheme. It would have made more sense for the culprit to distance themselves from the whole situation. Why in the world would they impersonate their victim for over three years? One thing was clear. This was not a typical homicide, and the killer was not a typical suspect.

When it comes to female victims, *58 percent of the time* the killer is either an intimate partner or a family member, according to a 2018 global study published by the United Nations Office of Drugs and Crime (UNODC). Investigators, aware of the statistics, looked closely at David Kroupa. Not only was he the victim's boyfriend, he was the last known person to see her. But he'd been nothing but cooperative, and they quickly ruled him out. They found themselves focusing on someone else, a woman whose name popped up so frequently that it had to be more than a coincidence. The first time her name surfaced was just two days after Cari was last seen. On Thursday, November 15, 2012, a West Corp supervisor received a text from Cari's phone: *I won't be coming back. I'm taking a job in Kansas. Sorry for the short notice. I am sending someone out to you to fill the position. Her name is Shanna Golyar.*

Those who knew Cari best insisted she wasn't one to make capricious decisions and that she'd never move away without her son. And she knew she couldn't hire her own replacement. West Corp had a rigorous hiring process, first screening resumes of promising applicants before inviting the most impressive in for a series of interviews. "Cari's" recommendation was especially ludicrous because Shanna had no training in computer coding. A manager at West Corp forwarded the message from "Cari" to his superiors, adding his own comment, "I'm not putting a lot of faith in the recommendation." Shanna filled out an application a few hours after the text was sent to the West Corp supervisor. Under reference, she listed Cari Farver. She did not get the job.

As detectives studied the endless emails and texts, signs of Liz's obsession with Dave began to emerge. Both he and Liz had allowed downloads of their phones early on, and investigators now became familiar with the strained dynamics of their relationship as they read the thousands of words that had passed between them. The messages attributed to Cari were strange. They found the email from the January 2013 kidnapping hoax, the one with the attached photo of the bound woman in the trunk that "Cari" claimed was Liz. The metadata on the photo revealed it was taken with an LG spectrum cellphone, model number, VS920, identical to one of the phones Liz owned.

They viewed a YouTube video, allegedly uploaded by Cari, and discovered by one of Cari's friends who'd forwarded it to police. The video, "My Husband's Cheating Place," features an apartment building as the videographer walks toward it. The detectives ran the plate numbers of parked cars, visible in the video, and traced them to residents of Dave's former apartment complex. The cars' owners weren't involved in the case, but the plate numbers verified the video was made outside of Dave's Omaha apartment. The detectives now knew *where* that video was made but couldn't prove *who* had made it. They needed more information and submitted a search warrant to YouTube.

Nancy Raney was brokenhearted. Her daughter had been missing for two-and-a-half years, and she was certain something terrible had happened to her. She had tried repeatedly to make authorities listen. In the beginning, when police reported that Cari was breaking into houses and vandalizing property, Nancy had been shocked. Cari had never done such wretched things. But they'd been so adamant, that Nancy had begun to wonder if it were possible. As the weeks melted into months, and Cari's family and friends continued to be taunted with bizarre texts, Nancy knew the truth. Her daughter was not a criminal. She was a *victim*.

On May 8, 2015, Detective Doty went to see Nancy. When he appeared at her door, she steeled herself to hear more negative things about her daughter, and she admits she wasn't very friendly. But then he said something she wasn't expecting. "I want you to know that I don't think Cari left on her own."

All of Nancy's anger was swept away in a wave of relief. *Finally!* Someone believed her! Overwhelmed with gratitude, she hugged the detective. When he asked to download the contents of her Samsung cellphone, Nancy granted permission at once. He was particularly interested in the image of the check the texter had sent as proof of payment for the furniture in Cari's house. That image, of course, had proven to be a picture of a check that Shanna claimed Cari had stolen from her garage. Until now, no one had considered comparing the signature on that check to Shanna's actual signature. Doty explains, "I looked up several traffic citations, issued to Shanna Golyar in the past, and looked at the signatures." The signatures he found were nearly identical to the one on the check. It appeared that Shanna Golyar had indeed written that $5,000 check. It was enticing evidence but not proof she'd harmed Cari.

The investigators found it odd that not only had their suspect tried to take Cari's job, she'd also tried to steal her furniture. She'd been so confident she wouldn't be caught that she'd blatantly linked her own name to both schemes, signing the check without attempting to disguise her handwriting and applying for the West Corp position under her real name.

It was as if Liz believed she could slip into Cari's shoes and take over her life. Though they'd yet to prove it, the detectives suspected Liz had stolen Cari's phone and had set up numerous social media and email accounts in her name. While she hadn't succeeded in stealing Cari's job or furniture, Liz *had* managed to steal her boyfriend. But Liz could never hold onto Dave for long. The detectives realized Liz was fixated on him, desperate to make him commit. Had Liz's obsession driven her to kill? Evidence suggested that, but all of it was circumstantial. They had no body, no crime scene, no murder weapon, no confession and no witnesses.

The January 2013 downloads of Dave's and Liz's phones had produced endless pages of data, and the investigators stared at it till their eyes watered. If the evidence was there, they were determined to find it. But there were not enough hours in a normal work week to sift through everything. Detective Avis estimates he put in an extra 500 unpaid hours, often taking work home, and though his wife, Angie, was understanding and supportive, he knew he wasn't giving his family the attention they deserved and confides, "Our marriage was suffering drastically."

On Memorial Day weekend of 2015, the Avis family took an out-of-state trip to visit relatives. It was supposed to be a relaxing getaway, but Ryan Avis was obviously distracted. While his family slept, he sat up until 2 A.M., studying Liz's phone data. Something caught his eye. Liz had made six calls to a landline, five on November 6 and one on November 7, and each time, she'd first punched in star 67 to block caller ID. *The calls had been made to Cari Farver's home!* Liz had called Cari about one week after she'd interrupted Cari's first date with Dave and about a week before Cari vanished. The longest call had lasted thirty-three seconds.

The 2013 phone download had also captured pictures Liz had taken, including one of a Ford Explorer, identified as Cari's car, via the plate number. Investigators felt a chill as they noted the date. *Christmas Eve, 2012.* That picture was snapped while Cari's car was still officially missing, two weeks before it appeared in Dave's parking lot. Very interesting, but not proof of murder. They needed stronger evidence to make a homicide charge stick.

As Detective Doty studied the report on the recovered SUV, he was intrigued by the unidentified fingerprint on the mint container. He contacted Katie Pattee and asked her to compare it to Shanna's known prints on file. Pattee soon reported back that the prints matched! It was an exciting find but no smoking gun. A defense attorney could argue that Dave might have picked up the container and carried it to Cari's car. It was more circumstantial evidence. Each piece was weak on its own, but collectively, it was gaining strength.

Meanwhile, Liz had no idea detectives were closing in. She had other things on her mind. Garret, wary of her games, had asked her to move. She refused, claiming she couldn't afford it. While she continued to live in his home, their romantic relationship ended in the autumn of 2015. Convincing Liz to move wasn't easy. Gabe told Garret, "Dude, I'll come over and kick her out." Garret could kick her out as easily as Gabe. Getting her out wasn't the problem. It was what might happen *afterward* he feared. He wasn't afraid Liz would harm him, but he worried about what she'd do to his home.

Dave, too, became fed up that fall. Liz's jealousy was wearing him down. The tension escalated on Thursday, November 26, Thanksgiving Day, a holiday she'd asked him to spend with her. He'd agreed, but their plans were derailed. "There was a blizzard, and Amy asked me to drive Mason to the emergency room." The baby had a respiratory infection with a fever of 103 and was having difficulty breathing. Amy was afraid to drive on the icy roads, but Mason needed immediate care.

Liz was not pleased when Dave ran to the rescue, and she picked a fight with him. He was disgusted by her selfishness. How could she expect him to sit down and eat turkey when Mason was so ill? He would have dropped everything to help *any* child who needed help, and this was his kids' baby brother. Dave told Liz it was over, and this time he meant it.

Shortly after that, Dave went to bed alone one night and woke the next morning to discover nearly every female on his cell phone contact list was mad at him. He stared at their hostile texts, baffled. It soon became clear they were responding to texts *he* had sent. Though he'd been deep asleep in his usual coma-like slumber, he'd somehow managed to start fights with some now very angry women. "I went to sleep with my phone plugged into my charger next to my bed and woke up to find that someone had texted these women on my phone and started some shit."

The riled-up women included Amy, and she had retorted with an angry text of her own. Apparently, he'd also texted a number of women and was "really rude and calling them whores!" Dave was not in the habit of walking or talking in his sleep, and he'd certainly never *texted* in his sleep. He couldn't see what he'd supposedly written because all of his outgoing messages had been deleted, but the recipients filled him in after he sent apologies and explained that he wasn't the one who'd texted them in the middle of the night.

Only one woman in the bunch had become suspicious. Her name was Jane, and Dave barely knew her. They'd only recently began talking. She'd received a text from his phone, sharing a very personal thing: "I had sex tonight."

Jane responded: "Yeah. And? What do I care?"

He appeared to reply: "Doesn't that make you mad?"

Jane didn't care if Dave had sex, though it was weird that he'd text to brag about it. She knew if they decided to date, it wouldn't be exclusive. They'd discussed that in one of their first conversations. The odd texts now filling up her phone sounded nothing like the guy she'd been getting to know. After a rapid exchange of messages, an outgoing text from Dave's phone said he wanted nothing to do with her. "Fine," Jane replied. "Fuck you." But she wasn't really all that offended because she doubted Dave was the one texting her. Jane had picked up on an anomaly. "There was a word I always screwed up when texting her," Dave recollects. "And all of the sudden, I was texting it correctly."

While the hoopla with Jane wasn't disastrous, he cringed when he learned some wayward texts had reached into a corner of his past, kicking up dust in a most humiliating manner. The contact info of his old high school girlfriend was stored in his phone because he sometimes texted her a friendly birthday greeting. The lady, married with four kids, had received a vulgar text.

"We hadn't talked in forever." Dave points out that she no longer knew him well enough to realize he was a rational person. While she seemed to accept his mortified apology when he claimed he hadn't sent the texts, he couldn't be sure she believed him. "Who knows? Maybe I'm off my rocker! More than anything, I think her husband was irritated, wondering why I was texting his wife at 1:30 in the morning, talking shit. And, of course, I'm like, 'It wasn't me!' He's responding, 'Okay, it wasn't you. It came from your phone.' That doesn't fly, so, I gotta explain the whole stalking thing, and that sounds like bullshit unless there's a news article to go with it."

In addition to the embarrassment and trouble caused by the rude texts, the situation gave Dave a serious case of the creeps. The stalker had come into his locked apartment and stood over him while he slept. How did she get in? Did she sit on the floor by his bed as she sent the dozens of inflaming messages?

Dave could protect himself from any female who meant to cause him physical harm, unless she had a weapon, or he was asleep. Asleep, he was as vulnerable as a newborn infant. As he lay dreaming, the nut who'd bragged about stabbing people had been close enough to slit his exposed throat. Was she capable of murder? He didn't know and didn't want to find out. Days later, "I woke up one morning, and my phone was totally done. It didn't work. It didn't turn on." Had the stalker crept in and broken his phone? Or had it simply conked out on its own? The only thing he knew for sure is that it never worked again.

Dave spent Sunday afternoon, November 29, visiting his kids. When he returned, he discovered something alarming. "I went into my bedroom and opened the door to my closet, and the box my pistol resides in was hanging out over the ledge of the shelf. I grabbed the box, and there was nothing in it." The box of ammunition was still there, but the gun had held two loaded clips. Dave reported the theft to the Council Bluffs police. His shotgun, stored next to the handgun, hadn't been touched, and nothing else was missing.

How had the thief gotten in? There was no sign of forced entry, but there was an ongoing issue with the lock on his front door. Sometimes it didn't work. The crazy texter who'd borrowed Dave's phone and the gun thief could have gotten in because of the deficient lock. He suspected, of course, that they were one and the same, but he couldn't be certain. There was no question his stalker was the mad texter, but the thief could have been a lucky burglar who happened upon a door with a faulty lock. If so, it was odd that only the gun was taken. It was as if the crook had known exactly where it was and had walked right to the closet to get it.

CHAPTER TWENTY-FOUR

IN DECEMBER 2015, Detectives Avis and Doty were dying to talk to Liz. But they couldn't risk spooking her, so they continued to investigate from afar. And then on December 4, Avis recalls, "We were given a gift." He was stunned to see Liz, walking down the hallway of the Sheriff's Office. He'd studied her for months, but it was the first time he'd seen her in person. "It was like seeing a famous person!"

Avis learned that Liz had come in to file a harassment report against Amy Flora. He followed Liz to the parking lot and explained he'd been appointed to assist her. He went to her home to take the report. He knew everything about her life and all of the characters in it. He was well aware of the fact she lived with Garret, but she told him that only she and her children lived there. Twice more during the interview he asked who lived there, and each time she failed to mention Garret.

Liz explained she was worried because Amy had been stalking her on Facebook. Avis played dumb, an act reminiscent of the clever 1970s TV detective, Columbo, as he asked her to repeat the names he knew so well and then deliberately stumbled over the spelling.

Liz explained that Amy was Dave Kroupa's ex.

"Dave Cooper?"

"Kroupa," Liz corrected, and patiently spelled it for the detective.

He was fascinated by the fact she was suddenly shifting the blame to Amy after years of accusing Cari. Liz told him, "Not even two days after we broke up, his apartment was broken into, and his gun was stolen. So, I told the police officer I was kind of worried since she has a key to his apartment." She now realized it didn't make sense for Cari to stalk Dave. "Like I said, they only dated for two weeks, and I don't understand why a person would still be stalking him almost three years later."

"Cari and Dave dated for two weeks?" Avis asked.

"Mm—hmm," Liz answered. "I would find it much more reasonable to believe that the kids' mom is the one that was stalking him."

Avis was unaware of the gun theft because the Council Bluffs Police Department maintains a separate database from the Sheriff's Office. Liz stressed that only three people other than Dave had keys to his apartment: Amy and the kids.

"What kind of gun is it?" asked Avis.

Liz told him it was a 9mm Smith & Wesson, silver and black, loaded with two magazines. She was anxious to press harassment charges against Amy. If the detective needed evidence, that was no problem. Her phone was full of threatening texts. For the second time in three years, Liz signed a consent form, allowing detectives to download her phone. She followed Avis's instructions to remove her phone's passcode, putting it into airplane mode. The procedure, Avis explains, "preserves the phone as is, so when I return it to her, it's like taking a step back in time. When she takes it out of airplane mode, all the messages that she was getting will start to come through again."

Downloads typically take between two and six hours, and the phone would first be delivered to the county's task force office and placed in a Faraday box, a strong box that blocks signals. Named for Michael Faraday, the British scientist who invented the container in 1836, also known as a Faraday shield or cage, the contraption shields items from electromagnetic fields. Detectives sometimes opt to use Faraday shields for confiscated cell phones to prevent digital evidence from being deleted or altered remotely. Special Deputy Anthony Kava, from the IT department, would handle the download.

Avis told Liz he would speak to Dave and Amy about the harassment and gave her his work cell phone number, inviting her to call should any issues arise over the weekend. The next morning, Liz forwarded him more threatening messages, claiming Amy had just sent them. The detective acknowledged her concerns and assured her he'd speak with Amy on Monday. But by then, everything would change.

It was late Saturday afternoon on December 5, 2015, and Amy Flora was at her apartment, settling in for the evening. Her two older kids were spending the weekend with their father, so she and little Mason were alone. Though it wasn't quite 4 P.M., night comes early in Iowa in December with the sun setting by five. Soon it would be dark, and it was cold outside. It had been a long day, and Amy was tired and glad to be home in her cozy apartment. She'd been out to lunch with her friend Dustie, and the ladies had shopped for Christmas presents afterward.

Mason had conked out in his car seat on the way home, and she'd carried the sleeping boy inside and tucked him in for his nap. She showered, pulled on her flannel pajama bottoms and a tank top, and got comfortable. With a full-time job and three kids, she didn't often have time to relax. There was only one thing she felt like doing. "I sat on the couch, playing games on my iPad."

About three miles southeast of Amy's apartment, Garret Sloan was at home, watching TV with the kids when Liz announced she was going to Walmart. Garret stared at her, surprised she'd bothered to inform him of her plans. "Typically, Liz never told me where she was going, and I never cared enough to ask," he says, adding that she often insinuated he had an obsessive need to know her whereabouts. It wasn't true. Frankly, he didn't care what she was up to, as long as it didn't involve him.

Liz watched Garret expectantly, waiting for him to acknowledge her plan to go shopping.

"Okay. Whatever," he said, and she went out the door.

Council Bluffs' Big Lake Park is not normally viewed as a place of mystery. The 163-acre park is a rolling terrain of grassy hills and grand old trees. Features include three lakes, tennis courts, playgrounds, and a hiking trail that loops around Gilbert Pond, a tiny lake stocked with rainbow trout for those who fish off the dock. Few visitors are aware of two strange incidents that frightened some folks away. Each occurred on a chill December evening, and each involved lights in the sky—though the first incident *began* with lights, and the second incident *ended* with them.

On December 17, 1977, at quarter to 8 P.M., a peculiar thing appeared in the sky over Big Lake Park. Eleven people witnessed it, and their descriptions were somewhat varied. Some insisted it hovered for a moment before rocketing toward the Earth. One witness described a ball of fire, while another said it resembled a shooting star. Still another said the object had rotating lights. They all agreed on one thing. It did not remain in the sky.

The Unidentified Flying Object (UFO) crashed to the ground near Gilbert Pond. Firefighters rushed to the scene, shocked to find a mass of metal, melted and boiling and running down the edge of the embankment. After the largest pieces had cooled, the firefighters gathered them up and whisked them away.

Authorities were stumped. Where had the thing come from? What in the world was it? Experts at Iowa State University examined the molten fragments and determined they were a mixture of metals, including iron, nickel, and chromium. The largest chunk retrieved was approximately fifty pounds, but some UFO enthusiasts suspect that the pieces scattered near the lake were just a bit of rubble from an alien spacecraft. The ship itself, they theorize, plunged into the water and sank to the bottom of the lake. Skeptics insist it was nothing more than space debris, but that contradicts eyewitness testimony of a hovering ship with rotating lights. The mystery remains unsolved.

The woman at the center of the second incident had been just a toddler in 1977 when the Big Lake Park sighting earned Council Bluffs a spot on UFO maps. She probably had never heard of the freaky occurrence and was *not* pondering spaceships and aliens when she went to the park "to think" on the night of December 5, 2015. Creatures from outer space or not, few women would not be wary of visiting a deserted park alone after dark. Liz Golyar, however, was unexpectedly bold, *especially* for someone who'd just reported a stalker was after her.

The park is a peaceful place to walk or jog in the daylight but creepy after sundown. Two large parking lots sit on opposite ends of the grounds, and neither is lit. At night, the park is awash in an inky sea of darkness. It was 6:41 P.M. when a 911 operator was alerted to trouble at Big Lake Park. The caller gave her location, and she sounded scared. "I've been shot in the leg!" she cried.

"Where are you in the park, ma'am?"

"I'm in one of the parking lots on the, um, left hand side. I have a little red Toyota, and I'm laying next to it."

"Is the assailant still nearby?"

"I don't think so. I took off running."

"How many people were there?"

"Oh, I, I don't know," the victim stammered. "I only heard one."

"Do you know if it was male or female?"

"A female." The caller sounded certain of that.

"Is there more than one wound?"

"Um, I think it's just one. They shot out a couple of shots. They only hit me with one, I think." Clearly distressed, the woman cried, "Um, my, my pant leg is filled with blood. *Oh, Jesus.*"

The Pottawattamie County Sheriff's Office is one-tenth of a mile from Big Lake Park and can be seen from the south parking lot where Liz Golyar waited for help to arrive, but the first responder was with the Council Bluffs Police Department. Officer Dave Burns, a ten-year veteran with CBPD, pulled his cruiser into the dark lot and noted a single vehicle, a small car, in the northeast corner. The driver's door was open, spilling light onto the woman who sat on the ground, her back to the door jam. She held a cellphone to her ear as she talked to the 911 operator. Burns observed no one else in the vicinity as he approached the injured woman. Shot in her left thigh, she was obviously in pain. Burns reassured her that medics were on the way and asked, "Who shot you?"

"I don't know." Pale and distraught, she was going into shock. Was the shooter still in the area? For all Burns knew, somebody could be hiding behind a tree, watching them, planning to shoot again. Despite the fact the parking lot had no lights, tonight it was somewhat brightened by the moon and the light from the victim's car and the police cruiser.

"Where were you when you were shot?" the officer prodded.

She indicated a bench, about 100 yards north. "I went there to think," she volunteered. Suddenly her fuzzy memory cleared. "It was Amy Flora! Amy Flora shot me!" She told Burns she'd been lying on the bench when someone named Amy had suddenly appeared and blurted, "So, you like fucking Dave?" After asking the crude question, the assailant had shot her and vanished into the night. She said she hadn't seen the shooter leave and had no idea where she went. Officer Burns wrote down her description of the incident, including her assertion that she and this Amy had been involved with the same man.

Medics and another officer soon arrived. Liz was rushed off to CHI Health Mercy Hospital while police cordoned off the crime scene. Officer Burns and other police searched the park for the shooter, and Omaha PD sent their Able-1 Helicopter team to assist. If the armed attacker was on foot, she couldn't have gotten far. Anyone else she encountered could be in grave danger.

People driving by the park on nearby North 8th Street were startled by the jarring clatter of the chopper and its glaring spotlight as it scoured the park from above. For just a flash of a second, one passerby admits, he mistook it for a UFO and feared aliens had returned to Big Lake Park. Some Council Bluffs' residents had been frightened back in 1977 when they read the newspaper reports on the bizarre thing that had burst into flames over the park. Now, news of the shooting was about to make local headlines, and some people would once again be wary of visiting the beautiful park.

There was no sign of the attacker, and it didn't seem possible that the shooter could have fled on foot and exited the park before the Able-1 team swept in. The helicopter crew aimed their infrared camera at the dark park below. The device detects body heat, and sure enough, they got a hit. They radioed the location to the team on the ground, and officers rushed to the scene with guns drawn but encountered only startled homeless people, camping in a tent they'd pitched near the park. The camera detected no other warm bodies, no one trying to flee. It seemed the shooter had melted into the shadows.

CHAPTER TWENTY-FIVE

IT WAS ABOUT 7 P.M., and Amy was still sitting on her couch, playing games on her iPad, when she was startled by noises outside. It sounded like someone was bumping up against her door. "Whose there?" she called out.

"Open up! Police!"

She opened the door and was stunned to see three police officers with guns aimed at her. "I was terrified!" she confides. "One of them told me that Shanna Golyar had been shot, and it took me a minute to realize who that was. I knew her by Liz, but I'd heard she went by Shanna." Once she realized who the cops were referring to, Amy had just one question, "Is she all right?" It was the most frightening moment of Amy's life, but her first concern was for the woman who'd been making her life miserable.

The cops told Amy that Shanna was alive, and what they told her next hit her like a bucket of ice cubes. "She said *you* did it!"

If Amy hadn't been so terrified, she might have laughed. She hated guns! The idea of her shooting *anyone* was ridiculous. "I was in shock," she remembers. "I didn't expect to open my door and have police there with guns pointed at me." She burst into tears as the officers scrutinized her.

"It doesn't look like you just shot someone," one of them said.

"Of course, I didn't!" Amy exclaimed, stressing she'd been home for hours. "My son just woke up from his nap!"

They asked if they could look around, and Amy stepped aside.

"Do whatever you have to do," she said. The sooner this nightmare was over, the better.

Council Bluffs PD Detective Matthew Kuhlmann interviewed Liz at Mercy Hospital. She appeared drawn, her face pale against her long black hair, splayed out on her pillow. The bullet had gone straight through her thigh. She was lucky it had missed major arteries and bone. Even so, Liz was in pain. Shaken but coherent, she told him she'd been nervous earlier that night when she noticed a silver car parked near her house. It looked like Amy Flora's car, but by the time she got outside for a closer look, it had vanished. The whole story came pouring out—the years she'd suffered as the stalker tried to destroy her, the constant threats, the vandalism, the arson, Dave's stolen gun, and now *this*.

Asked if they could search her car, Liz gladly signed a waiver. While still at the hospital, Kuhlmann got a call from Officer Jarzynka, one of the officers who'd confronted Amy. "He advised me that it didn't appear she was involved, and I mentioned that to Liz."

"Well," Liz told him. "It sounded like her."

When Liz called Garret to tell him she'd been shot, he was shocked. How did that happen on a trip to Walmart? She asked him to come to the hospital, but he wasn't about to leave her kids alone. He didn't know what kind of trouble Liz had gotten herself into but suspected the shooting hadn't been random. What if the shooter came to the house? Garret called Dirk, who was understandably alarmed and rushed over to get the kids.

At the hospital, Garret "walked in and saw Liz there, and one of the first things I said was, 'Does this have something do with the Dave and Cari thing?' She started bawling. She pulled out some real tears." He'd hit a nerve. Liz was on the verge of hysteria, so he dropped the topic. "I didn't want a scene at the hospital." But he had to know why she went to the park at night. "I asked her, 'What the hell were you doing there?' It's not a place people go at night!" Liz had no reasonable answers and was getting groggy from the pain medicine. She asked him to retrieve her car and bring her some things from home.

He figured Liz had gotten "mixed up with something and pissed somebody off." He'd give her time to heal, but Liz had to go. As he gathered the items she'd asked for, he found something he hadn't expected to see again, something that strengthened his resolve to make a clean break. Liz wanted her Samsung Tablet to play games on, and he found that quickly, but the charger was missing. He descended into her unkempt quarters to search for it. When he peered under her bed, he was stunned to see his Gateway laptop that had been stolen in the burglary two years earlier. He still had the box with the serial numbers printed on it and admits he opted for "a passive-aggressive" approach rather than a confrontation. He left the box next to the laptop where Liz would see it. "Of course, she didn't find it till she got home, and then I got a text. She said, 'Oh, damn, sorry. I guess I'm out five hundred bucks.'" She wanted him to believe that in an incredible coincidence she'd purchased his stolen laptop from a pawnshop. He knew it was a lie. Police had given the computer's serial number to the pawnshops, and they were required to report known stolen items.

Garret had begun to suspect Liz was behind the burglary when he'd noticed her wearing Gabe's distinctive Notre Dame sweatshirt. He'd had a chance to examine it when he'd found it crumpled on the bathroom floor. He showed it to Gabe, who instantly recognized it. While a missing sweatshirt could be explained away as a borrowed item, there was no good argument for why his stolen laptop had materialized beneath her bed, though she'd made a feeble effort with the pawnshop story.

Dave Kroupa was just as shocked as Garret to learn Liz had been shot. "It was awkward because we were done, and I didn't have any desire to rekindle that, but I also didn't want to say, 'Oh, that sucks you got shot. I don't care. Tell somebody who cares,' so I went down to see her." Looking back on that visit, he doesn't remember if Liz told him Amy was the shooter. "If she did tell me, I absolutely would not have believed it." Amy was kind and gentle, and she *hated* guns! The whole incident had left Amy thoroughly rattled. "Amy was pissed and scared. Probably more so than I'd ever seen her before."

If the most frightening moment of Amy's life was opening her door to find three cops with guns pointed at her, the *second* scariest was just hours later. Police asked Amy to take a lie-detector test, and she agreed. She had nothing to hide and wanted to cooperate. It didn't occur to her that she could *flunk* the test!

She was shaken when the examiner said she'd failed. He angrily confronted her, pounding his fist on the desk, shouting, "We know you shot her!" Amy was terrified, not for herself, but for her kids. If she went to prison, they would grow up without a mother. She knew what that was like, and she'd vowed to always be there for her children.

Amy had assumed, as most people do, that the test results would be accurate and prove her innocence. But the polygraph, often referred to as a lie-detector test, can't really confirm whether or not a person is lying. The machine measures physiological reactions such as blood pressure, perspiration, and breathing rate, responses that are heightened under stress, and the assumption is that lying causes stress. While that is usually true, just taking the test can make some people so nervous they fail.

According to a September, 2018, *CNN* report, the National Polygraph Association (NPA) claims that polygraph results are accurate 87 percent of the time when examiners follow proper procedures. Critics insist that number is too optimistic, but even if the NPA's percentages *are* correct, that means that at least one in ten times, the results are wrong. Some honest people, including Amy, can appear to be deceptive, while some liars outsmart the machine.

Despite the fact she failed the polygraph exam, Amy was quickly eliminated as a suspect. Her neighbors verified she'd been home all evening. And within minutes after the shooting, a cop had felt the hood of Amy's car. It was ice cold. It was clear she'd not driven for hours.

CHAPTER TWENTY-SIX

WHEN MOST PEOPLE THINK of Anthony Kava, the first word that comes to mind is "genius," but his official title in December 2015 was Information Technology Supervisor. He'd been working that full-time job for Pottawattamie County since 2003 and is also known as Special Deputy Kava, toiling countless hours for the Iowa Crimes Against Children Task Force, but it isn't the extra pay that motivates him. He earns *one dollar per year* for that second full-time job. "Iowa Law prescribes that reserve peace officers be paid at least a dollar per year to make them formal employees of a law enforcement agency," he explains, adding that this allows for legal benefits such as qualified immunity. He is driven by the fact that victims need him. Most often, those he helps are children. Imagine, he says, if "the worst moment of your life is captured and replayed over and over again." The cyber exploitation of innocence via Internet videos is rampant, but thanks to Kava's investigations, multiple pedophiles have been arrested and countless children saved.

Deputy Kava's expertise in digital forensics was essential to nabbing Liz Golyar, who had used electronics to both commit and conceal her crimes. But even with his extensive skills, it was no easy task. Like Detective Ryan Avis, Deputy Kava was also a married father with young children, and there were not enough hours in the day to be a perfect father and husband *and* do all of the work necessary to get justice for Cari Farver. It was a frustrating dilemma for investigators dedicated to their work, and they constantly struggled to create a balance but admit their families were shortchanged.

When Liz walked into the Sheriff's Office on December 4 and handed over her phone for download, she was unaware deleted data could be recovered. Back in January 2013, a *logical* download of her phone had found only existing data, but now Deputy Kava performed an all-encompassing *physical* download and soon found himself staring at incriminating evidence that Liz believed was gone forever. She had used an app called Textie, tying it to fake email accounts she'd set up in Cari's name and then sent hundreds of threats to Dave while pretending to be Cari. Liz had deleted those messages, but Kava revived them. When he realized what he had, he immediately stopped searching and asked Avis to get a search warrant, so he could legally scan the phone's data for evidence to use against Liz in the murder of Cari Farver. The warrant was in place within a few days, and he resumed his search.

Liz's voluntary 2015 phone dump was "the major development that opened doors for us, in terms of probable cause to get dozens of search warrants," says Deputy Kava. The investigators submitted warrants to sites used by the Cari impostor, including Facebook, Yahoo, Google, Microsoft, PayPal, MeetMe, OKCupid, Twitter, Etsy, Pinger, Amazon, Pinterest, and LetterMeLater. They sought information on IP addresses, associated email addresses, and the dates accounts were created. The warrants were sealed to prevent them from becoming public record, and the investigators added a *second* seal to prohibit managers of Facebook and other sites from tipping off their suspect. Without that extra seal, users of social media sites are often warned about pending warrants and immediately rush to delete evidence. Detective Doty stresses, "We were working the case on the downlow because we didn't want her to know we were looking into her."

Liz Golyar had no idea that the investigators were on her tail, and they wanted to keep it that way. She believed she could outfox detectives, perhaps because she'd so far managed to troll the Web unfettered while hiding her identity and Internet Protocol (IP) address. An IP address is a unique identifier, assigned to each device engaged with the Internet and contains a string of numbers, separated by periods. Liz often used proxy servers to conceal her IP address, and also Virtual Private Networks (VPNs) to make it appear that her device's IP address was tied to a remote computer.

By the time the investigation was done, Special Deputy Anthony Kava would put in over 3,000 unpaid hours, unraveling Liz's web of deception as he tracked her Internet activity and sorted through over 20,000 emails and texts. Liz had dozens of email addresses via various servers, and this created a tremendous amount of work for him. While it takes minutes to create a fake email account, it takes *hours* to debunk it and trace it to its source.

Faced with a staggering mountain of data, Deputy Kava realized it was too much for his computer. "There's no 'Microsoft Homicide' type product," designed to sort a deluge of digital evidence. "Midway through the case, I built a new machine with sufficient capacity. I ended up creating a database from scratch and writing code to input the tens of thousands of emails, texts, social media logs, etc. into a system that I could query to find correlations between accounts, dates, IP addresses, and other details. I called the system DEX, as in 'index,' of course, but also a reference to *Dexter*." It's a deliciously ironic twist that a machine named for one of Liz's favorite shows would assist in her downfall. Liz was captivated by *Dexter,* the Showtime series about the blood-spatter expert who worked both sides of the law, solving murders and killing people he deemed worthless.

Did Liz draw inspiration from *Dexter*? Perhaps it's just a coincidence that in a case of "life imitating art" Liz's actions echoed Lila's, a character obsessed with Dexter, just as Liz was obsessed with Dave. In episodes that first aired in 2007, Lila, a dark-haired beauty who vaguely resembled Liz, set fire to her own loft to gain Dexter's sympathy when he drifted away from her. Lila stalked Dexter, staged catastrophes to get his attention and attempted to frame people close to him for crimes they didn't commit. Lila and Liz, and Dexter and Dave, even shared first name initials. Deputy Kava had no inkling that Liz was a *Dexter* fan when he custom designed the machine to aid in her demise. In early December 2015, Kava was still months away from breathing life into DEX and was just beginning to decipher data that Liz was certain she'd destroyed.

The first week of December had come and gone, and Cherokee realized it had been a while since she'd talked to Shanna. "When I don't hear from her for a while, I text her and say, 'Are you okay?' If she doesn't hear from me, she does the same thing. We would call it, 'checking in with assholes,'" Cherokee says, explaining that it was a standing joke between them. She never expected Shanna to *not* be okay. Usually she'd text back and say she'd been busy. This time, however, Shanna had alarming news. *Someone had shot her!*

Cherokee rushed to Shanna's house and found her propped up in a living room chair, cleaning her wound. "It was gross. She was pulling out gauze from the inside of it and putting in more gauze." Cherokee listened to the terrifying story but found nothing unusual about the fact Shanna had visited the park at night. "She told me she and Dave got into an argument, so she was trying to clear her head, gather herself together." Shanna seemed to be in a lot of pain, wincing as she shifted in her chair, and Cherokee's heart went out to her as she asked, "Why would someone *shoot* you?"

It wasn't a robbery, Shanna explained. And it wasn't a predator planning to rape her. In fact, her attacker was a *female*. "All I saw was her shadow," Shanna said. "I heard a female voice. She said to get on the ground, or she'd shoot me. I got down on the ground, and she shot me anyway!"

"Who would do something like that?"

"I can't be certain," Shanna said slowly. "But I think I recognized the voice. It sounded like Amy."

"That crazy assed bitch!" Cherokee shuddered, picturing Shanna as her attacker's shadow loomed over her. It was like a scene from a scary movie! Cherokee didn't realize that Big Lake Park was not lit. At night, it was engulfed in one big shadow, and there was no way for a single shadow to emerge.

When Cari's car was discovered in January 2013, crime scene technician Katie Pattee was instructed to process it as a recovered stolen vehicle. Now, investigators asked her to take another look. "This time they wanted it to be processed to see if we could locate some latent blood inside of the vehicle," explains Pattee. "This time, specifically, in that rear cargo area."

The Explorer had been sold, and the new owner lived in Malvern, Iowa, about a thirty-mile drive southeast from Council Bluffs, but he granted permission, so Avis and Doty picked up the car and brought it the Pottawattamie County Sheriff's Office on Tuesday, December 8, 2015. The first time Pattee had seen the Explorer, nearly three years earlier, it had been exceptionally clean, but now the opposite was true. The car's new owner had dogs, and they'd tracked in mud and shed so much that everything was coated with fur. Pattee removed the vehicle's contents and photographed both the exterior and interior. She sprayed every accessible inch of the interior with Bluestar, a blood detecting chemical reagent. "When Bluestar indicates a positive reaction for blood, it will luminesce a blue color." She dimmed the lights to observe the results. In the cargo area, near the latch, she spotted an eerie blue glow. "That reaction ended up being a false positive. I located some small copper wires in that area. Bluestar will have a false positive reaction with copper." No new evidence was discovered, and the SUV was released back to its owner.

While Sheriff's Office detectives worked the Farver case, CB Police investigated the shooting. On the same day Pattee reexamined Cari's Explorer, Liz agreed to go back to Big Lake Park to help with the CB Police probe.

Detectives Kuhlmann and Harris drove her to the park. They pulled into the parking lot, stopping where her car had parked on Saturday night. It was easy to find the spot. The pavement was stained with her blood, a stain that would remain for years to come. Liz told them she'd left her phone in the car when she'd ventured into the darkness and had had to hobble all the way back to her Toyota to call for help.

Detective Roberts and Investigator Salter soon arrived, armed with a metal detector. They hoped to find projectiles, casings or maybe even the weapon itself if it had been discarded in the park. In order to make the ordeal easier on the injured woman, Kuhlmann had parked in the lot closest to the bench where she'd told Burns she'd been shot. That bench was about 100 yards away, and Liz limped in that direction, but she surprised them when she passed it and led them to the other side of the lake. There was a bench there, too, and another parking lot. They scoured the area but found nothing. There were no projectiles, no casings, and no weapons.

Liz's story shifted, changing a little with each telling. In some versions, she'd spotted people on the trail before her attacker appeared. In one version, she'd seen a truck in the parking lot, and in yet another, it was too dark to see other vehicles. Sometimes she indicated she'd been shot on the bench, and other times claimed she'd been on the ground. In one telling, she'd seen Amy running away, and in another, she'd not actually seen anyone but had heard a familiar female voice, coldly ordering her to get down on the ground.

Both Council Bluffs PD and the Pott County Sherriff investigators suspected Liz had shot herself. "We were concerned for Amy Flora's safety at this point," Doty emphasizes. A blond wig had been found in the backseat of Liz's car on the night of the shooting. They realized the wig could be a disguise, part of an abandoned scheme to shoot Amy. Had her original plan been thwarted? Had she shot herself out of desperation because, for whatever reason, her murder plot had gone awry?

Amy was still in the crosshairs of Liz's wrath, and police made a plan to protect her. A warrant allowed them to place a Global Positioning System (GPS) tracker on Liz's vehicle. They covertly secured the magnetized tracker to the underside of her car on December 11. Doty explains, "With the GPS program, we put a geofence around Amy's apartment complex, so if Shanna's vehicle entered that complex, we'd get text notifications."

The tracker alerted them many times each day. Liz usually looped through Amy's parking lot and left. The safety plan counted on the CB Police. If Liz should pause for "an extended period of time" near Amy's apartment, officers would rush to the scene. Meanwhile, Amy was going about her business, still rattled by the accusations made against her but oblivious to the fact her life was in danger.

CHAPTER TWENTY-SEVEN

A FEW DAYS AFTER THE SHOOTING, Shanna told Cherokee that police suspected she had *not* been shot by Amy. "They think I was behind it," said Shanna. Cherokee stared at her quizzically. Shanna was the *victim*. How could she be behind the shooting when she was the victim? "They think you shot *yourself*?"

"They think *you* did it—that you were my accomplice!"

The idea was so nutty that Cherokee laughed. It didn't occur to her to worry she'd be arrested for shooting her friend. She was confident she wouldn't get in trouble for something she didn't do. She was right about that. No detectives contacted her.

Though most of the cops suspected Liz had shot herself, none of them had accused her. Pott County Sheriff investigators were keeping their suspicions close to the vest. They were excited when Deputy Kava found proof that Liz had been impersonating Cari Farver, but their work was far from done. It was compelling evidence but not enough for a murder charge. They needed more. *Much more.* Ideally, a suspect will confess, but they doubted Liz would do that, not unless they *tricked* her into it. "In this case, we had to understand that what was driving Liz was her obsession with Dave, so once we knew that, we could flip that on her," Detective Doty explains.

The investigators had a huge advantage. They'd studied her for months and knew what made her tick. But Liz had no idea who she was dealing with and believed she could outsmart the detectives. "We knew she'd think that because she'd tricked a few cops in the past," Detective Avis confides. "Luckily, she ran into someone smarter than she is."

On December 14, 2015, Liz was invited to Doty's office. Recently hired by an Omaha pet food company, she stopped by on her way to work and wore gray scrubs with her hair pulled back into a ponytail. It was Doty's first meeting with her, so he introduced himself and explained he was working on a missing person case and that they'd found some remains. "We're waiting on the lab results to make a positive I.D., but the initial indication is these remains are Cari."

Liz appeared cooperative but gave the impression she knew little about the situation. Doty gave no indication that he saw Liz as anything other than a potential witness as he said, "I'm going to tell you some stuff that I would hope would stay in this room, okay?" In reality, nothing had been found. The detective was putting on a performance. He had *literally* set the stage by adding a prop—an x-ray that now sat atop a stack of papers on his desk. It wasn't connected to the case, but he knew it would trigger her interest. Asked if she'd met Cari, Liz described the encounter at Dave's place. "I didn't know he was dating anyone else at the time. So, she came out, and I was going in. And she made a smart comment to me."

"What did she say to you?"

"Called me a bitch. And it wasn't a big deal. I didn't really care at the time, I just wanted to get my stuff, and then I left and went home." Liz insisted it was the only time she'd seen Cari and suggested that Amy was the *real* stalker. "She was with him for twelve years. And she still goes in and out of his life all of the time."

"So, you think she could have been the person who did some of that stuff?"

"I'm just saying as another person who would be possessive of Dave, it would be her," said Liz. "So, I mean, I wouldn't put it past her."

"I'm thinking if she was bold enough to go and shoot you, okay, she could have easily been bold enough to have done something to Cari."

While Liz was probably jumping for joy inside her head, she appeared calm as Doty said he hoped to build a case against Amy but didn't have enough evidence. If he had evidence that Amy had made threatening statements or inferred she'd done something to Cari, that would be "like gold to me."

Four days later, Liz forwarded an email to Doty, claiming Amy had sent it to her. The subject line was: "I shot you."

I shot you, Liz, to make sure Dave stayed away from you . . . I got rid of the gun. Looks like the police haven't arrested me. No one has proof it was me . . .

Liz had stepped right into Doty's trap. Just as he'd hoped, she'd impersonated Amy and confessed. But she'd confessed to the *wrong* crime! Investigators wanted her to reveal facts about Cari's murder, but instead, "Amy" had confessed to shooting Liz. She was eager to see Amy arrested, but Doty explained that the park shooting wasn't even his case. It took awhile for her to comprehend that the Pottawattamie County Sheriff's Office was an entirely different agency than the Council Bluffs Police. The CB Police were investigating the shooting. Doty needed information about the *murder.* "I need specific details of Cari Farver's murder to build a case," he told her.

Liz knew exactly what had happened to Cari. She knew her manner of death, and she knew what had happened to her remains. And now, Liz believed those remains had been found. She'd watched enough crime shows to realize that if cops had found a body, they knew a lot about Cari's demise. Liz realized she had to make "Amy's" confession fit the actual scenario. Unless "Amy's" emails contained authentic details, the police wouldn't believe it. On December 20, Liz forwarded another email to Doty, and this time "Amy" gave details about the murder. It was a long, rambling letter but portions of it were clear and to the point: *When I met Crazy Cari, she would not stop talking about Dave and him being her husband. She tried to attack me, but I attacked her with a knife. I stabbed her three to four times in the stomach area. I then took her out and burned her. I stuffed her body in a garbage can with crap. She was carried out to the dumpster, probably when Dave took my garbage out for me.*

So be glad I did not do you that way, Liz. I will never admit to Dave or police, no one. Maybe I'm drunk now and just telling lies to you. Dave will always take care of me and protect me, so I will never go to jail. When I followed you that night, I shot you. I left Mason

*home because he was sleeping. Made sure I called Dave and texted
him for my alibi, so you can never prove it was me.*

Possibly as farfetched as the notion Amy could shoot someone
was the idea she'd leave her baby home alone. Amy was a devoted
mom and very picky when it came to choosing babysitters. She certainly would not have left Mason alone for even a moment.

Half an hour after the stabbing confession, "Amy" confessed to
arson, too. The email's subject line was "Fucking crazy bitch" and
began, *Now that I got your attention, don't ever come back around
my kids, Dave or me. Just like your house getting burned was me.
That's another thing that Dave won't believe either . . .*

In crude terms, "Amy" wrote that she and Dave still had sex and
that no one would believe Liz if she reported her crimes. The idea
that Amy would confess to Liz was preposterous. The two weren't
friends. And if Amy *were* a killer, it would be downright stupid for
her to put her evil deeds in writing. What were the odds that "Amy"
would confess immediately after the detective asked Liz to help him
find evidence? None of it made much sense, but either these things
didn't occur to Liz, or she assumed the cops were too dumb to question it.

Amy would no more confess to Liz that she killed Cari than Gloria
Munson would confess to shaking Cody. Both Amy and Gloria were
Shanna's adversaries. The prosecutor had encouraged Shanna to tell
the story about Gloria's so-called confession, and had also encouraged
her to read aloud letters that were very likely forged. If Shanna had
gotten away with lies about confessions and forged letters as they
pertained to Cody's death, it's understandable that she would believe she could get away with it again.

On December 21, Liz told Doty she wouldn't be able to help him
for a while. She was too busy moving. *Finally*, Garret had convinced her to leave! After the shooting, he'd explained to her that he
simply could not be involved in whatever dangerous drama she'd
been swept up into. "I was so desperate to get her out that I rented a
U-Haul truck for her stuff and gave her the money for the deposit
and rent for an apartment. I told her, 'If it doesn't work out, don't
come to me. Don't ever come back.' "

He had virtually supported Liz and her kids for almost two and a half years and was now investing his time and money to help her get a new place, but she continued to behave like a victim. "She went running to Dirk to tell him I was kicking her out." Liz found an apartment in Persia, Iowa, a tiny town in Harrison County about thirty miles northeast of Council Bluffs. Surrounded by farmland, Persia has a population under 400, so it's understandable that the businesses in town didn't appear to be thriving. At least one storefront was boarded up, but most of the homes in the area were lovingly cared for. Liz's apartment was on the second floor of a somewhat creepy 1912 brick building, originally the town's mortuary. Erected after the 1905 fire that destroyed many of Persia's buildings, it was built to last and was a landmark on Main Street, a long, straight road on a gradual uphill slope.

In early January of 2016, Garret helped Liz move mattresses to her new place, loading them into a pickup truck she'd rented and lugging them up the steps, into the new apartment. They managed to fit most of her other possessions into the U-Haul, and Garret breathed a sigh of relief when he dropped off the last load. She couldn't take her pets to the apartment, and that was fine with him. They were used to his place, and he'd grown fond of them.

Cherokee, apparently unaware that Garret, too, assisted Liz in the move, remembers that they packed Shanna's stuff into a small caravan of two SUVs, and "I moved her to her new place in Persia and stayed the night." Shanna was still hurting from her gunshot injury, so Cherokee did most of the heavy lifting. Afterward, "We drank, and watched TV," Cherokee recalls, adding that she felt bad for her friend and tried to help her as much as possible.

Liz briefly talked with Detective Doty a couple of times over the next weeks and forwarded him more incriminating emails from Amy. Liz was frustrated that it was taking so long for the idiots to get off their butts and arrest Amy. She'd practically delivered "Amy's" confessions to Doty on a silver platter. What more did the guy want?

CHAPTER TWENTY-EIGHT

LIZ WAS A MASTER MANIPULATOR, but she had met her match. The investigators were now pulling her strings, and she was their obedient puppet, dancing toward her doom, oblivious to the fact she was performing exactly as the "dumb cops" had planned. Dave Kroupa, too, was about to be manipulated and would unwittingly share her stage as detectives choreographed *his* next move.

Investigators needed Liz to share more details about the murder. The best way to accomplish that was to push their suspect to the brink of despair. What did Liz want more than anything? *Dave.* Who did Liz hate the most? *Amy.* What possible scenario would stir Liz up into the frenzy of all frenzies? *Dave and Amy, together again!*

When Doty deceived Liz, he'd made a show of taking her into his confidence and told her, "I hope this information does not leave this room," but he knew that asking Liz not to tell Dave that Amy was a murder suspect was like asking a fish not to swim. As anxious as she was to tell Dave, she was likely showing restraint because she wanted him to learn about it *after* Amy was arrested, so Amy would be caught off guard. But it was taking way too long for the cops to get around to that, and Liz could wait no longer to tell him the marvelous secret. The mother of his children was a killer! *Finally*, he would see that he must cut ties with the greedy woman who took all his money and forced him to spend holidays with her!

In late January, the detectives received the call they'd been waiting for. Dave sounded shell-shocked as he asked about the secrets Liz had been so eager to share. Detective Avis grimly advised, "I'd be damned moved in with Amy, if I were you." Avis gave the impression he was doing Dave a favor, sharing confidential information because he, too, had a family. Man to man, father to father, Avis's tone implied that Liz was dangerous as he stressed, "Since Liz did come and tell you this, I would avoid her like the plague right now."

Dave was confused. Liz was manipulative, she was possessive, and she could be extremely annoying, but Avis's suggestion she was dangerous made him dizzy. Liz had been telling him *Amy* was dangerous, that she'd followed her to Big Lake Park and shot her and might have done something to Cari. The idea that Amy could harm anyone was even more farfetched than the suggestion Liz was violent. He'd known the mother of his children far longer than he'd known Liz. There was absolutely *no way* Amy had done the things Liz claimed.

He'd always figured Liz's issues were due to insecurity, and he'd been patient as long as he had because he felt a little sorry for her. She was a tiny thing, and could seem so vulnerable. She'd appeared genuinely frightened when "Cari" terrorized her. Whenever Liz looked up at him with her brown eyes brimming with fear, he'd instinctively put his arm around her and tried to reassure her.

Dave didn't realize it, but he'd been suffering from "confirmation bias." *Every* human experiences this phenomenon of the mind, and most of us are unable to comprehend what's happening until long after we've been set straight and have had both time and distance away from whatever influenced us to accept falsehoods as truth. Also called "*confirmatory* bias," this trick of the mind is exploited by cult leaders who use it against followers to keep them in line. But most of the time, we dive in on our own. It occurs after we've formed an opinion about a particular subject, and it prompts us to embrace information that supports our initial belief and disregard facts that don't. It narrows the perspective of people, no matter how intelligent, so that they dismiss anything negating their viewpoint. The longer it goes on, the harder it is for us to see the truth.

Dave's confirmation bias had begun to take root in November 2012 when he received the first hostile texts from Cari's phone number. For over three years, he'd been inundated daily with fake emails and texts, each one confirming his belief that Cari was stalking him.

Liz had worked very hard to make sure Dave never doubted that the woman he'd once been infatuated with had turned into a monster. The longer Liz kept up the charade, the easier it was for those she'd fooled to believe the lies. The first round of detectives working the case were also influenced by their confirmation bias, but no one had been led deeper into the abyss than Dave Kroupa.

He was at work shortly after his phone conversation with Detective Avis when Detective Doty showed up. "He had a marshal with him," Dave recalls. The two men sat him down for a serious talk. "Doty told me he was certain that Liz was the one making all the threats." While the men couldn't tell Dave everything they knew, they made it clear they believed Liz was extremely dangerous, that she was behind Cari's disappearance, and that they feared Amy and his kids were in danger.

He was numb as he picked up his phone, called Amy and repeated what the police had told him. "I told you so!" Amy exclaimed. Yes, she *had* told him so. *Again and again.* He'd always known Amy wasn't fond of Liz but figured she'd been a little jealous. The fact Amy didn't like Liz "didn't raise any red flags for me." But any "red flags" waving at him would have had to have been on fire for him to take notice because he'd wholeheartedly believed Liz was a victim, and Cari was the stalker.

Dave couldn't focus on work after learning about Liz. "I went and sat down by my tool box and did nothing for two hours." The past he'd believed was real had been nothing more than an illusion. How had he allowed himself to be fooled? When he learned that Liz had used a LetterMeLater app, he realized that had played a large part in the deception. He'd initially been convinced Cari was the stalker, because not only were the texts coming from her number, he'd been with Liz when they both received them. He'd had no idea it was possible for a person to send themselves a text to arrive at a specific time.

When he realized the truth, Dave describes it as "like walking through a dark forest, unable to see anything, and then the sun comes out." Suddenly everything was clear. *Painfully clear.*

Dave immediately moved in with Amy, just as the investigators had hoped. It was part of their strategy to drive their suspect to the edge of despair. If the plan worked, Liz would come unglued. She'd be so desperate to get rid of Amy that she'd reveal incriminating clues. Dave had no idea he'd been manipulated by detectives. The police were watching over Amy and didn't need his help. They'd been honest when they said Liz was dangerous but had twisted the truth when they said he needed to move in with Amy to protect her. While it might seem like a dirty trick to deceive an innocent person, their motives were pure. Amy was not at risk at the moment, but ultimately, she *would* be if Liz remained on the loose. When Dave moved in with Amy, it *was* to protect her, even if it wasn't in the way he believed.

The detectives realized their strategy had worked when an enraged Liz called Doty on February 1, 2016. Half sobbing, she cried, "Looks like the only person that benefitted was her! So, she gets to shoot somebody, and then she gets to kill another person! And then she gets to move in with Dave, and she gets to be free, and you guys aren't arresting her!"

"I'm sorry," said Doty, though he really didn't sound very sorry. He explained that he needed more specific information in order to build a case against Amy. "It's really tough right now, because Amy's not really talking," he stressed.

If the dumb cop could not build a case from everything Liz had sent them, she would just have to make it easier for him. *Doty wanted Amy to talk?* She'd talk all right! "Amy" would talk her way right into a cold, gray prison cell and Liz would do a celebratory jig as the doors clanged shut behind her. She rolled up her sleeves, prepared to write a confession that would leave no doubt Amy was the killer.

She decided that Doty would be more impressed by "Amy's" confessions if *he* discovered them himself. Later that day, she dropped by his office to offer access to her Google account, explaining it was too much trouble to forward Amy's emails. Liz gave Doty her password, and he began to monitor her emails.

Within hours, more confessions from "Amy" appeared. Some of it sounded like pure fantasy, but a few details were chillingly accurate. The killer described Cari's tattoos, including a yin-yang image on her thigh. While Cari's missing person flyer indicated she had four tattoos, the yin yang symbol was not mentioned. In fact, investigators were unaware of it until they read about it in the "Amy" impostor email, penned by Liz. Cari's family verified that she did indeed have a yin-yang tattoo, but it was in a private area, and no photos of the tattoo had been posted on the web, and no posts referenced it. Anthony Kava thoroughly searched the Internet to rule out the possibility that the letter writer could have learned about the tattoo in an innocent way. He concluded that only someone who'd come in close contact with Cari would know about it. The emails also described the inside of Cari's home—the small, all-white bathroom, the leather couch and loveseat, and the wooden bedroom furniture. Doty knew the description was accurate because he'd seen the photos Phyllips had taken.

"I noticed several consistencies in the emails after reviewing them all," Detective Doty recalls. "Cari was stabbed in the chest or the stomach area, the incident happened in her vehicle, the body was burned, it was disposed of in the garbage, the vehicle was cleaned after the fact, the vehicle was returned to Dave's apartment, the perpetrator posed as Cari after the fact, she contacted Cari's mother after the fact, she went to Cari's residence and took some of her possessions."

As more details came to light, the investigators realized that the murder had probably occurred in Omaha. That meant it was under the jurisdiction of Douglas County, Nebraska, and couldn't be prosecuted without cooperation from their friends across the river. On February 10, 2016, Deputy Kava and Detectives Avis and Doty gathered at the Omaha Police Department's Homicide Unit to brief Detective Dave Schneider.

A member of OPD's cold-case squad, Schneider is investigating three to four dozen murders at any given time and doesn't mind admitting they sometimes "move me to emotion." He feels special empathy for parents of victims, maybe because he's a father himself. He and his wife Kendra, an administrator for a public-school district, have three children and make their home in Omaha, where Dave Schneider was born and raised. His father worked in management in the heating, ventilation and air conditioning industry (HVAC), and his mother did clerical work for a grain company. They lived in a middle-class neighborhood in West Omaha where a good night's sleep was never interrupted by gunfire.

"There was definitely a different world out there that I didn't know about," he stresses. "When I was working in North Omaha in the middle of the night, it would be quite common to hear gunshots go off." He went to work for Omaha PD in 2005, patrolling a high-crime area and often saw the aftermath of violence, something he hadn't planned on while earning his B.A. in Geography at the University of Nebraska. He played baseball there until he injured his shoulder and was admittedly uncertain about his goals. After graduation, he worked part-time at his old school, Omaha's West Side High. He coached, worked security, and ran errands for the dean. The school resource officer encouraged him to take Omaha Police Department's application exam. He followed his advice, aced the test, and after three years working patrol was promoted to detective. In the beginning he approached the job with the competitive spirit that had motivated him when playing sports. "I want to be the best. I want to solve the case. That's how I went into it." But his attitude evolved as he learned about the victims, and he realized, "This is somebody's loved one." He felt for the victims' families. Cracking cases was no longer about ego. "You do everything you can to solve it for *them*."

By the time a cold-case file makes it to Schneider's desk, it's been pored over and picked at and pretty much discarded. Some cases are so old that the detectives who first worked them are dead or retired, but because they carefully preserved evidence, Schneider can use new DNA technology to finally get justice.

When the Iowa team brought the Farver case to him, Detective Schneider was impressed. Despite their lack of experience with homicides, they were handling the case like pros. Schneider was immediately on board, and they worked together to plan their next steps. Schneider agreed that at least one of the confessor's claims was true: *I really did kill Cari, and I did it in her own car.* Katie Pattee hadn't found blood in the car, but she hadn't been looking for evidence of a stabbing. Now, as she learned about the new suspicions, she suggested they remove the covers on the seats. If a significant amount of blood was shed by a driver or passenger, it would have seeped into the seats.

About two months had passed since Pattee's last search of the vehicle. The SUV's owner again allowed access, but it was broken down outside his parents' home in Malvern. Doty and Pattee drove there on Thursday, February 18. Doty used wrenches to remove the front seats. They set the seats on a tarp, and when they peeled back the cloth cover on the driver's seat, Pattee says, "I used Bluestar and sprayed the foam area underneath the cloth seat." They saw nothing unusual, but then they peeled back the cover on the passenger seat. Doty will never forget the moment they saw the large red stain saturating the foam seat. Pattee sprayed Bluestar on it, and they were rewarded with an undeniable luminescing reaction.

Though the SUV's owner had agreed to the search, investigators now secured a search warrant to make it official and had the Explorer towed to their headquarters. Somebody had bled profusely on the passenger seat. It was possible someone other than Cari had bled there, maybe before or after she had the car. Without proof it was her blood, the evidence was useless. They didn't have her DNA profile for comparison but hoped her mother had saved a relic, perhaps a toothbrush or a hairbrush Cari had used.

Doty and Pattee went to see Nancy Raney the next day and learned most of Cari's possessions were in a storage unit in Oakland, Iowa, a few miles from Macedonia. They drove Nancy there and watched as she picked through boxes until she found three hairbrushes with strands of her beautiful daughter's hair caught up in the bristles, along with a headband with hair still clinging to it. The few strands of hair might be all that was left of the vibrant young woman, the only thing containing her DNA profile. Pattee swabbed the insides of Maxwell and Nancy's cheeks to get DNA samples for comparison. Max's father in Colorado also cooperated and submitted his DNA for comparison with Maxwell's so that through the process of elimination, they could determine that the blood was Cari's. Pattee submitted the new evidence to the Iowa Division of Criminal Investigation for testing.

On Sunday, February 21, Dave Kroupa was napping on Amy's couch in the middle of the afternoon when a rock sailed through the dining-room window. Amy was in her room and came running when she heard the glass shatter. Dave was sleeping so deeply he didn't stir until Amy shook him awake. Once they'd called police and swept up the broken glass, they had a good laugh as Dave poked fun at himself. He'd moved in to be the fierce protector but had slept right through the commotion.

The hidden tracker on Liz's car placed her at the scene of the crime, and she was arrested. She pled guilty, paid a fine, and was released. Three agonizing weeks had passed since Dave moved in with Amy, and Liz's rage was building. She'd thrown a rock in broad daylight, too furious to wait for nighttime when she could hide in the shadows. She would have been caught even if she *had* waited till dark, but she didn't know that. Investigators were concerned about their suspect's escalating rage. She had killed before and would kill again if she got the chance. She had to be stopped. *Soon.*

February 25, 2016, was a landmark day for investigators. They'd been granted search warrants for Liz's Persia apartment *and* for the home she'd recently shared with Garret. His involvement with Liz made for a sticky situation. Not only was he a Pottawattamie employee, Anthony Kava was his *boss.* Because they worked together in the IT department, Garret interacted more frequently with Kava than he did with the detectives.

"We liked Garret. We trusted Garret," stresses Detective Doty. "But we didn't know how well Liz had her claws into him, and if he found information, what he would tell her."

Kava, too, thought highly of Garret, but it was an unusual circumstance. "It had become clear to me that we needed to put Garret on administrative leave. He was too close to this case, and as an IT technician, had access to Sheriff's Office systems, including ones with information about the case," Kava explains, adding they wanted to be sure that digital evidence brought to trial couldn't be attacked on the grounds that Garret could have planted evidence.

Garret was put on paid administrative leave. His employers made it clear he'd done nothing wrong but banned him from using county computers "until otherwise directed." It wasn't fun for Garret to be "escorted out" of the building, and he was shocked to find himself barred from work. He was done with Liz and would never have betrayed the investigators but understood why they were required to take precautions.

The team waited until Liz left for work before they invaded her apartment. They weren't about to give her a chance to delete digital evidence, something that can be done remotely on some gadgets. As for the search of Garret's house, he invited them in and helped move furniture as they looked for clues Liz might have left behind. It was already an awkward situation Kava emphasizes, and as Garret's boss, he didn't want to make it "even *more* awkward if I went through his sock drawer." With that in mind, Kava stayed away from Garret's place and joined the team in Persia as they picked through Liz's messy apartment.

While the investigators didn't find anything of interest at Garret's place, they hit the mother lode in the Persia apartment. They confiscated every electronic gadget there, including a number of cell phones and two items that had once belonged to Cari Farver—her camera and camcorder. Liz believed she'd deleted Cari's videos, but Kava was able to retrieve one made by Cari in April 2012. It showed a friend of hers, sawing a fallen tree in her yard.

One of Liz's confiscated cell phones revealed it had been used to call Cari's mother on April 17, 2013, the same day a man had phoned Nancy, identified himself as Dave Kroupa, and told her that her daughter was at the Siena/Francis House. Dave had denied making that call, and now there was proof it had originated from one of Liz's phones. Nancy was certain she'd heard a *man's* voice. Had Liz enlisted a guy to help with the hoax? Maybe. Or she might have used one of the popular voice changer apps. Nancy had probably spoken to Liz Golyar, herself, as the killer used an app to deepen her voice.

CHAPTER TWENTY-NINE

GARRET SLOAN DIDN'T LIKE missing work. He was still being paid, but he was restless and had too many empty hours to ponder the mess Liz had dragged him into. He wished he didn't have to think about her, but it wasn't easy to put her out of his mind when his privacy had just been turned inside out by investigators searching his home. They were courteous and seemed embarrassed for him as they rummaged through his things. Even so, it was a violation of his personal space, and he realized if he'd never met Liz, he wouldn't be in such an awkward spot.

As painful and humiliating as the experience was, Garret would do it all over again because of the role he played in trapping a killer. Of all the men in Council Bluffs who Liz could have chosen to use and abuse, she'd picked one of the few guys whose computer system was tied to law enforcement's. Garret's Virtual Private Network (VPN) connected him to Pott County's computer system. In normal circumstances, "IP addresses change, and providers don't keep records forever," Deputy Kava explains. "We had a long-term record, thanks to Garret's log-ins."

Liz had used Garret's Internet and WIFI when she lived with him, allowing Kava to track her activity and tie it to the impersonations of Cari and Amy. While Kava believes Liz would have been convicted even if she hadn't used Garret's Internet, the evidence was *much* stronger with proof that the activity was connected to her residence.

Garret's relationship with Liz had been a disaster, but he has the satisfaction of knowing that the proverbial joke is on her. She'd found one of the nicest guys she could have ever hoped to meet, taken advantage of his kindness, turned his basement into a garbage dump, burglarized his home, lied to him, and cheated on him. She never contributed a dime toward the utility bills. And using Garret's Internet service had cost her nothing—*nothing except her freedom!*

The Internet service she'd enjoyed under Garret's roof would soon help to snare her in her own snarled web of deceit.

Detective Dave Schneider was eager to talk to Liz Golyar. Interrogation was his favorite part of the job, probably because of his talent for coaxing confessions from reluctant subjects. Liz was still at work, halfway through her shift, unaware investigators had pawed through her possessions and unearthed her secrets.

Liz was arrested at work—not for murder, but for a traffic citation she'd neglected to pay. It was only a misdemeanor but an arrestable offense if a cop wanted to be hard-nosed about it. She was escorted to a small room at the Omaha Police Department where she met Detective Schneider for the first time. Her hair was twisted up into a bun, and she wore neon pink pants and a patterned smock over a long-sleeved dark shirt. She sat in a chair facing Schneider, her pose defensive, arms folded over her middle and legs tightly crossed.

Liz had believed *she* was in control in her recent meetings with police. But now she'd been placed under arrest and brought, *against her will*, to an interrogation room, and she wasn't pleased. Schneider Mirandized her, and she agreed to chat with him, probably assuming she could talk her way out of whatever trouble she faced. Schneider spoke to her in his usual calm manner, explaining he wanted to talk about a missing person. Did she know who he meant?

"Uh, Cari?" Liz's voice was strained. "I'm not sure of her last name."

"Farver. Does that sound familiar?"

"Yeah."

"Okay. Did you know her at all?"

"I ran into her for like two seconds at Dave's apartment. She was coming out. I was going in. I don't know exact dates. It was right around the time when they first started seeing each other."

"And Dave is?"

Liz explained he was her "boyfriend at the time," and when Schneider asked if he'd cheated on her with Cari, she said, "Well, I don't know what the whole situation was. I just know that that night when I was try-ing to get my keys from him, he was with her. So, she left so that I could go in and get my stuff. And I packed up all of my stuff that was at his apartment, and I left. That was the only time I ever saw her."

Schneider asked if Liz had ever called Cari, and while she at first vehemently denied it, when he continued to question her, she said she might have if Cari had called her first, but it was hard to remem-ber details from so long ago.

"So, do you know anything about where she's at, where she's gone to?"

"When this whole thing started, I had thought it was weird be-cause they had dated for like two weeks, is what Dave said, two or three weeks," she answered evasively. "And I don't understand how a person who dated him for two or three weeks would stalk me. Like break out my windows and spray-painted whore across my garage."

Schneider asked about Cari's car. Had Liz ever seen it, driven it, or ridden in it? The answer was no. He gently asked, "What do you think happened to Cari Farver?"

She raised her shoulders in an exaggerated shrug, and after a long pause began to speak rapidly, her voice high pitched. "I don't know. I don't know if what Amy is saying is true. I don't know. I'm more scared that something is going to happen to me, and my kids aren't going to have anybody."

"Like what?" he asked. "What do you mean?"

"Because the emails that she sent, they're pretty graphic."

Investigators had kept Liz in the dark for months, and she had no idea they were stockpiling evidence against her. Now, Schneider was ready to divulge it all, and he kept his voice level, as he pref-aced each revelation with explanations and details that Liz was probably too shocked to fully comprehend. But she knew she was in trouble and swiped tears from her eyes, sniffling, as Schneider said, "Okay, at the beginning, I kind of told you a little bit about how I'm working with the Pott County Sheriff's Office. This has been going on a while now. Obviously, we handle a lot more homicide investi-gations than they do."

Liz said, "I don't know about the police department. I just went to them and told them I wanted something to be done."

"Let me just explain a couple of things to you, so you understand where I'm coming from," he said. "I'll simplify it down. As part of homicide investigations, we do some things that are pretty routine. Process crime scenes, process evidence, collect the evidence and examine it. Evidence nowadays includes digital forensics, stuff like that. Digital forensics could include cell phone records." Schneider explained that cell phone towers can use triangulation to pinpoint a phone's location. "These cell phone companies keep these records, and we can obtain them through a search warrant. And that's routine, what we do on all homicide cases now."

Liz was quiet.

"The reason why you're in this chair, right now, today, is because you have a lot of questions you need to answer for me. Very important questions. You're in a very serious position here. For almost four years now, this woman's son hasn't had his mom, a mom hasn't had her daughter—"

"I know!" Liz interrupted. "That's why I'm concerned, too. Because, I'm just like, she's missing and for her family—"

"It's tragic," Schneider cut her off. "They're all tragic, but some are worse. The reason I want to talk to you specifically is her phone was at your house right after she disappeared."

"*My* house?"

"Yeah, her phone, when she went missing was at your house. The location data showed specifically it was at your house on 116th. I want to ask you how you can explain that to me, please."

"She's never been to my house."

"Exactly. So, after she's done disappearing, her phone is at your house. When her vehicle is located, guess what was found inside her vehicle?"

"Hmmm," said Liz.

"Your fingerprints are inside her vehicle. If you've never been inside her vehicle, how would your fingerprints be inside her vehicle?"

"I don't know. Because I've never been in her car."

"For years and years, people have been sending emails under Cari's fictitious accounts. The location on that data sometimes is masked by different apps, but we have ways around that. A lot of times it wasn't masked. The IP addresses show up to whose house? *Your* house. Okay. Liz, this is where I want you to think hard, okay, about what direction you're going to go in here. Are you going to sit in this chair and be remorseful? Are you going to sit in this chair and be cold-blooded? Because right now, after four years, this family's been looking for answers." Schneider reminded her they had her prints in Cari's car and could place Cari's phone at her house. He said they had proof she'd impersonated both Cari and Amy, adding that he'd read all of the messages and noticed that the writing style and grammar in the impersonations was nothing like Cari's. "That doesn't matter," he said. "The physical evidence is what matters. Inside her car, we found, guess what? Besides a print, what else do you think would be in a homicide investigation?"

Agitated, Liz snapped, "I don't know, but I've never been in her car. I don't even know what car she drives."

While Schneider continued to speak in a manner so calm it was almost soothing, Liz was talking faster and faster, her voice higher pitched as she grew more irritated. Schneider explained, "Now, when you give permission to download your phone, they can extract deleted data from those things. There is a picture of Cari's car that you had deleted on your phone."

"What car? I've never seen Cari's car."

"Her Ford Explorer. A picture of her car, with her plates, her Explorer, is on your phone."

"I've never seen her car!" She was emphatic. "Ever!"

"You've been in her car. You drove her car."

"No, I didn't!" Liz's voice rose in anger. "I've never been inside of her car. I've never been around her car! *Ever!*"

"Your fingerprints are in there."

"No, I haven't! I'm not lying. I've never been around her car. I've never even *seen* it! I had to ask a sheriff."

"Where do you think the IP addresses come back to?"

"What IP addresses?"

"When Amy Flora sent these emails to you, these confession emails—let me just give you a head's up. The Pott County Sheriff's Office, has got your phone right now. They've done warrants on your house. They've seized this morning while you were at work. They've seized all of this data. All of this information. They've downloaded it. They know where these emails were created from specifically. The ones that you've been forwarding to him from Amy. You created all of those."

"No, I didn't."

"You can't explain that."

"No, I didn't."

"Why would you create all of these emails?"

"I haven't created any emails!" Her fury had escalated to rage, but Schneider continued speaking softly, as he said, "They're coming from you."

"No, they're not!"

"All of these have been coming from you, over the years."

"No, they're not!"

"All of these have been coming from your—"

"No, they're not."

"Your house."

"And I'm not going to be accused of something I didn't do."

"The finger's pointing right at you."

"Then I'm done talking, and I'm going to have my attorney, because I didn't do anything."

"Okay." The interview was over.

James Martin Davis is one of Omaha's most celebrated attorneys. Voted the city's best criminal lawyer for nine years in a row, he was also a highly decorated Vietnam combat veteran and a former Secret Service Special Agent whose duties included riding in parades with U.S. President Richard Nixon—a job memorialized in a framed 8 x 10 photograph hanging on his office wall. After over thirty-five years of practicing law, he's defended his share of clients, but none has been as secretive as Shanna Elizabeth Golyar. "I've never had a client who kept things as close to the vest as she did," he notes. In fact, Golyar was *so* reticent, she revealed very little to him about her involvement in the case when he was called upon to help in her February twenty-fifth arrest. JMD, as he is affectionately known in the Gateway to the West, quickly took care of the matter with the unpaid citation, and Shanna was released from jail.

Shanna had stood firm with Detective Schneider and refused to admit anything. Maybe she thought he was bluffing and that she'd won. Maybe she thought the trouble would blow over. She'd gotten away with evil deeds for such a long time, why shouldn't she believe she could continue to do so?

Chapter Thirty

Garret had changed the code on his burglar alarm immediately after Liz moved, and he hoped to never see her again. When she called to ask about items she'd left behind, he was wary. "I told her to contact the Sheriff's Office to make arrangements to meet me in a public place, and I would bring her the rest of her stuff. She asked why, and I told her because I was being investigated because of her."

Liz was unsympathetic, and when he added that he was off work because of her, she snapped, "Don't blame me for your problems!"

She was surprised to learn he still had the pets. She seemed unable to grasp the idea he'd grown attached to them. It was the last time she contacted him. Though both Garret and Dave had dumped her, Liz's dance card was full. Cherokee recalled a couple of young guys Liz dated. "She got together with Charlie for a little bit. He was a younger kid. He just wanted to get laid." Both guys were in their early twenties, and Liz worked with one of them at the pet food company.

While Liz often pretended to be monogamous, she usually had many boyfriends. Even as she'd begged Dave for the thirty-day commitment in October 2012, she was sleeping with two other guys. There was Garret, of course, and there was also Fred. Investigators learned about him after downloading her phone. Liz had spent the weekend with Fred, just a few days before Cari vanished. She had gone out of her mind with jealousy over Cari, and all the while, Liz had multiple sex partners. Fred wasn't the only surprise detectives discovered in the phone data. As if tormenting all of Cari and Dave's friends and relatives wasn't enough, Liz had also broken the heart of an Omaha woman. To this day, Sandra is unaware that "the guy" she'd exchanged love letters with for eight months was actually Liz.

Investigators aren't sure if they spoke, but if they did, Liz would have used a voice deepening app. Avis felt horrible for the cat-phished lady because "They even said 'I love you,' to each other." Liz and Sandra exchanged nude photos, but Liz, of course, didn't send photos of herself. The images of the naked man were either random photos she'd pulled off the web or pictures of one of her lovers.

Sandra was a single mom in her mid-thirties, eager to settle down and believed she'd found the man of her dreams. Then one day, Liz simply vanished from her life with no explanation. Liz, who couldn't bear rejection, had gone out of her way to cat-phish and reject a stranger. Sandra was hurt and confused. Avis considered contacting her to reveal the truth but feared it would make her feel worse.

In March 2016, detectives received Cari's Rolling Hills Bank records. "We noticed two transactions that posted on November 19, 2012," remembers Doty. "One was for Family Dollar, and one was at Walmart. And we continued to try to get these records. Family Dollar didn't have records going back to 2012. Walmart did." The purchases had actually been made on November *16*, but reflected the approximate three-day delay before the bank posted the transactions. Both stores were in Omaha, and records revealed that Cari's debit card was used for a $167 purchase at Family Dollar. No other details were available. But the information for the Walmart purchase was very specific. Three days after Cari vanished, someone had strolled into the huge discount store, filled a shopping cart and at 11:48 A.M. swiped Cari's debit card at the cash register.

The Universal Product Code (UPC) identified the items purchased. The mysterious shopper's loot included winter clothing, cleaning supplies, and a shower curtain featuring huge black and white flowers. That curtain—or one exactly like it—was visible in photos Liz had snapped in her bathroom, two days after the Walmart purchase. "What stuck out is that that shower curtain seemed to be new because you could still see the folds in it," says Doty. But lots of people shopped at Walmart, and thousands had purchased that same shower curtain. The shower-curtain evidence could be explained away as a coincidence.

A few weeks had passed since Pattee sent samples to the lab for DNA tests on the blood found in the car. The results were in, and the news was far more compelling than the revelations about the shower curtain. There was only *a one in 288 trillion* chance that someone *other* than Cari had bled in her SUV.

Cari Farver had been attacked in her car and probably died there. Now they had a crime scene. *Kind of.* The evidence indicated she'd been stabbed in her vehicle, but no one knew the location of the car at the time. The phone pings suggested the attack had occurred in Omaha. But *where* in Omaha? At least one of Liz's emails claimed the murder had happened in a Walmart parking lot, but that seemed too public for a clandestine crime. Maybe the killer had driven to a secluded area. Or maybe it had happened in Liz's garage. For all they knew, the Explorer could have been racing down the highway when Liz attacked, though that scenario was rife with complications.

Investigators had yet to find a body, a witness, or a murder weapon. Detective Schneider realized few prosecutors would be willing to take on such a difficult case. This very peculiar, twisted crime demanded the attention of someone who thrived on challenge and was so passionate about justice they would draw upon every ounce of energy to put a killer behind bars. He knew just such a person. Brenda Beadle. Schneider had worked with her on several cases and watched her convict killers he had captured. She'd successfully prosecuted a number of high-profile Douglas County homicides.

Beadle was intelligent, articulate, and determined. Admittedly skeptical when she heard about the Golyar case, she recalls, "When it was first pitched to me by Detective Schneider, it was hard to believe it was true." Eventually, Schneider convinced her that Shanna Golyar was a diabolical killer.

Brenda Beadle joined forces with fellow prosecutor Jim Masteller. He was known for his honesty, even temperament, and ability to tackle complex cases. Beadle had earned her law degree from Omaha's Creighton University—the same school where Masteller had earned his undergraduate degree, though he achieved his law degree at the University of Chicago. The two had worked together for years at the Douglas County Attorney's Office. "But this was the first time we prosecuted a case together," Brenda reveals. Their styles are different but complement each other. "I think Brenda is very empathetic, but I don't think I'm nearly as much," Masteller admits. Beadle points out that, "He's structured, organized, and methodical."

Brenda Beadle had worked with and trusted Jim Masteller and Dave Schneider, but admits she was apprehensive about the Iowa investigators. Violent crimes were rare in Pott County, and Detective Doty had assisted in just one prior homicide investigation. The Golyar case was Avis's first. Would their lack of experience with homicides be a hindrance? She soon realized that Doty, Avis, and Kava made a phenomenal team. "It was a pleasure to work with them. They would do anything we asked. They were very, very good at what they did."

Even with an extraordinary group of professionals working to get justice for Cari Farver, it wouldn't be an easy case to prosecute. Jim Masteller stresses that in a typical homicide, "Someone hears gunshots, they look outside to see a body on the ground, the police show up, and right off the bat, you know when the crime happened, you know how it happened, and you know where it happened. These are things you take for granted." With the Golyar case, "We didn't know when it happened, we didn't know where it happened, and we didn't know how it happened. One of the things we have to show beyond a reasonable doubt is venue—that the crime occurred in Douglas County, Nebraska," he explains, adding there were also challenges in proving premeditation with no witnesses. "How do you do that when you don't even know how the person died?"

While the pinging of Cari's phone helped establish location, Beadle emphasizes that Cari's last Facebook post is "what we hung our hat on." Investigators strongly suspect that Cari was intercepted at Dave's apartment, shortly after signing onto Facebook. Liz had a key to the apartment, and could have entered when Cari was in the shower. But the team doesn't rule out the possibility that Cari was confronted as she was getting into her car. It's also possible Liz feigned illness and asked Cari for a ride home. Kind hearted Cari would have had no reason to suspect Liz was dangerous, and it was in her nature to help someone in need.

The killer left a digital trail as damning as bloody footprints in the snow. Not only were Liz's cyber activities helpful in tracking her travels, some of it reflected premeditation. Days before Cari vanished, Liz posted a "joke" on Facebook: *My doctor told me to start killing people. Well, not in those exact words. He said I had to reduce stress in my life, which is pretty much the same thing.*

To Ryan Avis, the Golyar case seemed like "a slam dunk." It seemed obvious that Liz had killed Cari. "But I started to lose faith around Beadle and Masteller. They'd say it was going to be tough. I'd say, 'Your doubt is making me doubt that this can be accomplished.' Maybe I went into it naïve. I knew it so well, that I thought there was no way people wouldn't believe it."

If they moved too fast and arrested Golyar before there was enough evidence to convict, she could get off scot-free. She had a constitutional right to a speedy trial, and could be prosecuted only once for Cari's murder. If Liz was found not guilty because of lack of evidence, there would be no do-overs, no matter how compelling evidence found in the future might be. Beadle and Masteller weren't confident they could successfully prosecute. They didn't have enough evidence. *Not yet.*

Homicides without bodies are notoriously difficult to prosecute. But they couldn't wait too long for remains to be recovered. Liz's rage was building. Her regular loops through Amy's parking lot made everyone nervous. Brenda emphasizes, "Amy is lucky she wasn't another victim."

Anthony Kava was working every possible minute to gather more digital evidence to prove that Liz was the stalker and that she had been impersonating Cari for the past four years. Kava's new evidence, together with the blood in the SUV, Cari's possessions found in Liz's apartment, and the confession emails made their case strong enough that the State was finally ready to go forward.

Thursday, December 22, 2016, was the day investigators had been waiting for. "I was at work that morning when I got the call we had an arrest warrant," Kava remembers. "By 11 A.M., Avis and I were in position watching Liz's apartment." Doty, Schneider, and Ambrose arrived with a Harrison County deputy around noon. Six cops to arrest one small woman! The men filed up the narrow stairway to Liz's apartment. When she opened the door, it was obvious they'd woken her. She didn't resist or even appear surprised to hear she was under arrest for first-degree murder. Kava remembers, "Doty put the cuffs on Liz, and he later notched them as a memento."

Liz was in the most serious trouble of her life. She was eligible for a public defender but wanted Omaha's best. She asked JMD to defend her, assuring him she could afford it. "She showed me her tax returns," he says wryly. According to the form, Liz had earned a huge sum of money via her cleaning business and was expecting a hefty refund. It was another of her forgeries and probably never filed. But it convinced JMD that she was good for the money, and he agreed to wait for payment. He laughs now, admitting she stiffed him.

Most of Liz's deceit had played out in cyberspace as she hid behind her computer screen, but she could hide no longer. Inquisitive eyes watched as she took center stage at the Douglas County Courthouse. The Omaha landmark on Farnum Street is a stately beige structure built in 1912 in French Renaissance style. Designed for justice, it has also seen *injustice*, most notably in September 1919 when an innocent man was denied his day in court. Willie Brown, a black man falsely accused of assaulting a white woman, was attacked by vigilantes who stormed the courthouse and abducted him from the fifth-floor jail. The mob also set fire to the building and hung Mayor Edward Parsons Smith from a lamppost when he tried to intervene. The mayor was cut down before he was strangled to death, but poor Willie was murdered by the mob. The old courthouse still bears the scars of the horror, though few who pass through the grand entryways are aware of the bullet holes in the marble walls. The interior of the six-story courthouse is stunningly ornate with enormous murals depicting scenes from the city's past and a central rotunda reaching 110 feet high to a domed stained-glass skylight. But Liz was probably not appreciating the beautiful architecture that day. She listened quietly as the judge set bail at five million dollars.

Murder defendants are rarely allowed bond, and JMD told reporters the judge's decision indicated the State had a weak case.

"How can you charge somebody with first-degree murder when you don't have proof of death, you don't have a body, you don't have murder weapons, and you don't have eye-witnesses?"

The prosecution, too, realized that the judge was sending a message that he had little faith in their case, but they'd known from the get-go it was convoluted and difficult to explain. They didn't blame the judge for failing to comprehend it in the brief time he'd had to consider the confusing facts. It had, after all, taken them a long time to get their minds around it. But they weren't worried about Golyar making bail. She had no wealthy friends lining up to help.

On Wednesday, January 18, 2017, Douglas County Judge Craig McDermott oversaw Shanna Golyar's preliminary hearing, a process that lasted nearly four hours. A brilliant litigator, Masteller expertly presented the State's case. Judge McDermott ruled that Golyar would go to trial on a first-degree murder charge. Her arraignment was eight days later, at 2:30 on a Thursday afternoon, and by then the media had caught on that something big was going down. TV news cameras were rolling in the hallway outside of District Court Judge Timothy P. Burns's fifth-floor courtroom as the defendant appeared, clad in the infamous orange jumpsuit, chains around her waist, wrists, and ankles. She wore glasses, and her long dark hair had been woven into a single braid. Flanked by two female guards, the prisoner glanced at the cameras and quickly looked away. She did not look happy.

Shanna waived her right to a jury trial, choosing instead to allow a judge to decide her fate. Judge Burns tentatively set the trial for May 10, 2017. The defendant was excused and remanded back to the custody of the Sheriff. It was 2:33 P.M. The entire process had taken three minutes.

May 10 was less than four months away! Beadle had hoped for more time to prepare. "On murder cases, it's not uncommon for us to go to trial maybe a year after we file, and maybe longer, but certainly not four months." She understood JMD's strategy. "He didn't want us to find the body or have more evidence come forward. We were going to have to push hard. Thankfully, we were very lucky that Pott County gave us the guys at our beck and call, and they were awesome. They had lived with this case for years, and we were just coming in. We had so much to quickly learn and get up to speed on."

Kava was eager to help. "Corporal Avis and I were approved in March 2017 to be one hundred percent dedicated to trial prep, and he moved into my office. Later, the two of us began working out of the Douglas County Courthouse to prep, a few weeks prior to the trial." The longer the team worked together, the more they respected each other, and, in fact, felt genuine affection for each other. More than one of them notes, "We became like family." Everyone was concerned about one member. Deputy Anthony Kava had a serious health issue. He'd learned about it in August of 2013, when he began to see aurae around lights, and his doctor ordered an MRI. The visual anomaly turned out to be "some transient thing, like an infection" and quickly cleared up, but the scan revealed an unrelated problem—a tumor, "near my brainstem, sheathed around a nerve—a schwannoma."

The fleeting infection had been a lucky thing. Without the MRI, the tumor could have remained hidden until it did real damage. Schwannomas are usually benign and often operable, but the proximity of Kava's tumor to his brainstem made surgery riskier. Doctors monitored the tumor with regular MRIs, and when it began to grow, "I received radiation treatment with the understanding that surgery would likely be the next step." By the spring of 2016, he suffered headaches as the tumor expanded, but he was immersed in the Golyar case, still unraveling her tangled web as he prepared for trial. Kava was to be the State of Nebraska's star witness and was adamant that justice for Cari Farver should take precedence over his health.

When Brenda Beadle learned he was delaying treatment until after the trial, she urged, "You need to get on this." But Kava was steadfast. "I wasn't going to do anything that might jeopardize the case. Certainly, someone could read my report and give testimony about the findings, but I felt I knew the material best." With surgery, "I could expect short-term neurological issues that might affect my memory and ability to concentrate. I did not want to risk losing what was in my head that I intended to turn into testimony," he stresses, adding that if he testified while recovering from brain surgery, a defense attorney could "argue I was not in my right mind."

Beadle asked Detective Schneider to learn what he could about Liz's past, so he traveled to Battle Creek, Michigan, over six hundred miles east of Omaha, for a surprise visit to Liz's adoptive family. The Parsnoll home was outside of town, reachable only by a decidedly creepy, narrow dirt road. The tips of the branches on the rows of trees on either side of the road laced together, creating a leafy tunnel that blocked the sun. The Parsnoll house was nice, but appeared to be in the middle of a remodeling project. He pulled into the driveway where two Cadillacs and an SUV were parked. When he got out of the car, he was confronted by a woman in her late fifties, accompanied by a pretty teenage girl.

"What do you want?" the woman demanded.

"I'm Detective Dave Schneider from the Omaha Homicide Unit."

"We wondered if you'd show up!" said the woman, her tone now friendly. "I'm Nannette Parsnoll." She apologized for greeting him so rudely and explained that the teens she fostered had a bad habit of meeting men on the Internet. "We have these strange men show up here every once in a while, because of these kids!"

They went inside, and before he could start asking questions, Nannette had one for him. After they talked, could he speak to the girls about the dangers of meeting strangers on the Internet? He was a little surprised by the request but agreed.

Liz was so diabolical that everyone working the case had wondered about her background, and they expected the Parsnoll family to have answers. Were there early signs she was disturbed? Had she ever harmed animals, stolen things, or lied?

"All of these kids are liars," Nannette replied, unconcerned about the foster kids within earshot. Schneider glanced at them, wondering if they'd take offense. He read nothing on their faces, and Nannette didn't miss a beat as she explained that all of the foster kids were trouble, all were liars. None of them could be trusted. She had nothing specific to offer about Liz. The whole lot of foster kids seemed lumped together in her mind. While she was very cordial, Detective Schneider got nothing useful from her, and neither did this writer. When I called, Nannette politely explained that she "really appreciated writers," but was going to support her biological daughter, Patsy, in her decision to shed no light on possible warning signs in Liz's childhood. Only three people know anything, she insisted. "Mickey, Patsy, and Nannette."

Confused, I said, "Nannette? I thought you were Nannette."

"Yes, I am," she replied, and I realized she'd been referring to herself in the third person. In her lovely, almost musical voice, Nannette said that the three people with key information about Liz's childhood had vowed to say not one word about it. Mickey had apparently been a foster child who'd grown up with Liz and was privy to the secret details along with Patsy and Nannette. "He's a cancer survivor," Nannette volunteered and warned me not to call him, because he'd likely be rude. It's the Parsnolls' right, of course, to keep their secrets to themselves, though their refusal to speak does make me wonder if they're hiding something. But Nannette seemed sincere in her interaction with Detective Schneider. It's possible that the Parsnolls never noticed alarming behavior in Liz and that they're simply very private people.

Before he left, Detective Schneider granted Nannette's request to lecture her foster daughters on the dangers of meeting people on the Internet. The teens listened and nodded, but somehow, he didn't get the feeling his warning made an impact. It was a little ironic, considering that he'd traveled there to get information on the *very* dangerous person whose meeting of Dave Kroupa on the Internet had resulted in murder. Whether or not Nannette Parsnoll noted that irony, she did not say.

The Parsnoll family seemed to be decent folks, though some members had a different perspective on the world than Schneider did. When he visited the home of Liz's adopted sister, Marcy, he was greeted by her husband, who sidled up to him, dropped his voice in a conspiratorial tone and confided, "I'm armed too. I just want you to know, I'm progun, too."

While his job requires him to carry a gun, the detective is adamant that it's not a political statement, emphasizing, "I'm probably the least pro-gun cop you could meet."

As the trial drew near, Schneider, Doty, and Avis continued to interview those close to Liz, while Kava's time was consumed with deciphering Liz's electronic trail. He stopped in to see Kroupa at Hyatt Tire on February 1 and asked about electronic devices they might have missed.

"I think there's a tablet in storage," said Kroupa. He'd rented a storage unit during his last move, and it was filled with boxes of stuff he hadn't gotten around to sorting.

"Could you see if you can find it when you get a chance?"

Kroupa said he'd look for it, but Kava didn't expect much. He had no idea how important that forgotten tablet would turn out to be. Dave soon located it, and handed it over to Kava, who discovered it contained an SD card with multiple images erased. He retrieved the deleted photos, his pulse quickening as he realized he recognized many from an earlier search of Liz's phone. The SD card from the tablet had at one time been inserted in Liz's cell phone!

Liz had apparently deleted the photos from her phone and then re-cycled the SD card, plugging it into Dave's tablet. Kava found himself staring at images Liz believed were gone forever. There were photos of her kids and lots of selfies, some in the nude. As he scrolled through the photos, he paused as he saw something strange. It appeared to be a close up of a tattoo, and as he studied it, he noticed veins around it. He couldn't be certain, but it looked like the tattoo was on a foot.

When detectives asked Nancy if she had a photo that showed Cari's bare feet, she didn't ask why. She supplied the picture, and it was soon confirmed that Cari's tattoo matched the one in the photo. *Had Liz taken a photo of Cari's foot?* If so, it was proof she'd been near the missing woman, near enough to snap a closeup photo. But there was something very disturbing about that photograph. The detectives sought the opinion of another expert, and the news she gave them was extremely helpful to their case. It was also horrifying.

Chapter Thirty-one

WHILE CARI'S LOVED ONES, the investigators, and the prosecution team all felt certain that the vibrant woman no longer walked the earth, there would be no justice for her unless it could be proven she was deceased. Murders without bodies are notoriously difficult to prosecute, but many "no-body" trials do result in convictions. When Charles Manson was convicted of the 1969 murder of Donald Jerome "Shorty" Shea at a Chatsworth, California, ranch, the victim's body had yet to be found—a point the killer emphasized when he appealed his conviction in June 1977. A judge in the higher court denied Manson's appeal, stressing, "The fact that a murderer may successfully dispose of the body of the victim does not entitle him to an acquittal. That is one form of success for which society has no reward."

Six months later, in December 1977, Shea's remains were recovered when Manson's incarcerated accomplice, Steve Grogan, drew a map for authorities. Unfortunately, many victims are never found. The judge who made the Manson ruling had an excellent point. Why should killers enjoy victory for successfully concealing their victims' remains? But there is a flipside to the argument. About a hundred miles southwest of Omaha, in 1887, William Marion was executed for the murder of his best friend, John Cameron. The two had left Beatrice, Nebraska, together to look for work on the railroad, but when William came back alone wearing his friend's boots, authorities concluded he had killed John. A crowd gathered to watch as William was marched up to the platform and a rope was looped around his neck.

He swore he was innocent, but everyone assumed he was lying. About a year after his execution, John ambled back into town, looking for his pal.

One hundred thirty years later, as Douglas County prosecutors prepared to go to trial, they were quite certain Cari Farver would not come strolling back into town as John Cameron had. The trick, however, was *proving* that. Anthony Kava's latest discovery had just made their jobs a whole lot easier. He'd been right about the disturbing image he'd found on the memory card. Forensic pathologist Dr. Michelle Elieff studied the photograph and concluded it depicted a tattoo on a foot—a foot that was in a state of decay.

The killer had snapped the photo, Brenda Beadle realized, as a gruesome souvenir of her sadistic crime. Cari's remains might never be located, but the photo of her lifeless foot with the unique tattoo proved she was no longer alive.

Cari had four tattoos, including a large sun between her shoulder blades and the yin yang symbol on her hip that investigators had learned about when Liz wrote the confession in Amy's name. As it turned out, Liz had also photographed Cari's hip tattoo. Anthony found that photo while extracting deleted images on the memory card from Dave's tablet. The foot tattoo was special to Cari, and she had told her mother that the inking process had been very painful. (Some tattoo artists refuse to work on feet because the procedure is excruciating for clients and risk of infection is high.) But Cari had withstood the agony and proudly sported the Chinese symbol for mother.

Mother. It was a role she loved, and, of course, she loved her own mother. How perfectly fitting that this symbol of the thing most sacred to her would be the single most powerful piece of evidence to emerge. Cari's family and friends were so lost without her. Her mother and son, especially, needed justice before they could move forward with their lives. Cari had gotten the tattoo to honor them, but as she endured the hours of pain at the tattoo parlor, she had no idea that the new symbol she wore would one day bring them peace.

Liz, too, had tattoos, and the inked message on her left bicep was ironic, considering her evil deeds: "True Beauty lies within the heart." She had fooled many people into believing her heart was pure. Well aware now that the killer's heart was anything but pure, some wondered if a conviction would result in the death penalty. Each state has its own death penalty laws, and Nebraska is one of thirty states that currently allow it.

Nebraska executes by lethal injection, but in the early part of the twentieth century, the Cornhusker State had preferred to dispatch its killers via hanging. After 1920, convicted murderers sizzled in the electric chair. One of Nebraska's most infamous killers, Charles Starkweather, who took the lives of eleven people, was electrocuted in Lincoln, Nebraska, in 1959. His fourteen-year-old girlfriend, Carol Ann Fugate, was considered his accomplice and also convicted of first-degree murder, though she was spared execution. Carol served seventeen years in the Nebraska Correctional Center for Women in York, Nebraska, and was paroled in 1976.

The death penalty was abolished in Nebraska by legislators in 2015 but reinstated a year later by voters, just in time for Liz Golyar. But fair or not, juries have a tough time stomaching the idea of executing females. While four people have been executed in Nebraska since 1976, *none* were female. The numbers are conservative, compared to Texas with 474 executions since 1976, including six females. According to Jim Masteller, Liz Golyar was never a candidate for execution. "In our state, in order to obtain the death penalty, you have to have at least one aggravating factor," he explains, stressing that it's usually not even considered without several aggravating factors. Nebraska's Statute 29-2523 lists nine aggravating circumstances that allow prosecutors to seek death, including previous murder convictions, offenders who knowingly create a great risk of death to multiple people, the murder of law enforcement officers, and murder for hire. Liz didn't fit the criteria, and the most her detractors could hope for her was life behind bars.

The prosecution had a huge responsibility. They knew Liz was dangerous, that she'd killed Cari Farver, and that she'd most likely kill again if allowed to go free. Beadle and Masteller had each successfully prosecuted multiple murderers and excelled at their jobs. This case, however, presented more challenges than most. For one thing, there was so much evidence it was almost impossible to keep it straight. Liz had sent *20,000* texts and emails while impersonating Cari. For the first time, the prosecutors asked a judge to allow a detective to sit with them at trial. Nebraska law allows it, but it's extremely rare for Douglas County prosecutors to make the request.

When the trial began on the morning of Wednesday, May 10, 2017, Detective Ryan Avis was seated at the prosecution table with Jim Masteller and Brenda Beadle. Avis knew the details of the very complicated case by heart. "He had his laptop in front of him, with the entire case file on it," Masteller says, adding that whenever they needed a particular photo or other info, Avis located it instantly.

Shanna Elizabeth Golyar not only faced a first-degree murder charge, another count had been added—second-degree arson for the fire at her rental home. Cari's loved ones packed Judge Burns's courtroom on the fifth floor of the Douglas County Courthouse. Cari's friends Amber Jones and Holly Drummond were among those attending. Holly had met Cari when they worked together years earlier in Council Bluffs at Claire's, a chain retail store, specializing in costume jewelry and accessories. The loss of her friend cut deeply. "Cari was a great friend," she says, stressing, "always nonjudgmental." Holly felt sick as she stared at the back of the defendant's head. "She never once turned around to look at us."

She had interacted with the defendant online when Liz was impersonating Cari, and Holly had demanded that she tell her how they met. It was a test. "Few people knew we'd met at Claire's," she explains. Holly knew the messenger was definitely an impostor when she responded, "I'm not going to play games." Holly felt a chill as she sat in the courtroom and realized she was breathing the same air as the twisted woman who had ended her dear friend's life.

The Golyar trial was huge news in Omaha, a case so bizarre it had caught the attention of media from around the world. Reporters from local news outlets vied for space with NBC's *Dateline* crew, who set their cameras up in the vacant jury box.

Nancy had vowed to be there for every moment, no matter how painful.

But Nancy was a witness, and except in rare cases, witnesses are barred from the courtroom until after they've testified. Nancy spent the first day of the trial sitting on the hard wooden bench in the corridor.

She'd known before she arrived that day that she wouldn't be allowed in but felt she owed it to her daughter to be nearby. The prosecution scheduled her testimony for as early as possible, so she wouldn't miss much. It wouldn't be easy to listen to some of the witnesses, and Nancy was grateful to Brenda Beadle for her sensitivity. "Brenda was very good at warning me when something bad was coming up."

JMD's assistant, Cheyann Parr, sat between him and Shanna at the defense table. In her twenties and a mother of a toddler, Cheyann was extremely pretty and appeared much younger than she was. When the photograph of the trio at the defense table appeared in the newspaper, Cheyann heard through the grapevine that some who'd seen it assumed *she* was the defendant and had commented that she looked too sweet and innocent to be a killer. Either the caption had misidentified her, or people hadn't noticed the frumpy woman beside her. Shanna wore street clothes, appearing the first day of trial in a red shirt, black skirt, black jacket, and white tennis shoes. Her frizzy hair was partially pulled away from her pale face. Glasses completed her schoolmarm look.

Both Garret and Dave would later comment that Liz had gotten fat. The weight gain was likely due to lack of activity and too many calories consumed. Jailexchange.com, a website providing comprehensive information on detention facilities, reports that the Douglas County Jail meals fed to inmates total 2,500 calories daily, far more than the recommended caloric intake for a woman of Liz's height. If she cleaned her plate, she could easily have put on twenty-five to thirty pounds in the nearly five months she'd been incarcerated. Liz had once delighted in denigrating "fat asses," and now, she received the cold kiss of karma as she grew into what she despised.

Judges typically warn spectators to behave, especially in cases that attract so many curiosity seekers, and before the trial began, Judge Burns advised the gallery, "You cannot just get up and go when the case is proceeding or we're in trial. You're here until we get a break, then you can leave and come back before we start again. But if you don't get back in time, you will not be allowed back in the courtroom. I expect everybody to sit quietly and listen, no reactions. And if you do have reactions, it may require me to remove people from the courtroom . . ."

It was not the first time the prosecution and defense had faced off in an Omaha courtroom to argue a peculiar case involving a love tri-

angle. In 2010, 19-year-old Ryan Carson killed his father, Brian
Carson, when he learned he'd slept with his girlfriend. Investigators
suspected that Ryan's mother, Teresa Carson, conspired with him to
murder Brian, Teresa's ex-husband.

Teresa was JMD's client, and he'd made a valiant effort to defend
her. He insisted she'd been a battered wife—a victim with no
knowledge of Ryan's plan. But Beadle had statements from witnesses who'd overheard Teresa, prior to the murder, discussing a
life-insurance payout for Brian's death.

Teresa was convicted and sentenced to 18 to 20 years for helping to
cover up the homicide.

While JMD lost that case, his winning streaks have broken records.
Juries, especially, are charmed by the sense of humor and abundant
charisma of the seasoned attorney with the shock of thick, white hair.
But JMD's magnetic personality could do little to distract jurors from
his client's unbelievably cruel deeds. She was not on trial for tormenting Cari's mother, killing her pets, or cheating on her boyfriends—de-
spicable acts that JMD knew would infuriate ordinary people if her
fate was left in their hands. While judges are trained to separate
emotion from the law, a jury of her peers "would have jumped out of
the jury box and strangled her," he states. He had wisely advised her
to choose a bench trial.

JMD did not have a monopoly on charm. Both Brenda Beadle and
Jim Masteller were likeable and attractive people. Masteller was
more reserved than Beadle, and his well-trimmed beard and mous-
tache gave him a distinguished air. Brenda, with high cheekbones
a model would envy, was a striking blonde and looked smart in a
black blazer and skirt as she began her opening statement. "This is a
bizarre and twisted case of a fatal attraction. It's about an obsessive
woman that would stop at nothing to get what she wanted, and in
this case, what she wanted was a man, and it wasn't just any man, it
was Dave Kroupa."

That was Liz's motive, plainly stated by Beadle in her opening
line. The prosecution was not *required* to prove motive in order to
convict Liz of murder, but it always made a case stronger when they
did. They also didn't have to know or prove exactly how Cari had
died, though the blood found in the car and the references to stab-
bings in the impostor emails indicated the weapon was a knife. That

knife was never found, and while it would have been helpful to have the weapon, it was not a prerequisite for a conviction. Witnesses were waiting to testify about Liz's maniacal infatuation with Dave *and* about the things that absolutely had to be proven, such as premeditation and venue.

Beadle promised they would spend the next days "delving into the warped and diabolical actions and behaviors of the defendant. We will attempt to unravel the web of deceit the defendant has spun." She introduced the cast of characters and outlined the sequence of events that culminated with Cari Farver's disappearance. She touched on evidence they would present—including the blood found in Cari's car, the fingerprint on the mint container, and the fact that Liz had referenced a tattoo of Cari's she could not have legitimately known about. She described Liz's efforts to make it appear Cari was alive, and her endless harassment of innocent people. The story was so complex, it took over an hour to lay out the basics. Brenda Beadle did an excellent job, simplifying a long and complicated story.

JMD was equally prepared. He wasted no time conceding that Liz would not win any citizen-of-the year awards but stressed that didn't mean she'd committed murder. "Judge," he began. "We've just heard an hour-and-a-half opening that can be probably titled, 'Death by supposition and homicide by innuendo.'" The questions prosecutors could not definitively answer were endless, and JMD painstakingly listed them. "Was there a death? Where is the body of Cari Farver? What's the cause of death? Was it a homicide? Where did the homicide take place? What's the venue for these charges?"

If Cari was no longer alive, that didn't mean his client had killed her, and JMD reminded the court that it was the State's responsibility to prove it was Liz's fault. "But even if there was a death, they have to prove that death was caused by an unlawful violent or negligent act. What does that mean? An unlawful violent act: That my client killed her either intentionally or during the commission of some other unlawful act. And they have to prove that those acts took place in Nebraska."

Liz probably felt hopeful when she heard how confident he sounded, but it was hard to guess what she was thinking. Her reactions were minimal throughout the trial, but Cheyann remembers that on breaks Liz would often ask, "How do you think it's going?" Cheyann tried not to discourage her, even when she felt things weren't going so well for the defendant. While she was not exactly a fan of Liz's, she made a point to be professional in her interactions with her. Cheyann knew her boss did everything in his power to defend his clients, and as his assistant, she did what she could to help him.

She remembers that Liz had few people left who had faith in her. While the State had thirty-two witnesses, the defense had none. Liz's new boyfriend, Joshua Stemmer, believed fervently in her innocence, and if it would have done her any good, he would have taken the stand to testify, but there was nothing he could say to help her. Back in 2012 when Cari vanished, Joshua had been just a teen and hadn't even met Liz yet. Now, at 22, he was devoted to her. He'd dutifully shopped for her trial clothing and delivered outfits and shoes to JMD's office. He visited her often in jail and accepted her collect calls. Inmates' personal calls are recorded, and when investigators listened to the conversations between Liz and Joshua, they noted that she was definitely the boss in the relationship, often speaking harshly to the young man as she gave him orders.

Detectives Doty and Avis were familiar with the Stemmer family. As far as they knew, Josh had never been in trouble, but some of his relatives had a reputation for drinking too much, and it was not uncommon for neighbors to call police to complain about rowdy behavior. The family lived in a small Pott County town on the Nishnabotna River, about thirty miles from Council Bluffs, and both Doty and Avis had been dispatched to Stemmer's home on more than one occasion. Joshua's father, Henry, had a record for offenses that included assault and drunk driving and had spent time in jail, but he and his wife were nevertheless alarmed to discover their son was involved with an accused murderess nearly twice his age.

Liz had fooled Josh, just as she had fooled many of the State's witnesses. Spectators noticed that some of the professionals Liz had duped seemed uncomfortable during their testimony. Tricked by a killer, they were embarrassed, and at least one of these men sweated profusely, face flushed as he answered questions that made it clear a deadly woman had pulled the wool over his eyes. More than one cop had ignored Nancy Raney's concerns and now realized they'd made a mistake.

One by one, witnesses took the stand, and the shocking scenario took shape. Witnesses included firefighters, arson investigators, crime scene investigators, detectives, and Cari's coworkers. Detectives Jim Doty, Ryan Avis, and Dave Schneider gave detailed testimony about the investigation, answering questions about everything from the shower curtain purchase to the download of Liz's phone. As a professional and an integral part of the case, Avis was allowed to remain in the courtroom for the entire trial, despite the fact he was a witness.

Both Cari's mother and son testified about their last days with her, their anguish when she vanished, and the years of torture they endured as the killer taunted them. Nearly everyone listening cried or wanted to cry. But Liz sat, quietly listening, without a flicker of emotion registering on her pale face.

CHAPTER THIRTY-TWO

FOR EVERY BIT OF EVIDENCE the State presented, Shanna's attorney had an argument. Cari Farver had not been seen since the November morning in 2012 when Dave left her in his apartment to go to work. No one had heard her voice in over four years. Multiple witnesses verified this, including Cari's friends and family and her coworkers at West Corp. JMD had no witnesses to contradict them, so he focused on the fact no remains had been found and referred to it often. He dismissed the blood in the SUV, stressing that there wasn't enough to indicate exsanguination—the immense bloodshed that results in death. He mentioned the lack of blood spatter evidence and the fact that only two things were known about the blood. "Number one, it was Cari Farver's blood, and it was on the passenger side seat in her car. That's all we know. We don't know when it was shed, how it was shed, or if anybody else was involved in it being shed."

While blood can be tested to determine whether or not it's the result of menstruation, JMD knew that had not been done in this case, and he suggested the stain was a result of Cari's monthly cycle. Beadle nipped that in the bud when Nancy took the stand, first determining that the car had not been in Cari's possession before August 2012. "It wouldn't have been menstrual blood," Nancy testified. "She had a hysterectomy in March of 2012."

As for the fact Shanna knew about the yin-yang tattoo, something she revealed while concocting the Amy confessions, JMD scoffed at the notion his client couldn't have learned about that tattoo from somewhere other than an encounter with Cari. Perhaps David Kroupa had mentioned it to her, he ventured. A prosecution witness expressed serious doubt about that. Why would Dave mention the tattoo on the missing woman's thigh to his very jealous girlfriend?

JMD also shrugged off the fingerprint evidence. So what if Liz's print was found on the mint container? "There is no indication that my client is the one that put the mint container in the car." The mints happened to be a brand Cari favored, and the same brand and flavor had been found in a drawer at her house, documented by Deputy Phyllips's camera when he'd searched her home in April 2013. Investigators believed that the mints had been in Cari's vehicle and that Liz had thoroughly cleaned the car after her vicious crime. She'd likely picked up the container to scrub the console, and then set it back down when she was done, not realizing she'd left a perfect, crisp fingerprint for detectives to find.

JMD emphasized that his client's prints were not found on the car itself. Not "on the dash, on the steering wheel, on the windows, or on the doors." He was not impressed by a print on a small, easy to carry tin that Liz might have handled in Dave's apartment before he picked it up and left it in Cari's car. JMD stressed that significance should be placed on "the *absence* of all the other fingerprints that would have been there, should have been there, could have been there if my client was in there and committed a homicide there."

That argument would have been much stronger if the car had not been wiped clean. Nobody's fingerprints had been found on the vehicle itself, not even Cari's.

Other evidence presented by the State included the photo from the January 2013 kidnapping hoax. Dave had not been certain that the bound woman in the trunk was Liz because her face was turned away in the image sent to him. But Liz had taken several photos before she selected that one and was recognizable in the rejected images Kava had recovered. When investigators found those practice photos, they realized Liz had placed duct tape over her own mouth, crawled into the trunk of a car, looped rope around her wrists, and posed as a damsel in distress. She'd apparently set the camera's timer to give herself time to pose.

JMD didn't dispute it was a bizarre game. But it didn't prove his client was guilty of murder, and he stressed that Liz was not on trial for stalking or for the burglary of Cari's home. The State could choose to charge her with burglary later, he noted, emphasizing that it had nothing to do with the murder charge. He was adamant that the so-called confessions Liz had written to frame Amy were nothing more than fantasies, He also brought up the size difference between Liz and Cari. Liz was 5'3" and 110 pounds, while Cari had been 5'7" and 145 pounds. How could Liz have overpowered the larger woman? And how could such a petite lady dispose of a body all by herself? It was actually not that difficult to imagine, but JMD was casting shadows of doubt wherever he could. No one could say he did not give his best effort. He was on his toes, quick to object to hearsay testimony and the occasional leading question by the State.

Liz could have made her attorney's job easier and spared herself grief if she hadn't lied to him about insignificant things. It was clear that she had misled her own attorney on the third morning of the trial, shortly after Garret took the stand. Brenda Beadle asked about his relationship with the defendant, and he explained they'd met in September 2010, been together for five years, and that he'd believed the relationship was exclusive. Beadle questioned him about his awareness of the alleged harassment of Liz. Had she told him about the vandalism in the garage? Did he know Liz had made a police report about that? Did Liz tell him that a stalker had photographed her daughter through her window? Had she mentioned threatening emails?

The answer to each question was "No." Liz had told him nothing about being terrorized. The prosecutor asked about texts exchanged with someone claiming to be Cari. "After you get a text from this Cari, do you then go back and tell the defendant, who is your girlfriend at the time, about these texts from Cari?"

"I'd mentioned it to her, yeah."

"What did she say to you?"

"Essentially she corroborated what Cari was telling me—that they were friends."

"And Liz told you that?"

"Yes."

When it was JMD's turn to question Garret, he was at an awkward disadvantage. Liz had told him that their romance was a figment of Garret's imagination. "Good afternoon, Mr. Sloan. Now you indicated that you thought Shanna was your girlfriend. True?"

"Yes."

"But during the entire time she lived with you, you had sex with her, what, maybe three times?"

"During the entire time?"

"The time she lived at your house."

"No, it was more than three times."

"Not many, though, right?"

"It wasn't often, no."

"Once in your apartment and then maybe once or twice a year while she lived with you?"

"No, it was more than that."

"You can't tell us any specific numbers?"

"No, I didn't keep a tally of it."

"Well, before she moved in, you said she never stayed over at your house or apartment, right?"

JMD had planned his strategy based on Shanna's lie that Garret had only imagined their romance. If indeed Garret had been delusional, he could have discredited him and everything he said. Why Shanna didn't want her attorney to know she'd had an ongoing sexual relationship with Garret was anybody's guess.

Her lie backfired, and she slid a sheet of paper to Cheyann with a note on it. "It said maybe she *had* had sex with him more than a couple of times," Cheyann remembers. Shanna might have had the best defense attorney in Omaha working for her, but she wasn't helping herself by misleading him. JMD was unable to discredit Garret. If anything, the questions he asked Garret made it appear that Shanna had lied to her own attorney—and of course, she *had!*

Garret's testimony included a tidbit prosecutors knew would inspire a disturbing image. Investigators believed that Cari's remains had been burned, and not only had they found photographs of burned tarps concealing something the size of a body among Liz's deleted images, they had noted a consistency in the confession emails Liz had written to frame Amy. She had made multiple references to burning her victim.

Beadle asked Garret about something he'd mentioned during the January 2013 interview with detectives—the same meeting when they'd revealed Liz had labled his photo "fat ass." "Do you some-how mention to them in the course of the interview something about a fire at the defendant's house?"

Garret acknowledged he'd told detectives he'd smelled a burning odor at Liz's house.

"And that's obviously prior to the arson that happened in August at her house, correct?"

"Yes." Unfortunately, he couldn't recall the date he'd noticed the odor. He remembered only that it had been during the fall or winter of 2012. Cari had vanished in mid November, within the time frame Garret had indicated.

Investigators had varying opinions about the burning. Some believed her remains were only partially burned and then thrown in the garbage, while others suspected she'd been cremeated in a burn barrel in Liz's backyard. It was a horrific thing for those who loved Cari to contemplate, but it was a grim reality that had to be addressed. The subject came up again during Battalion Chief Michael Shane McClanahan's testimony. Jim Masteller asked him about a burn barrel discovered in Liz's backyard after the August 2013 fire. It was visible in a photograph admitted into evidence as Exhibit 194. "It's a black metal barrel, approximately fifty-five-gallon drum," Chief McClanahan acknowledged. But no one had searched the barrel for human remains. By the time Liz became a suspect in Cari's disappearance, almost two years had passed since the fire, and the barrel was long gone by then.

Detective Schneider thinks it's unlikely that Liz would have been bold enough to burn a body in her backyard. While her yard was so overgrown that neighbors couldn't peek over the fence, there was nothing to stop a neighbor from ambling over to see what she was up to. Detectives Doty and Avis, however, lean toward that possibility. No one but Liz knows for sure.

Jessica McCarthy testified after Garret, and she gave details about the week of terror she'd endured when she'd friended Dave on Facebook. It was difficult for spectators not to gasp when she read aloud the threat, "I will cut your kids' throats, and yours, while you sleep."

Liz, however, appeared unmoved. Cheyann noticed that Liz showed emotion only twice during the trial. Her eyes lit up when a slide of the Freaker's Ball was shown. Liz and Dave appeared on the screen,

a cozy couple in matching togas. Liz stared at the image, mesmerized, as Beadle emphasized that the night had been special to the defendant. It followed the 30-day commitment she'd forced upon
Dave, and she'd pinned all of her dreams on what she hoped would
be a magical evening.

Obviously moved by the photo, Liz perked up even more when
Dave himself appeared. She was clearly still infatuated and gazed at
him longingly as he was sworn in. He was extremely uncomfortable.
It had taken him a long time to accept the truth. The woman he'd
feared and despised for years was actually the *victim*. The woman
he'd felt obligated to protect was the real monster. When he realized
an innocent person had died because of Liz's obsession with him,
the guilt ate at him. He was forced to glance at Liz to identify her for
the record. She'd been staring but quickly looked away.

When Beadle asked about his dating situation in early 2012, he
said, "I was not in a committed relationship of any type. I was seeing multiple women."

"Is that kind of how you rolled then?"

"Correct."

He described their relationship as, "Casual, on and off. We would
be hard and heavy for a month or two, and then I would back way
off. And generally, we would break up for a little while, and pretty
soon we'd be back together again for a little while."

"During the time you were on with her, were you seeing other
women as well?"

"Correct."

A picture of their tumultuous relationship emerged as Dave answered questions about the breakups and makeups, and his desire
for freedom as Liz pressured him to commit. He was handed emails
Liz had sent and asked to read them aloud. Some she'd sent as herself, but in others she impersonated Cari, and the wording was
crude. Conscious of Cari's mother watching him, he tried to censor
the foul language, but Beadle explained he had to read the letters as
is. He cringed inwardly and forged ahead.

On cross exam, JMD said, "I think you indicated that you met
Shanna Golyar in 2012?"

"Correct."

"And that was on Plenty of Fish?"

"Correct."

"And although you saw Cari Farver at Hyatt, you also saw her on Plenty of Fish, right?"

"Correct."

"That's where you did your fishing, right?"

"There you go."

"You didn't know there were sharks in the water, though, did you?"

"Apparently not."

JMD brought up Dave's texts with other women. "There were texts going back and forth with Sue, right?"

"Yep."

And Pam, right?"

"Yep."

"Joanne, right?"

"Yep."

"Kelly, right?"

"Yep."

JMD went on, naming multiple women Dave had known, and then went through the names again, asking if they'd had threats made against them. This group of women had not been threatened. With that shrewd line of questioning, Liz's attorney demonstrated that she had known about many other women, and nothing had happened to them.

He asked Dave if he'd ever been afraid of Liz, and he said no.

As uncomfortable as it was for Dave to testify, it was worse for Amy Flora. "It was the scariest thing I ever had to do," she confides. "I was having panic attacks. Brenda told me, 'Don't look at Liz. Look at us. The only time you have to look at her is when you're asked to point her out.'"

Amy's testimony came about halfway through the ten-day trial, on the morning of Tuesday, May 16. She fixed her eyes on Jim Masteller as he asked about her Internet server, her email address, and her cell phone number. She answered easily, but his next question stumped her.

"Now," said Masteller. "You said you have Internet access at your residence. Do you ever use VPNs?"

"I don't know what that is," she replied.

"Have you ever used a Surf-Easy VPN?"

"I have no idea what that is."

"How about Hotspot Shield VPN?"

"No."

Amy didn't know what a Virtual Private Network was because she had no reason to hide her location. *Liz* had sometimes used VPNs when impersonating her. It was clear that Amy had not sent the confession emails. She hadn't even *heard* of some of the technology Liz had used to conceal her crimes.

Amy dreaded reading aloud the confessions Liz had written in her name. She was worried Cari's family would believe the letters—that they would think *she* had harmed Cari. Even if they knew she was innocent, Amy didn't want Cari's family to have to picture the things described by the killer. *Not ever.* And yet, there they sat, in the front row of the gallery, waiting for Amy to read words that would hurt them.

Everyone in the courtroom seemed to be holding their breath. It was so, so quiet, and when Amy began to read, she hated how her voice cut through the silence. She wanted it to be over, and without realizing she was speaking too quickly, she read, "My last email got deleted, just so you know it's me—"

"Whoa! Whoa!" JMD interrupted.

"Sorry," Masteller apologized to Amy. "The court reporter is going to have to type everything you say, so you're going to have to go really slow."

It was bad enough that she had to speak such horrible words! Now she had to read slowly! "I did meet up with Cari at a local place here in Council Bluffs. I have a family that won't let me go to jail. So, when I met Crazy Cari, she would not stop talking about Dave and him being her husband."

"Let me stop you right there," Masteller interrupted. "Is it hard to read this email?"

His question was about the misspellings, not about Amy's state of mind. She knew what he meant and replied, "Yes, the spelling is terrible."

"Yes, please continue."

"She tried to attack me, but I attacked her with a knife. I stabbed her three to four times in the stomach area. I then took her out and burned her. I stuffed her body in a garbage can with crap. She was carried out to the dumpster, probably when Dave took my garbage out for me. So be glad I did not do you that way, Liz. I will never admit to Dave or police, no one. Maybe I'm drunk now and just telling lies to you. Dave will always take care of me and protect me, so I will never go to jail . . ."

While Cari's family and friends understood that Amy had not written the emails, they realized that much of what Liz had written had actually happened. One line in particular would forever haunt them. "When I killed Cari, you know she begged me to call Dave at work, and she begged me to talk to her family before she died." As Amy read, she heard Cari's mother cry, and it broke her heart.

Though Judge Burns had warned spectators they could be ordered to leave if they showed a reaction, he did not reprimand the grieving mother. Her pain was raw and real, and she obviously had no control over her anguished sobs. If a jury had been present, he would have been forced to consider the effect Nancy's reaction could have on them. Emotional outbursts from the gallery can influence a jury, sometimes causing mistrials. But Burns was a professional and would not let emotion influence his ruling.

CHAPTER THIRTY-THREE

ANTHONY KAVA, the State of Nebraska's star witness, took the stand in mid morning on Thursday, May 18. No one else had his grasp on the complex digital evidence tracing Golyar's covert activities. It was not only difficult to comprehend, it was difficult to *explain*, because IT terminology can almost sound like a foreign language to laymen. But Kava was not only brilliant, he had superior communication skills. He'd prepared a PowerPoint presentation with thousands of slides to illustrate his testimony. A rudimentary understanding of the cyberworld and vocabulary associated with it was necessary for the evidence to make sense. Everyone in the courtroom got a crash course in digital forensics.

Over his next three days of testimony, Kava painted a vivid picture of Liz's crimes, describing everything from the fake emails she created in Cari's name to how she used proxy servers to hide her location. He explained how he revived the deleted evidence from Liz's cell phone, and he showed the images she thought she'd destroyed.

Perhaps most telling was the activity on Cari's Facebook account on the morning she disappeared. Kava determined that someone had logged onto Cari's page from Dave's apartment at 6:42 A.M. That would have been a legitimate log-in by Cari. The next Facebook log-in was at 9:54 A.M., and Dave Kroupa was unfriended. *That*, investigators maintained, was Liz invading Cari's Facebook page, probably after she'd attacked her. The pings from Cari's phone, the unauthorized use of her debit card at Walmart, and the curious Facebook activity had all occurred in Omaha. That evidence was crucial to establishing venue.

Liz had used Cari's phone the first time she'd logged onto Cari's Facebook page. Cari's computer was never recovered. Cari had a very long password she'd guarded jealously, and Liz had probably discarded the laptop when she realized she couldn't crack her code. Kava traced Liz's steps in her creation of the Sam Carter and Amber Mildo fake Facebook profiles she'd used in her attempt to lure Cari into her trap—a clear indication of premeditation.

Sam Carter was a made-up name, but the photo was real. It belonged to a doctor who lived on the East Coast. He had no idea a killer had borrowed his handsome face to use in her twisted games. As for Amber Mildo, Liz had created her years earlier and had used her many times in online deceptions. Kava's investigation revealed that around the time Cari vanished, Miss Mildo had tried to friend 15-year-old Max on Facebook but had accidentally sent the request to the wrong Max Farver.

While Kava's testimony was the most comprehensive, the most shocking revelations came from the State's last witness. On May 22, Omaha forensic pathologist Dr. Michelle Elieff testified she had performed over 2,500 autopsies and had seen bodies in every stage of decomposition.

The startling photo Kava had found appeared on the screen, and Eileff was invited to step down to point out the features consistent with a foot. "This is the top part, or what we refer to as the 'dorsum' of a human foot, and it includes several blood vessels—the greater saphenous vein, an arch, and the lesser saphenous vein; and digital and branch vessels that come out to the toes and the distal, or farthest away from the body, toe area of the top of the foot."

The photo had been taken when decomposition was underway, and few people could have glanced at it and understood what they were looking at. Masteller asked, "Now, in your experience of bodies that you've examined postmortem, in which the bodies had tattoos on them, when the skin sloughs off of a portion of the body that actually contains a tattoo, does the tattoo itself slough off?"

"It does not."

"Why is that?"

"The tattoos go into the deeper layers of skin, and it's the superficial or top layers of skin that get sloughed off and may get very discolored. Sometimes when the body is undergoing skin slippage or blistering of the skin on top of a tattoo, that area can be wiped off, and the tattoo can be clearly visualized."

JMD requested a voir dire examination and established that it was Dr. Elieff's *opinion* that the tattooed foot in the photo belonged to a deceased human. The doctor could not say with absolute certainty that the image in the photo was a foot, Liz's attorney stressed. "I object to any opinion." He was overruled.

Liz Golyar had photographed her victim's body, according to prosecutors, so that she could have a "trophy" of her vicious crime. When she deleted that photo, she had no idea it would come back to haunt her.

Closing statements began a little after 9:30 on Tuesday morning, May 23, and Jim Masteller brought up Liz's sick souvenirs. The tattoo photos weren't the only keepsakes important to her. There was also the shower curtain she'd purchased with Cari's debit card. It, too, was a trophy. Investigators had found nude selfies of Liz, posing in front of it. She had taken it with her each time she moved. First to Garret's home and then to Persia. The prosecutor pointed out, "They're not particularly expensive. They get dirty, of course. Why wouldn't you just leave it?"

It's hard to imagine the kind of dark thoughts that emerge from a killer's mind, but Masteller may have had a perfect grasp on it as he explained what the shower curtain meant to Liz. "This is something she's proud of, something she's able to look at every single morning and think about how she killed Cari Farver and got away with it. It's hiding in plain sight."

In his closing statement, JMD started by congratulating the prosecution for doing an impressive job but then pointed out that their case was built on circumstantial evidence. He referenced email exchanges between Dave and his client where she seemed to calmly accept that they were "going to take a break" from their relationship. She certainly hadn't behaved as if she were planning a murder. "Dave Kroupa's a nice guy, but who can say he's worth killing for? And that's what they're saying."

JMD reminded the court that the case was not about stolen property and not about his client's bizarre behavior. He again listed the many things the State could *not* prove. "There's a hundred unanswered questions," he stressed. After touching on the evidence the State had presented and explaining again why it wasn't viable, he said, "We're going to ask you, based on all the evidence you've heard—and mostly based on all the evidence you *haven't* heard—to find my client not guilty of first-degree murder.

Brenda Beadle had the last word, and she spoke passionately about the victim she had never met yet had come to know so well. "For years, the defendant portrayed Cari as a conniving, jealous, obsessed stalker. But all along, it was her. *She* was all of those things." She nodded at the image of the smiling woman. "This is the real Cari Farver. She was a bright, beautiful, hardworking mother, sister, daughter friend, coworker. And her life was violently cut short by this defendant's twisted, obsessive, reprehensible acts of violence . . ."

Beadle asked the court to find Liz guilty. "Cari deserves justice, and so does Cari's family."

Judge Timothy Burns delivered his verdict on Wednesday morning, May 24. His eloquent speech touched the hearts of Cari's loved ones, those who'd worked so hard to find the truth, and the prosecution team who'd expertly presented the evidence. His verdict included the powerful revelation that, "Cari Farver did not voluntarily disappear off the face of the Earth. Very sadly, she was murdered. The Court finds beyond a reasonable doubt that the defendant intentionally killed Cari Farver with deliberate and premeditated malice on or about November 13, 2012, in Douglas County, Nebraska.

"The Court further finds beyond a reasonable doubt that during the defendant's twisted plot of lies, deceit, and impersonations through digital messaging, the defendant, on or about August 16, 2013, intentionally caused damage to her residence and property inside her residence located here in Douglas County, Nebraska, by intentionally starting a fire."

Jim Masteller had barely glanced at the defendant throughout the trial. He was too focused on his work to notice her. He looked at her now. Her expression was as placid as a lake on a breezeless day. Her only sign of distress was the scarlet hue creeping up her neck.

Garret had planned to be there for the verdict but arrived late. "I had to sit outside the courtroom," he remembers. He learned of Liz's fate when he saw her led away in cuffs. "I'll never forget, as she left the courtroom, I was the last person she saw. We briefly locked eyes while they took her away." Her eyes betrayed nothing, and he saw no tears. But there were lots of tears flowing among Cari's family and friends as they gathered outside of the courtroom with the investigators to hug and congratulate each other. The verdict was exactly what they'd hoped for, but it was not a time of celebration. A guilty verdict did not bring their Cari home. They were relieved, and they were grateful to the judge. He had recognized the monster, and now the healing could begin.

When JMD was approached by TV reporters, he praised his opponents as he admitted defeat. "In my three or four decades of practicing law, it's one of the most powerful presentations of circumstantial evidence that I've ever seen." He'd done everything he could to defend Shanna, but the truth had won.

Shortly after the verdict, he got a phone call from his client. "I want to take the plea deal," she announced. There had never been a formal offer for a plea deal. JMD recalls a vague reference to the possibility, with a prosecutor commenting that no deal would be considered unless Shanna revealed the location of the remains. JMD had mentioned that conversation to Shanna, but it was a moot point, because she'd insisted upon her innocence. He reminded her of that now. "Shanna, you told me you weren't guilty," he stressed, adding that even if she *had* been offered a deal, it was too late because she'd already been convicted.

Shanna Elizabeth Golyar was sentenced to life in prison for first-degree murder and eighteen to twenty years for arson in the second degree. Judge Burns ordered that the sentences run consecutively. She is currently incarcerated at the Nebraska Correctional Center for Women in York, Nebraska, the same prison that had once been home to Starkweather's companion.

Does her young boyfriend still visit her? Detectives assume her romance with Josh Stemmer cooled after Liz's conviction. They heard no more about it, and Doty and Avis last saw Josh's relatives a few weeks after the trial when they were dispatched to the Stemmer home to deal with a complaint about a noisy domestic disturbance.

Things had settled down by the time they arrived, and it wasn't necessary to arrest anyone. But Henry Stemmer was not a fan of police, and he sat on the front porch, quite intoxicated, mouthing off as Doty and Avis prepared to leave. Detective Doty turned to Henry and advised, "Tell your son to pick better ladies."

"What?" Henry asked. "What do you mean?"

"Liz Golyar," Doty said over his shoulder. "I put her in prison."

"Deputy!" cried Henry. *"Deputy, wait!* I want to shake your hand."

"Henry got up," Avis remembers. "He stumbled down the porch steps and fell into a mud puddle. He squirmed around in the puddle for a minute, and then he got up and shook Doty's hand." The detectives had finally earned the respect of one of their toughest customers.

In November 2017, James Martin Davis received two startling and anonymous emails from someone threatening to harm Liz's kids unless the convicted murderer revealed the location of Cari's remains. "Shanna will provide the location to police, or she will suffer for the rest of her life," said one letter, pointing out that Shanna was unable to protect her children because she was in jail and that "a hole in the ground" was waiting for one of her relatives unless she cooperated.

JMD alerted authorities, and many people suspected Liz was behind the threats, but no one knew how she'd pulled it off. While inmates at the York prison are allowed limited access to the Internet, those monitoring her activity found no evidence she'd sent the threats. The many people tortured by Liz's electronic harassment before her incarceration were outraged to learn she was allowed to use a computer, even if she wasn't responsible for the latest threats.

If Liz had sent the threats, how had she done it? Did she have access to a cell phone? According to a January 2019 article in the *Lincoln Journal Star*, an estimated 250 to 300 cell phones were confiscated in Nebraska prisons in 2018, and officials suspect inmates are hiding many more. Cell phone contraband is a growing problem in prisons across the country, one perpetuated by crooked guards who sell phones to prisoners at greatly inflated costs. Phones are also delivered to prison yards via drones, and inmates have been known to conceal them in toilet tanks, body cavities, and books.

The drama continues even with Liz behind bars. When Detective Schneider visited the York prison to interview an inmate about another case he was investigating, the woman mentioned Liz, claiming that Liz was either insane or pretending to be insane. Liz insisted that people call her Cari, said the inmate. It was startling news, but Schneider is uncertain of its veracity. No one else has come forward to confirm the story.

Liz Goylar filed an appeal with the Nebraska Supreme Court, requesting that they reverse her conviction. She used the same arguments her extremely competent attorney had—no one had witnessed the murder, and neither a body nor a weapon had been found. She also claimed that JMD had failed her by advising her to waive a jury trial. The Supreme Court unanimously ruled against Golyar in November 2018, concluding her attorney was competent, and, in Judge Stephanie Stacey's words, "There is no merit to Golyar's claim that the evidence was insufficient to support her conviction for first-degree murder."

AFTERWORD

MAXWELL FARVER IS ENGAGED to be married and has followed in his mother's footsteps, studying computer programing and coding at a university. He recently added "Data Science" to his major. Nancy and Mark Raney have remained close to the investigators who helped them, and think of them as sons.

Deputy Anthony Kava, Detectives Jim Doty, Ryan Avis, and Dave Schneider are frequently invited to speak to law enforcement groups about cyber-crimes and their involvement with the Golyar case.

James Masteller is now a district court judge in Nebraska's Fourth Judicial District, appointed by Governor Pete Ricketts in the autumn of 2018. Brenda Beadle is still winning cases for Douglas County. JMD was once again voted Omaha's best defense attorney.

While Garret has not dated since he broke up with Liz and is somewhat wary when it comes to meeting women, he insists he's content with his life and grateful for his family, friends, and pets. "I'm not depressed, lonely or desperate to make a 'love' connection—not that I'm not open to it. It's not a high priority right now." He refuses to let his experience with Liz "have power over me," and "I have forgiven—*not to be confused with forgotten*—her trespasses against me."

Amy Flora and Dave Kroupa continue to co-parent their kids and have no desire to reunite. Both participated in an autumn 2017 *Dateline* episode about the case. Dave plans to cooperate with every TV program Cari's mother chooses to participate in. "I got her daughter killed," he says sadly, explaining that the least he can do is support Nancy's decision to tell Cari's story. He's still overwhelmed with guilt over what happened to Cari. Nancy Raney doesn't blame

Dave. "He was pretty much at the wrong place at the wrong time like Cari was," she insists, adding that she hopes his feelings of guilt won't hinder him. "Cari wouldn't want that."

Dave admits that while he has cried, he's not allowed himself to fully grieve for Cari. He can't let his mind go there because "I can't bear it."

Melissa Strom earned a degree in the medical field, has a great job, and met and married a wonderful man.

Liz Golyar's children were understandably devastated by their mother's conviction, but reports say they are doing well. Trina lives with a supportive foster aunt, and Peter lives with his father.

Liz Golyar still insists she is innocent.

Author's Note

While most of those interviewed for *A Tangled Web* allowed their real names to be used, some requested pseudonyms to protect their privacy. Some professionals were also given pseudonyms to spare them possible embarrassment over being tricked by the killer.

A few of those quoted in this story were not actually interviewed by this author, but their quotes were pulled directly from trial transcripts. The transcripts were also the source of all emails and texts, each one written verbatim—though most punctuation and spelling errors were corrected to reduce confusion for readers.

My publishers are not fans of the cumbersome asterisk, often used to indicate a name change, but you can visit my website to see a complete list of the pseudonyms used. (The subjects' real names, however, will not be revealed without their permission.)

Please visit Deputy Anthony Kava's website for tips on staying safe in the cyberworld. Links to donate to The Cari Farver Scholarship Fund can be found on both of our websites.

Anthony Kava's website is https://forensic.coffee.

Leslie Rule's website is www.authorLeslieRule.com.

UPDATE, 2021

As of this writing, Cari Farver has been gone for eight years. While no trace of her physical body has been found, the investigators who worked so hard to get justice for her are determined that her memory will live on in a positive light. Detectives Jim Doty and Ryan Avis, and Deputy Anthony Kava established the Cari Farver Memorial Scholarship Fund in May 2019 via the Pottawattamie County Community Foundation. The first award went to a Council Bluffs student, enrolled in IT courses at the Iowa Western Community College in the fall of 2020.

Somehow, I think Cari would approve. I never met her but feel as if I know her because I learned so much about her from those who loved her. I think she'd like the fact that her memory will bring more smiles than tears as scholarships in her honor are awarded to students for many years to come.

Cari's family is proud that her legacy of kindness has inspired something that brings joy.

They're doing their best to remember the happy times and not dwell on the horror, but it takes a great deal of strength for the families of victims to embrace normalcy. It is also difficult for the families of killers.

I've stayed in touch with Liz Golyar's biological aunts, and I know their hearts broke when they read *A Tangled Web*. They've had to face the fact that their once-sweet little niece violently and viciously killed an innocent woman. They were also shocked to learn about their great-nephew, baby Cody, and his tragic death. Their sister, Dee, died years before her grandson was born, but they do not doubt that she would have adored him.

This is not the first time Liz's aunts have had family in prison, but it is the first time a relative was convicted of murder. They wondered and worried about their niece for decades, and in all of the scenarios they could have imagined, it never crossed their minds that she would grow up to be as cruel as her father. They worried about their nephews, too, of course, and I shared with them what I know, though I respected the privacy of Liz's three brothers while telling this story. The two older brothers—her half siblings, who she didn't know existed because the State of Michigan took them before she was born—are now 51 and 52 and were adopted together. They moved out of the area with their new family many years ago. While I found a way to contact them, I chose not to. It would surely be a burden for them to learn that they had a baby sister who grew up to be a killer.

Information I uncovered indicates that these brothers don't know their mother's maiden name but that they do know that she died and have enough details to recognize her if they happen to read *A Tangled Web*. If they do, and they contact me, I've gotten the okay from their Aunt Camila to reveal her real name and put them in touch with her. I hope if they read these words that they'll take comfort in learning that their mother loved them desperately and did not willingly give them up.

Three years after her murder conviction, Liz Golyar still insists she is innocent. She tried to convince me of this in a six-and-a-half-page letter, handwritten in green ink. She'd had the chance to express herself when I contacted her while researching *A Tangled Web*, but she declined. Months later she changed her mind, but she had waited too long, and the book had already gone to press by the time I received her letter. In addition to listing all the reasons why she couldn't possibly be guilty, her letter was riddled with complaints about her unfair treatment. "I have people who call me a monster!" she exclaimed, as if expecting me to be as offended as she was.

She is probably aware by now that I, too, referred to her as a monster. According to *Merriam-Webster's Dictionary*, the fourth definition of monster is "a person of unnatural or extreme ugliness, deformity, wickedness, or cruelty." Liz demonstrated that she is both unnaturally and extremely wicked and cruel when she murdered an innocent person.

But she claims she has never harmed a soul and that the *real* killer roams free. She expressed dismay because her family and friends have abandoned her—despite everything she'd done for them in the past. She'd let her sister Marcy live with her, but now Marcy wasn't there for her, she wrote. Her young boyfriend had dumped her, and even "my son's dad hates me." She'd once had "the best friendship" with Dirk, but her brother had "told my son's dad I wanted to kill him. That is a lie."

Many people had failed her, Liz moaned. At the top of the list was her attorney. "Mr. James Martin Davis did not do his job! All he kept saying was for me to calm down and let him do his job." He had done everything within his power to defend her, but there is only so much even an award-winning defense attorney can do when his client is guilty of murder. His arguments had not moved Judge Burns, but Liz repeated them in an attempt to influence me.

She had sat quietly in court, absorbing her attorney's argument that her small stature would have prevented her from doing some of the things she was accused of. Now she drew upon that idea, informing me that she "had a hard time lifting my kids when they reach [*sic*] 50 pounds. I had a physical done [and] was told that I shouldn't lift anything over fifty pounds. They are trying to say I lifted someone 5'7" and 150 pounds." Perhaps Liz's doctor *had* told her to avoid heavy lifting, but the prosecution had never alleged she had *lifted* Cari.

No one but Liz knows how the horrific drama played out, but overwhelming evidence indicates that a weapon, most likely a knife, was used. No matter the size difference between killer and victim, a weapon always gives the killer the advantage.

As disturbing as it is to contemplate, the disposal of a body can be achieved in many ways that don't require unusual strength. A body can be wrapped in a shower curtain and dragged, then rolled up a ramp into a vehicle or burn barrel, without the murderess straining her back or breaking a nail.

As for Liz's fingerprint, pressed neatly upon the mint tin discovered in Cari's car, JMD had stressed in court that "there's no evidence my client put it in there. It simply suggests that at one time—someplace, sometime, that my client touched it."

Now Liz elaborated on that, acknowledging that her print likely *was* on the mint container but emphasizing that there was a perfectly good reason for that. She'd been in the habit of purchasing mints for Dave Kroupa for his car, his work, and "wherever we went. When we broke up, he still had them. I did not like kissing him after he smoked."

Upon reading that I texted him, and he immediately replied, "I call B.S. on the kiss thing. I smoked a *lot,* and I don't remember her ever saying anything about it. Mints have never been a thing with me. I certainly didn't carry them around."

Liz added that not only was she repelled by his cigarette breath, but the guy had never meant that much to her. "I was never in love with David Kroupa, and I most certainly didn't want anything serious with him." In fact, she'd been happy he'd met Cari because "I always wanted him to find someone he wanted to be with."

Liz's true feelings for Dave are scorched into the *thousands* of emails and texts she wrote. No one has to read between the lines to see that she was driven by her pathological infatuation.

She also echoed her attorney's argument about the lack of evidence found in Cari's car. "Yes, I cleaned for a living, but I don't know how to clean a crime scene . . . they had to take the car apart to find blood."

Cari's Ford Explorer had been under Liz's control for nearly two months, plenty of time for a determined woman to wash away evidence. Who better to sterilize a crime scene than a professional cleaner and fan of the Showtime drama *Dexter*? Dexter Morgan, the fictitious but nevertheless creepy serial killer, is notorious for his immaculate crime scenes, and more than one real-life murderer has allegedly copied his methods.

Liz's letter also took swipes at Amy Flora as she mentioned the Big Lake Park shooting and implied that her nemesis could be the real culprit. Amy was long ago cleared as a suspect in the shooting, and investigators concluded that Liz had shot herself. But Liz insists it was impossible to shoot herself in the thigh, and she wrote, "I am right-handed, and the entrance is in the back of my thigh and the exit in the front."

Common sense dictates it wouldn't take a contortionist to accomplish that, but it's a moot point. The alleged attack in Big Lake Park had little bearing on her murder conviction. The shooting hoax was a failed attempt to get sympathy from Dave and frame Amy. Liz had faced no charges for the incident.

Liz denied that she had written the incriminating emails that Deputy Kava had diligently traced to her but admitted she had applied for Cari's job, explaining that she'd applied at West Corporation "several times through the years," and that "I had no idea that it was Cari Farver's job."

It's obvious that Liz put enormous effort into her letter as she covered all of the reasons that she hoped would prove she'd been unfairly convicted. Her explanations fell flat, but most telling of all was her phenomenal recall of a day that should have held no special significance for her if she were innocent.

If someone were to ask me what I was doing seven days ago, I could not give them a breakdown of every minute of my day. If they asked me about my activities seven *years* ago on a random day, I certainly could not pinpoint what I was doing at 7:15 that morning. Yet Liz claims to recollect her every move on the morning that Cari disappeared.

If Liz had been accused of murder within days or even weeks of November 13, 2012, then it would make sense that she could perhaps trace some of her movements that morning. But it was not until February 25, 2016, over three years and three months after Cari vanished, that Liz was accused for the first time, when Detective Dave Schneider interrogated her. Liz did not attempt to provide an alibi in that recorded conversation with Detective Schneider, but she gave me a detailed alibi—albeit with no witnesses—for the period when investigators suspect the murder occurred.

"On November 13th, I woke up at 6 a.m., took a shower and got dressed," she wrote. She woke her kids at 6:45 a.m. and called her neighbor at "about 7 a.m." to make arrangements "to pick up my car." She agreed to give her neighbor's son a ride, and "I got back to my house at 7:10 a.m."

Liz made the kids breakfast, "took my cleaners out to my car," and at 7:20 a.m., picked up her neighbor's son. She then drove to the elementary school "and sat there until 7:30," when the boys went into the school. Next she drove her daughter to the middle school, and "we got there about 8:15 a.m.," and Trina entered the school at 8:20 a.m. "I then went to McDonald [*sic*] at 8:30/8:35 a.m. to grab breakfast." From there, Liz traveled to Sarpy County, about twenty-five miles from Omaha, for a housecleaning job, arriving by 9 a.m. She cleaned until 1 p.m., she claimed, emphasizing "I can't be two places at once."

Had I been unfamiliar with Liz's case, I would have been more impressed with her letter. The tone was polite, and she made sure to acknowledge that she wasn't the only one suffering. While she didn't express sympathy specifically for *Cari*, she did sympathize with those who mourned her. "I know Cari Farver's families [*sic*] lives have been turned upside down. I feel very bad for her family," she wrote. "I am not guilt [*sic*] of this and hope one day they realize that."

Liz had the common sense to mention her victim and to pretend she cared. But I saw through her. I know her case far better than she realized, and in some ways, I know Liz better than she knows herself. I definitely know more about where she came from and some of her sadistic relatives, who helped shaped who she became—either through example or genetics.

Liz actually made one true statement on the last page of her letter when she wrote, "It's frustrating when no one will listen or believe me." I don't doubt that she *is* frustrated. For most of her life, she got away with atrocious behavior. She used people, she stole, and she lied. She hurt others in many ways. She probably believed that she would always be able to do whatever she wished with few repercussions. Perhaps she would have gotten away with her appalling acts indefinitely if not for the committed team of investigators and prosecutors who demonstrated excellence in their pursuit of justice.

Despite the fact she's serving life in prison, Liz Golyar still hopes for freedom. She insists that she is fighting for the truth each day she spends behind bars and vows, "I will not stop fighting until I am set free, and they find the right person."

I did not reply to Liz's letter. I considered it for perhaps 30 seconds but realized I have no desire to be her pen pal. *A Tangled Web* is complete, and there is no reason to continue correspondence. Frankly, I had never relished the idea of communicating with her but reached out because it was my duty as an author to make the attempt. If she had been willing while I was researching the book, I would have gone to the prison to interview her. I wasn't disappointed when she declined because I remembered the wise words of my mother. She often said that sociopaths don't reveal their true selves to interviewers. They lie and manipulate. She learned about her subjects not by talking to them but by talking to the people who knew them. While it might have been interesting to meet with Liz in person and peer into her eyes as she lied to me, I doubt it would have offered many new insights.

Revelations continue to emerge as people from Liz's past confide in me. One of the more chilling accounts came from Delmar, a one-time pal to Liz. An easygoing guy, he was a friend of Dave Kroupa's and met Liz through him. "I'd just broken up with my girlfriend," he remembers. He needed to vent, and he was grateful to Liz for listening, though he admits that she dominated most of their conversations.

One observer surmised that Liz latched on to Delmar in an attempt to make Dave jealous. Neither Dave nor Liz's longtime boyfriend, Garret Sloan, however, knew that she had sex with Delmar. "It happened just once," Delmar told me. It was clear to him that Liz didn't view him as boyfriend material, because his appearance embarrassed her. An attractive man, bearded with gentle brown eyes, he is self-conscious because a rare dental disease caused him to lose multiple teeth. He is certain that Liz shuddered at the idea of being seen in public on his arm. But he didn't take offense, and he accepted her as a friend. She got a job at the warehouse where he worked with Cherokee, and the trio often hung out together.

Delmar soon realized that as long as he agreed with Liz, they got along well. She was extremely opinionated when it came to Dave, Amy, and Cari, and she spent long hours criticizing the three "horrible people" who made her life miserable. Liz told Delmar that Dave was cheating on her with Amy and that Cari was stalking her. If Delmar balked, Liz's anger intensified as she demanded that he agree with her. Sheepish now, he admits that he allowed her to influence him. She was so passionate about the injustices she'd suffered, that he found himself sympathizing. He'd been sincere when he nodded along, assuring his pal that she had every right to be outraged. Liz could be very convincing, and he usually managed to see her side of things. It was easier that way.

But the truth is, Delmar liked Dave. During one of Liz's tirades, Delmar stuck up for him. Liz was livid, and she and Delmar got into a heated argument. It was the not the last time that Liz got angry at him. She was furious in the summer of 2016 when she learned he had gotten engaged. Liz texted him, asking if he was really getting married. He confirmed that he was, and she cut off all communication with him for weeks. She refused to answer texts and would not return his phone calls.

Delmar was baffled. Liz's reaction was that of a jealous girlfriend. He felt bad that she was upset, and he continued to reach out to her. His fiancée didn't mind. She trusted him, and his kind heart was one of the things that had attracted her to him. It was just like Delmar to be concerned about someone else's feelings.

Liz had made it clear that she didn't want him, yet she didn't want anyone else to have him. It made no sense to him, but he kept trying to smooth things over. He was relieved when she finally responded and agreed to go fishing with him. It appeared that she'd let go of her resentment. He drove to her apartment in Persia, Iowa, to pick her up for what he expected to be a relaxing excursion. He climbed the creaking steps to her apartment in the old brick building and rapped on the door. He was invited in, and the moment he stepped inside, he was gripped by an icy sense of doom. "I had chills and a creepy feeling. I felt like something bad was about to happen."

Liz's kids were there, and they sat in front of the TV, staring at a program while they ate. Liz was on her phone, texting, and she beckoned to Delmar who huddled near the door. "She tried to get me to come in and sit down," he remembers, but he was immobilized by terror. He was unable to move toward Liz. Instead, he ran away. He hurried to his car, leaving Liz behind. Too shaken to drive, he sat for five minutes, trying to calm himself. He finally managed to drive to his fishing spot, but the terror did not subside until he'd been there for half an hour or so.

His response was not logical. He'd gone to his friend's apartment in the midst of an ordinary day and witnessed her texting while her kids watched television. What was so scary about that? He knew only one thing. His fright had been so overwhelming that he'd had no choice but to obey his instincts and flee as fast as he could as if his life depended upon it.

Months later when he heard the news that Liz had been arrested for murder, Delmar remembered his reaction on that unforgettably eerie day. Suddenly, it made sense. He was not paranoid. He had been in the company of a killer and was about to spend the day with her. *Alone.* Yes, he'd been alone with her many times before, but things had changed. It would have been their first outing since his engagement—the engagement that had inexplicably enraged her. Did Liz have a malicious plan for him that day?

Danger can sneak up on any of us without warning, offering only a split second for a decision. Do we listen to our intuition and embrace lifesaving fear? Or do we shrug it off to avoid the possibility of looking foolish?

Delmar chose fear, and he does not regret it. We don't know, of course, if Liz had planned to hurt him. It might be that he simply sensed the darkness in her. While he will never forget the frightening day that he fled her apartment, he is most disturbed when he reflects upon the time she spent with his children. He remembers her fixing his young daughter's hair. Liz was being helpful, and the little girl liked the attention as her daddy's friend ran the brush through her gleaming locks. There was never a threat. No harm was done. But Delmar can't help but shiver when he recalls how close he allowed a killer to get to his child.

ACKNOWLEDGMENTS

I am thankful to those who made it possible to shed light on a horrific tragedy—a story that *needed* to be told to warn potential victims about the killers in our midst and the digital tricks they use to deceive us. Thank you for your willingness to reveal often personal and painful things so that readers can truly understand what happened, *how* it happened, and can recognize danger if they see it headed their way: Nancy and Mark Raney, Maxwell Farver, Dave Kroupa, Trish Kroupa, Amy Flora, Cherokee Montoya, Tim Verbeek, Ray Strahan, Amber Jones, Holly Drummond, Brandie Bates, Tayandy Braver, and Heather. I'm equally grateful to those using the pseudonyms: Garret Sloan, Melissa Strom, Gloria Munson, Camila, Victoria, Christie, and Jean.

I am forever grateful to the professionals who worked tirelessly to solve this case and seek justice for Cari Farver. Thank you for sitting down with me to share your insights, Detective Jim Doty, Detective Ryan Avis, Detective Dave Schneider, and Prosecutors Brenda Beadle and Jim Masteller. Special Deputy Anthony Kava, I'm in awe of your genius and so appreciate the fact you shared your materials with me!

Thank you to James Martin Davis and Cheyann Forester Parr for the enlightening lunch at The Omaha Press Club. Thank you, Barbara Bisbee Pedersen, Adam Farver, LuAnn Smith, Cynthia Weisz, August Siefken, Stefan Stroebel, Shawn Flanigan, Alison Clark, Ann C. Miller, Matt Wilber and Tayandy Braver for your help with the photos. The following demonstrated excellence in transcribing trial testimony: Leslie B. Anderson, Joyce Kelly, Roana Smith, and

Theresa Stevens. Thank you to Dhebi Siconolfi for flawlessly transcribing interviews. Kathy Lavato, I appreciate your insights about Omaha and Council Bluffs.

I'm grateful to my editor, Michaela Hamilton, for her wisdom, encouragement, and enthusiasm. I'm grateful, also, to production editor Arthur Maisel for his sharp eye and patience. And to my agent, Sheree Bykofsky, for always believing in me.

I couldn't have completed this book without the encouragement of my husband, Glenn Scott, who nourished me with the world's best Garden Burgers, so I would have the energy to write through the night!

Thank you, Cari Farver, for being the wonderful person your family and friends loved so dearly. I wish I could have met you.

QUESTIONS FOR READERS
TO EXPLORE

1. Despite horror stories about predators on the Internet, it is very common for couples to meet online. What precautions should be taken to insure safety?

2. Did the killer in *A Tangled Web* use electronic ruses unfamiliar to you? If so, which devices had you never heard of?

3. Dave Kroupa was unable to see the truth because he suffered from confirmation bias. Have you ever experienced something like this in your life? If so, how did you finally manage to see the truth?

4. What do you think about the fact that Neil Munson was questioned in the back of a police car when he was exhausted?

5. Do you think Liz was the real author of the letters she claimed Neil Munson had sent from jail? If so, why didn't anyone question this?

6. Why did so few people believe Melissa Strom when she told them Shanna was dangerous?

7. Some of the survivors in this story believe they are alive because they trusted their gut instincts. Why do we so often dismiss our own intuition?

8. Do you think the stalker in *A Tangled Web* was shaped by nature, nurture or a combination of both?

9. Did the stalker possess the willpower to overcome her obsession and become a mentally healthy person?

10. Why didn't the police believe Nancy Raney when she told them her daughter was in trouble?

11. In order to solve this case, investigators worked thousands of extra unpaid hours. In what way should investigators be rewarded if they work on their own time to solve a crime?

12. Is it possible that the stalker focused on females to vent her rage because she felt abandoned by her mother? Though she had no conscious memories of her mother, could the fact her mother left her life so abruptly at such a young age influence who she became?

Connect with U~s~

Visit us online at
KensingtonBooks.com
to read more from your favorite authors, see books
by series, view reading group guides, and more.

Join us on social media

for sneak peeks, chances to win books and prize packs,
and to share your thoughts with other readers.

facebook.com/kensingtonpublishing
twitter.com/kensingtonbooks

Tell us what you think!

To share your thoughts, submit a review,
or sign up for our eNewsletters, please visit:
KensingtonBooks.com/TellUs.